Getting Started with Information Technology: Practice and Applications

GETTING STARTED WITH INFORMATION TECHNOLOGY
Practice and Applications

Ravikant M. Deshpande
Bharati P. Rahangdale
Ranjana D. Bhoskar

Ess Ess Publications
New Delhi

Getting Started with Information Technology : Practice and Applications

ISBN: 978-81-7000-749-4

First Published 2015

Published by:
Ess Ess Publications
4831/24, Ansari Road,
Darya Ganj,
New Delhi-110 002.
INDIA
Phones: 23260807, 41563444
Fax: 41563334
E-mail: info@essessreference.com
www.essessreference.com

Cover Design by *Patch Creative Unit*

Printed and bound in India at Salasar Imaging Systems.

Dedicated to the memory of
ANJALI RAVIKANT DESHPANDE

CONTENTS

From Authors' Desk

Capitalizing on our experience of practical applications of information technology and related entities, we thought it wise to narrate in our own words, instead of 'forewords', written by some experienced professional, the practice we have followed during applications of IT and related technologies before august readers and why we felt the necessity of bringing out this book.

Right from early nineties of last century, I have been practicing the information retrieval in CDS/ISIS package which came without any user manual. Studying by myself, all the intricacies of CDS/ISIS like FDT, worksheet, display format and FST I was able to understand the information retrieval process. Then in1993 I shifted to library automation package LIBSYS after studying some prominent library automation packages from U.K. such as CAIRSLMS and Library Cooperative Catalogue. I managed to successfully automate the library services of VNIT library by 1994 with more than 20,000 usable records. All modules like acquisition, circulation, technical processing, serials control and OPAC were operational 20 years ago. As of now all the records of 1.2 Lac documents are in the database. Meanwhile Ms. Rahangdale and Ms. Bhoskar (my co-authors in this work) also joined me in my endeavours and started contributing with their knowledge and technical know-how to the overall development of applications of IT. Today we offer our technical help to library professionals around us. Getting inspired from our automation efforts done at VNIT, Nagpur, many professionals have worked towards achieving similar results in their own institutions with success. This movement has managed to create awareness among urban Nagpur and nearby towns like Wardha, Bhandara, Chandrapur, Amaravati, Yeotamal, etc. and has left positive impact on professionals around us to develop the skills of IT applications or at least commence efforts in this direction.

I hope that this book shall help all the readers in getting inspired to get started for their automation needs and would act as their source book for achieving the desired results.

Ravikant M. Deshpande

1

ICT Applications

Keywords : *ICT Applications, ICT outcome, Information Impact, Library products and services, Information Communication Technologies (ICT), LIS professionals.*

INTRODUCTION

The life is full of changes. The library and information area has undergone various changes from yester years till today. The advent of ICT has created revolution in libraries and information centres. The traditional services like circulation, reference, loose issues of journals, technical processing has been transformed into digital services based on the differcnt electronic resources. The conversion of book material into digital sources created altogether different environment of services. The reactive services have taken placc of proactive services. The whole book is not needed but a small piece of information running in few pages are required and requisitioned by users. Their demands have become dynamic in nature. The copying culture of the documents has undergone changes into different media such as pen drives, CDs, DVDs. This is all due to applications of ICT and other related technologies. Sooner we accept these changes better is for our future.

The applications of computers to libraries for

housekeeping operations i.e. such as Acquisition, Technical processing, Serials control and Circulation of material has become essential elements. The digital services, Network services, full text services, Referral services are on demand. The applications of RFID Technology, cloud computing technology in libraries are opening new gates of services in information sector. The impact of all this will be seen everywhere whether you like it or not. The technological enforcement has become the order of the day. We are here to study the impact of these technologies in information and knowledge management. Our functioning of library, appealing environment, behavioural adjustment and customer focus activities have become priorities. Let us study these and other aspects of changes in library and information setting that have become essential.

A) Applications in Working of Library

- Automated Library services
- ISO Practices in Library
- Customer focuses services.
- Requirement of Information rather than books.
- Dissemination of information in Digital format.
- Transition from Computer to laptops or to mobile
- Secured Technology based Information.
- Hassle free Transaction of documents
- Information in easily usable form
- Transfer of information irrespective of its place of storage.
- Healthy Housekeeping Services.
- Inviting Atmosphere in Library
- 24X7 reading room Facilities.
- Cafeteria Services.

B) Applications in Awareness of Technology based Services for Library Staff & Users

- Users Study of Clientele, What they want?
- Technology handling awareness
- Knowledge for Searching Information through System.
- Sensitization for search formulations.
- Knowledge of modern Information Gadgets
- Telecommunication Knowledge
- Hardware and software Knowledge
- Handling Knowledge of Components of ICT
- Continuous Learning Process for modern Equipments & Machines.
- No age Barrier.
- Redesign your Library Skills.
- Upgrade Leadership skills.

C) Applications in Behavioural Changes Among the Information Handling Personnel

- Complete Knowledge of the System installed or commissioned.
- Interpersonal Relationship
- Lend listening ear to users.
- Smart Talking, clear Pronunciation
- Project Confidence of working Knowledge
- Welcoming with smile on the face.
- Project clarity in Thoughts.
- Perfection in Information communication.
- Neat and clean dress up
- No under or over promising.

D) Mandatory Technological Impact

- Accept technological Changes or remain detached from mainstream
- Sound Knowledge of Technology, no half hearted efforts.
- Monetary provision for technological enforcement.
- Re develop yourself for emerging technology convergence.
- Know the Information or get informed where to get Information
- Abreast yourself for technological advancement
- Upgrade the Technological skills
- Try to remain on fore front for acceptance of technology
- Positive frame of mind for the advantages of Technology
- Be aware of Technological Obsolescence.

CHANGING ROLE OF ICT IN LIS

The information atmosphere around the world is changing every minute and growing at a tremendous speed due to the emergence of the web based Information and Communication Technologies (ICT), globalization of networks and Internet. Information is the lifeblood of democracy and it is considered as a vital source of power. So the accurate, valuable, up-to-date, quickly, timely and pin pointed information is required for its patrons. Library and information professionals are being affected by a range of digital developments and so find their roles changing worldwide. A Librarian with diverse talents and training and who is flexible, will be able to meet the challenges of future library scene. The container of information is not only the print materials but this is the age we are living where a huge rate of information born in digital format. Technology alone cannot help bring about the required changes. Attitudes, practices and policies need to change if libraries in India are to truly benefit themselves and their users by the application of new technologies and services.

LIS professionals have been playing a versatile role beyond their traditional job. They have to gather adequate knowledge of computer and communication technologies, networks and networking, operating systems, Internet concepts, database management systems, along with adequate practical exposure to handle technological devices. In mobilization of all kinds of information resources librarians are expected to work as pathfinders by assisting all users with varied backgrounds and abilities through information supportive environment and multiple strategies. Figure 1 shows clear cut idea of changing the vision & role of library components.

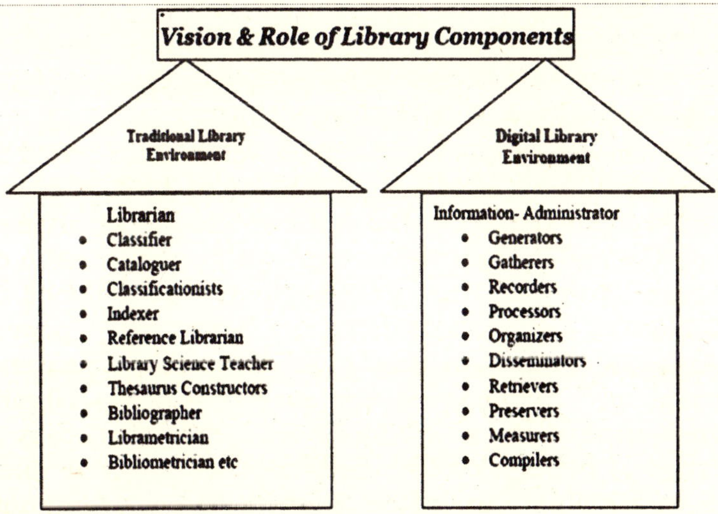

Fig. 1. Changing the Vision and Role of Library Components

EFFICACY OF LIBRARY PRODUCTS

E-resources mean electronic form of information

just like internet based information, online journals, online database, electronic books and useful effectively for user point of view. All newly techno-based products are very useful to our patron but it is our duty of assembling all the products in such a manner those are easily retrieved by every patron. Time is the main factor for this speedy age so designing of all library products is the demand of today's libraries and information centres.

E-Books

E-Books are the most useful product for our digital age users. Libraries and resource centres should be compilation of E-books in such a manner which is beneficial to our patron in finding according to their requirements. E-book offer advantages like portability, 24 hours access, text search, annotation, linking, and multimedia and self-publishing.

E-Journals

Electronic journals can be accessed via internet form any web enabled PC. One or more users can access the service simultaneously. Electronic journals also offer benefit of full text searching and downloading of articles. Technology based libraries can subscribe electronic journals through consortia, so that they can provide e-journal product to the users. Electronic journals are easily access by the users anywhere, any time.

E-Databases

E-databases are online collections of resources, like a collection of abstracts, newspaper articles, maps, online resource collections etc. Libraries and resources centres can subscribe according to patron needs so they can get the information as they required.

Audio Video Products

Audiovisual products are important sources for

information, education and entertainment. Many libraries particularly media libraries and large academic and public libraries hold audio visual material such as DVD, films, pictures and photographs etc. Libraries allow their members to borrow these.

e. g. Online lectures like NPTEL. NPTEL provides E-learning through online Web and Video courses in Engineering, Science and humanities streams. The mission of NPTEL is to enhance the quality of engineering education in the country by providing free online courseware. Therefore students can get information easily. This is more available right now VNIT provided this facility.

Standards

Library and information centres can be compile different categories of the standards which are very useful for the users. Standards are used to describe digital data using specific to a particular discipline. Standards are defined as data providing information about one or more aspects of the data, such as means of creation of the data, purpose of the data, time and date of creation, creator or author of data, location on a computer network where the data was created.

CD/DVD Collection

Libraries and information centres should be produce CD/DVD collection like guest lecturers, precious delivery of the prestigious personalities etc. When library users are not able to attending the conference, seminar and guest lecturers then they have the facility of same CD/DVD in the library. e.g If students are not able to attend regular class room lectures due to some reason he/she will be made available required lecture through DVDs.

Institutional E-Repository

An institutional repository is an online archive for

collecting, preserving, and disseminating digital copies of the intellectual output of an institution, particularly a research institution. Libraries and resources centres are includes material like academic journals, articles, digital theses and dissertations, administrative documents, course notes etc. again in addition to that learning object repository also provides better services to the patron.

Question Bank in PDF Form

The Library collects the question bank in previous exams and they provide to students in PDF form. Question bank in PDF format is a good idea for the user point of view. Users are easily accessible and clear the pattern of examination.

RFID Technology

RFID (Radio Frequency Identification) is the latest technology to be used in library theft detection systems. Unlike EM (Electro-Mechanical) and RF (Radio Frequency) systems, which have been used in libraries for decades, the RFID-based systems that libraries began to install in the late 1990s not only detect the unauthorized removal of library materials, but speed staff charge and discharge, simplify and speed patron self-charge and self-discharge, support electronic inventorying and shelf searching, and interface with materials handling systems. e.g. The NITs like VNIT, DNIT, Jallandar and NIT Surat have taken initiatives to implement RFID technology at their respective NITs for modernisation of library services.

Scanning

Scanning facility is playing important things for the patron because it is time saving, paper saving and convenient for speedy approaches to retrieve the information. Scanning of various documents, books and other study material will be helpful to users for further interest and studies.

Library Consortium

Library consortium product is a group of libraries who partner to coordinate activities, share resources, and combine expertise. For example Engineering students MHRD provides funds for INDEST Consortium in the collaboration of following core members IITs, IISc Bangalore, NITs, ISM, IIMs etc. NITs resource centres are well developed by computerization, digitization and in the development of computer and network infrastructure. Patrons of these reputed organisations are easily access e-journal products through libraries and information centres.

MODIFIED LIBRARY SERVICES

According to demand of present digital era it is the necessity of modification of traditional library services. Following are the some important technology based library services useful in the digital age.

Web OPAC service

Search Library Catalogue the entire Library collection including books, journals, etc. can be searched through the web enabled Online Public Access Catalogue (OPAC). Users can access the OPAC to find out the real-time availability of library materials from their own computer terminals. Faculty and students can reserve items, which are on loan. Faculty is also encouraged to send request for new acquisitions in thc Library though the OPAC. Web OPAC is a web based searching platform, developed with advanced information technologies for dissemination of information to the users.

E-mail

E-mail is the most universal application on the Internet and it can be used for direct communication with potential users. There are many benefits to using email as a promotional tool. Mail shots are an effective medium that creates personalized services, with information about library activities and events, membership renewal.

Instant Messaging

Library Help the patron enquiry answering service is trialling an online instant messaging service for answering enquiries. The service is aimed at library users with quick enquiries, and those users who may not be able to telephone us. Chat is available when the Library Research and Information Desk is open. Instant messaging using software such as AOL Instant Messenger (AIM), Yahoo! Messenger, MSN Messenger, and Google Talk.

E-Library alert

Library and information centres provides specific information services such as e-alert on upcoming day by day library progress, conference, seminars, refresher courses, workshops details etc. to the academic community. Mostly e-alerts are delivered by e-mail or by RSS feed. Alert services assist library faculty and students in keeping up-to-date with current research in specific areas of interest.

Bulletin Board

This is an offshoot of email and is a many-to-many email system. It is medium for messages of interest to a community of online users. This service can be used by libraries for disseminating information to online users.

Online Resource Sharing

Online Resource Sharing Services offers several options for providing access to materials held in our collections or obtaining materials available from other libraries or sources. Rear book collection can be shared through online resource sharing in any form. Cloud Computing will help patrons for access online resources from anywhere, any time. Libraries can build digital library, content management system, and institutional repository, inter library loan system and integrated library system form locally managed to vendor hosted environment, of their own with the help of cloud computing technology. There are no geographical boundaries for patrons for accessing any resources.

Subject Gateways

Subject gateways are Internet- based services designed to help users locate high quality information that is available on the Internet. They are typically, data bases of detailed metadata records which describe Internet resources and offer a hyperlink to the resources. Subject Gateways offer user an alternative to the generalized approach of the commercial global automatic "vacuum cleaner" type of search engines, as infoseek; altavista etc

Wi-Fi Service

Wi-Fi, short for Wireless Fidelity, is set of standards that enable to access the internet on your laptop or other supported device through wireless technology. Wi-Fi may offer some better services in the libraries and information centres. It provides access to the remote users, where user community can access the databases like CD-Rom databases, bibliographic databases and services like library web pages, off campus services through the library web pages. Though it offers good and tremendous services it may lacking with some other applications in libraries. Many advanced technologies have come like Wi Max, Skype etc.

Online display new arrivals

Libraries and Information centres are online display new arrivals through library webpage like new books, e-books, reports, e-journals, online databases, online reference works and DVDs arrive in regularly.

Newsgroups

Libraries can use newsgroups or discussion groups to build awareness among its clientele. It helps in building user interaction among the community. It will be definitely helping to upgrade the level of the society.

Blogs

Blogs are continuously-updated websites, created by individuals or organizations. They are generally free. A library can use blogs to promote its products and services by making it appealing and informative. Special alerts about new e-resources special services can be included in the blog entries. To get feedback, comments and suggestions can be invited from visitors.

E-commerce

A library can also sell its products online through online charging and credit facilities. E-commerce has redefined the way business is conducted. Well-known bookstores around the world are offering their holdings over the Internet. For example, Blackwell maintains a database of more than reaches many different countries, Maintaining a website is relatively cheap, and results in reduced prices, more competition, current information, quick access and sales caters to the customers wide and varied interests, saving travel time.

E-CAS & SDI

The E-Current Awareness & E-Selective Dissemination of Information Service provides the users with a list of latest E-documents and new issues of E-journals on specific subjects available in the library. Thus the user comes to know about the new collection of library. Library announces about the forthcoming conferences and also displays the subjects and areas of conferences. This electronic service facilitates that the user is getting the latest information regarding our core subject.

E-Query Services

E-Query Service is a Web-enabled contemporary reference service offered to the registered members of the Library together handle queries received in person or by e-Mail. E-Queries may sometimes need to be followed-up with telephone, fax, regular mail, or personal interactions. Library, appropriate and brief information gathered in response will be sent to the enquirer through e-Mail within three consecutive working days from the date of receipt of the query.

CHAPTER OUTCOME

In case, the library and information personnel grasp and accept the above changes in his/her working, there is no possibility of him being remaining out of the main stream. They must be enthusiastic to technological changes so that the impact factor will be minimal. If the case it is otherwise i.e. the library personnel are averse of these changes then they will be automatically side tracked. The earliest the changes are accepted better will be their future. Change is the requirement of the every person therefore it is very essential need of the every information & library professionals to hand shake with the newest upcoming technology for satisfy their patron. Above some important technology based services and products are very useful to introduce in the libraries and information centres. It definitely changes the vision and role of the library & information professionals as mention in the above figure. In this way we all have to play important role to uplift the national position in this digital age.

2

ICT Challenges and Skills

Keywords : *Information Communication Technology, ICT challenges, ICT skills, Library Professionals, Professional Competencies*

INTRODUCTION

Information and Communication Technology (ICT) is an umbrella term that includes all technologies for the manipulation and communication of information. Further, ICT described as the use of computer-based technology and the internet to make information and communication services available to wide range of users. Librarians are providing the strategies and tools to help users make the most of web-based information. Information overload, misinformation, fees, poorly designed navigation, and loss of brows ability all hamper the searcher. Library professionals have always been evolving, adapting to new technologies, new media, and the ever-changing needs of users, more recently these changes have accelerated to match rapid developments in information and communication technologies.

Library and information professionals today need to acquire knowledge and skills in information and communication technology (ICT) as the services of more and more libraries are now centring on information technology. In this age of globalization, the importance of

ICT to people generally and information professionals in particular cannot be overemphasized. In fact, it is now difficult to imagine a world without information technology. The provision and use of ICT is part and parcel of the entire system, to both the students, information professionals and the institutions. It is one thing to recognize the importance of ICTs and another to know if they are effectively used by professionals, students and academicians.

ICT CHALLENGES BEING FACED BY INFORMATION PROFESSIONALS

There are number of challenges being faced by information professionals on the use of ICT in information provision in Library Profession.

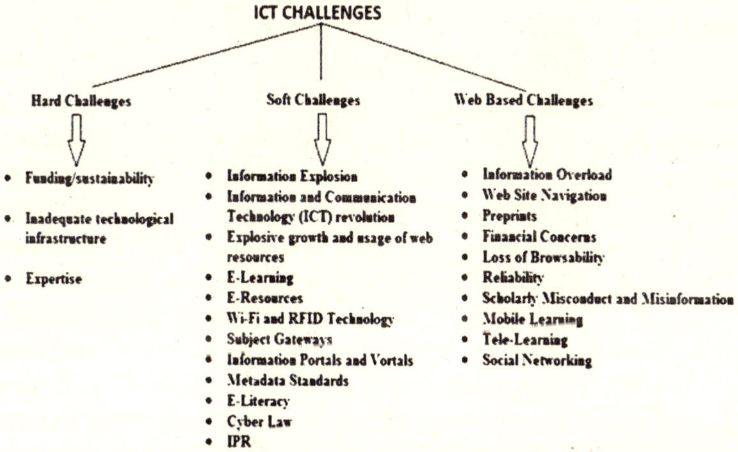

Fig. 1. ICT Challenges Faced by LIS Professionals

APPROACHES TO HARD CHALLENGES BY LIS PROFESSIONAL

LIS professionals adopt these hard challenges and implement emerging technology in its routine processes. For constructing better ICT implementation solution to hard challenges are essential. These are the hard challenges of LIS Professionals and without solving these challenges LIS Professionals do not build new technologies.

Funding/sustainability

Funding for the ICT technology is the major non-technical constraint in LIS schools. The unprecedented, phenomenal and multifaceted growth and development of the ICTs themselves pose another challenge. This rapid pace and transient nature of technological development requires sustainable funding. For centralisation of ICT services, funding had been found to be most essential factor. In absence of funding libraries & information centres may suffer development & use of technology. In order to solve funding problem, it is essential to tap out resources of funding & pursue them.

Inadequate technological infrastructure

Technological infrastructure is to support the integration of ICTs. This refers to issues such as poor or lack of national ICT policy, low internet connectivity, inadequate supply of electricity and inadequate number of PCs, etc. Internet access is now widely available, but the efficiency is poor in many libraries. The telecommunication services are the root cause of these downtimes in terms of, either, low bandwidth, technical faults or other network configuration problems. Thus there is urgent need for improved ICT policies and infrastructure in institutions of libraries.

Expertise

For the expertise issues are

(a) re-skilling lecturing staff so as to improve their ICT competency
(b) Lack of systems manager/support staff and/or ICT experts
(c) Low levels of students' epistemological access
(d) Observe the lack of ICT knowledge and skills among staff.

There is still a serious need for technical support with high level expertise in the maintenance aspects of

ICTs. The problem of technical expertise is two faceted. In the first place, there are not enough people qualifying or attaining ICT specialist skills at the speed at which the technologies are adopted.

SOFT CHALLENGES FACING KNOWLEDGE SOCIETY

Library Professionals are facing a variety of complex challenges from multiple sectors of the knowledge society. The major challenges are:

- Information Explosion
- Information and Communication Technology (ICT) revolution
- Explosive growth and usage of web resources
- E-Learning
- E-Resources
- Wi-Fi and RFID Technology
- Subject Gateways
- Information Portals and Vortals
- Metadata Standards
- E-Literacy
- Cyber Law
- IPR

Information Explosion

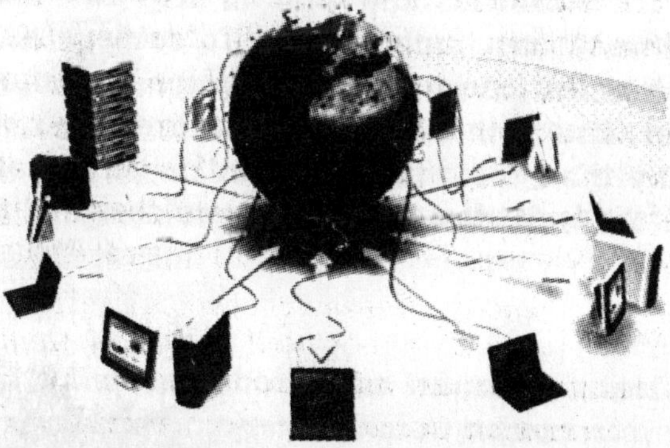

Fig. 2. Information Explosion through ICT

The information explosion is the rapid increase in the amount of published information and the effects of this abundance of data. As the amount of available data grows, the problem of managing the information becomes more difficult, which can lead to information overload.

Information and Communication Technology (ICT) revolution

Information and communication technology (ICT) has been identified as a revolutionary tool that can enhance multifaceted development of a nation. The Information and Communication Technology revolution has also brought about the increase in access to information and the sharing of research facilities. The impact of ICT has been so great in recent times that it is even affecting globalisation. All the arms of Libraries have all now been affected by the ICT revolution in an attempt to enhance the general development of the users.

Explosive growth and usage of web resources

The library faces these fundamental considerations as well as more complex challenges for delivering "quality information" and "trusted sources" and determined selection criteria to create collection resources valuable to its users. Library Professionals faces challenges of organizing information on the Internet. Librarians can provide the strategies and tools to help user make the most of web-based information. To retrieve electronic journal articles, users must navigate a vast number of web sites, and each publisher structures their web site differently than the next. This can be very challenging because the web sites are not always designed for easy navigation.

E-Learning

E-learning as an advanced system for learning through Information Communication Technologies (ICTs) is becoming an engine of innovation for users. This system also changes the library and information services, changing the role of information professionals and unwrap a new vista for effective and efficient environment for library profession. E-learning is now widely used to promote distance education in an effective way. The increasing demand of LIS professionals with the changing global scenario of job market requires facing the challenges with regard to survive in the competitive climate and to provide quality of LIS professionals is important programme.

E-Resources

E-resources are part of the "Invisible Web" which is essentially information accessible through the Internet. E-resources are not freely available to everyone on the World Wide Web and they may not appear on search engines like Google. Most E-resources subscribed by the libraries contain password-protected Web contents which are available only to staff and students via the Library portal such as e-books, e-journals and newspapers.

Wi-Fi and RFID Technology

Today, Radio Frequency Identification (RFID) technology is used for hundreds of applications in our daily life. For library aspect such as preventing theft of books, articles, searching of books misplaced, tools use as stock verification, controlling issue and return of books. Three new Wi-Fi technologies — 802.11ac, Hotspot 2.0 and Super Wi-Fi — will provide faster, seamless, more widespread and more secure connectivity.

Subject Gateways

Subject gateways are Internet- based services designed to help users locate high quality information that is available on the Internet. They are typically, data bases of detailed metadata records which describe Internet resources and offer a hyperlink to the resources. Subject Gateways offer user an alternative to the generalized approach of the commercial global automatic "vacuum cleaner" type of search engines, as infoseek; altavista etc.

Information Portals and Vortals

A portal typically has search engines and free email and chat rooms. A portal consists of web pages that act as a starting point for using the Web or web-based services. The word was first used to describe the sites of popular Internet access providers or search engines. Portal software has become a distinct class of web server software that acts as a platform for deploying portals. Some major general portals include Yahoo, Excite, Netscape, Lycos, CNET, Microsoft Network, and America Online's AOL.

A vortal is a vertical portal. An Internet site that provides a directory of links to information related to a particular industry. Vortal is a website that provides a gateway or portal to information related to a particular industry such as healthcare, insurance, automobile or food manufacturing.

Metadata Standards

Metadata is used to describe digital data using metadata standards·specific to a particular discipline. Metadata is defined as data providing information about one or more aspects of the data, such as means of creation of the data, purpose of the data, time and date of creation, creator or author of data, location on a computer network where the data was created, standards used. Using metadata electively in multi-million-volume collections poses special problems of scale. Solving these problems requires considerable application in library science.

E-Literacy

Information literacy is the ability to locate, evaluate, manage and use information from a range of sources for problem-solving, decision-making and research. Information literacy has its roots in library user education, where librarians inducted new users about the services offered by the library and taught them something about finding and evaluating information. With the rise of the internet and web technology there can be no doubting that access to information has improved.

Cyber Laws

Cyber laws are encompasses the legal issues related to use of communicative, transactional, and distributive aspects of networked information devices and technologies. Cyber laws refer to all the legal and regulatory aspects of Internet and the World Wide Web. Anything concerned with or related to, or emanating from, any legal aspects or issues concerning any activity of netizens and others, in Cyberspace comes within the ambit of cyber laws.

IPR

Intellectual property Right (IPR) is a very interesting aspect of law that is fast developing. The field of IP law is essentially the protection from theft of virtually all the intangible products of human intellect or creativity. It protects the exclusive rights of the author, inventor and researcher with a new research finding or other creator in the product of his intellectual or inventive ability.

CHALLENGES TO HARNESSING WEB-BASED INFORMATION

While accessing web-based information, research scientists face major problems including an overabundance of information, poor web site design, misinformation, and monetary concerns. These are web-based challenges discussed below.

Information Overload

E-books and e-journal articles, much scholarly information is available on other web sites and web-based databases and databanks. The lack of central organization and indexing on the web makes the information overload even more confusing because the precision of search engine results is often low (i.e. many irrelevant documents are retrieved). At the same time, no search engine can index the entire contents of the web, so searches also have poor recall with respect to all relevant information on the web.

Web Site Navigation

To retrieve electronic journal articles, users must navigate a vast number of web sites, and each publisher structures their web site differently than the next. This can be very challenging because the web sites are not always designed for easy navigation. Sometimes it is very difficult to determine what link on the crowded homepage leads to article content. Often the links to "subscribe today" are much more prominent.

Preprints

Scientific research is very competitive, and researchers must keep up with the latest developments in their field. Consequently, most of the articles read by scientists are less than one year old. In fact, researchers often want to know the results of a study before they are published. Preprints, copies of articles that have not yet been published, are sometimes available on the web.

Financial Concerns

Peer-reviewed articles are available on the web, but they are usually published in fee-based e-journals. Users access these resources via personal online subscriptions or, more commonly, institutional online subscriptions paid for by their libraries. For researchers not associated with an institution, such as retirees or independent consultants, these fees are barriers to information access. Even researchers with access to a small private library may be discouraged from requesting journal articles because of the cost involved. Some information resources are available at no charge, but they tend to be unreliable.

Loss of Brows-ability

The challenge to user is the loss of browsability of today's electronic journals. User's interest in electronic journals has increased dramatically in recent years, largely because of their convenience and the improved quality of figures that are now available in PDF format. The emphasis that today's users place on electronic journals may come with a corresponding loss of serendipitous readings. Electronic journals are not as browsable as print journals, and this may have a marked impact on the range of articles read by users, who have traditionally depended on browsing to find most of the articles they read.

Reliability

Print journals do not experience technical difficulties. However, when a publisher's server goes down, access to electronic content is temporarily lost. Compounding the problem is the fact that access to many electronic resources is rented rather than owned, so if the institution cancels a subscription, access to back files is lost. With a print journal, on the other hand, the previous volumes of the journal would still be available after a subscription was cancelled. Because of these issues, librarians and users cannot rely completely on electronic resources.

Scholarly Misconduct and Misinformation

Scholarly misconduct includes plagiarism, fabrication of results, and manipulation of data. Researchers have been known to manipulate numbers and even publish lies. In addition, many publications include incorrect bibliographic citations and other errors. It is already difficult for editors of print journals to detect scholarly misconduct and other errors, and the chance for misinformation to slip past an e-journal editor is even more likely given the faster turnaround time of online-only journals. Online journals may actually attract dishonest scholars who want to pad their resumes with quick, fabricated publications. In addition, scholars can publish results and papers on their personal web sites without peer review. Online discussion groups often contain biased information or information taken out of context. Thus, the potential for misinformation on the web is a real concern for research user.

Mobile Learning

Mobile learning tools are the result of two digital converging technologies mobile phones and computers. The use of mobile device for communication and information access to ICT applications has increased exponentially. Mobile learning tools are expected to make a significant impact on education and learning and to provide interactive content in previously unreachable and remote locations.

Tele-learning

The most common way of Tele-learning is by means of the Internet, but also be used on a smaller basis where a few local computers are linked up to a Local Area Network (LAN). Tele-learning is also be referred to as online education, e-learning, virtual learning or distributed learning. Tele-learning is very popular and easy accessible through the internet. Users are interacting with each other via text, graphics, audio and video.

Social Networking

Social network is an online service for communities of people who share an interest with one another to collaborate. A social network service consists of a representation of each user social links, and a variety of additional services. Most social network services are web-based and provide means for users to interact over the

Internet, such as e-mail and instant messaging. Online community services are sometimes considered as a social network service, though in a broader sense, social network service usually means an individual-centred service whereas online community services are group-centred. Social networking sites allow users to share ideas, activities, events, and interests within their individual networks. E.g. Facebook, Twitter, MySpace, LIS-Link etc.

PROBLEMS BEING FACED BY LIBRARY PROFESSIONALS

Information Communication Technology is advancing very rapidly. In order to keep pace with developments in ICT field library profession needs to move faster and gain competency in ICT use. Some major problems being faced by LIS professionals are as follows.

- Lack of dependable ICT infrastructure in libraries.
- Inadequate collection.
- Information gap.
- Leadership gap.
- Lack of proper reading space with necessary amenities.
- Lack of competency in the use of ICT gazettes.
- Lack of mechanism for training and retraining of library staff.
- Lack of awareness about the safe disposal of end-life ICT gazettes and peripherals.
- Lack of financial resources.
- Lack of supporting policy.
- Emphasis on teaching of traditional aspects by not giving enough scope for IT and practical aspects of library automation.
- Lack of coordination and cooperation between Librarian and Library staff.

- Inadequate human resources i.e. well equipped ICT laboratories.
- Lack of research experienced by the faculty members and librarians.

REQUIRED SKILLS FOR LIS PROFESSIONALS IN THE AGE OF KNOWLEDGE

Professional competencies needs of flexible knowledge and skills that allow the LIS professional to function in a variety of environments and to produce a continuum of value-added, customised information services that not easily duplicated by others. For upgrading above challenges and problems LIS professionals must have developed the following skills.

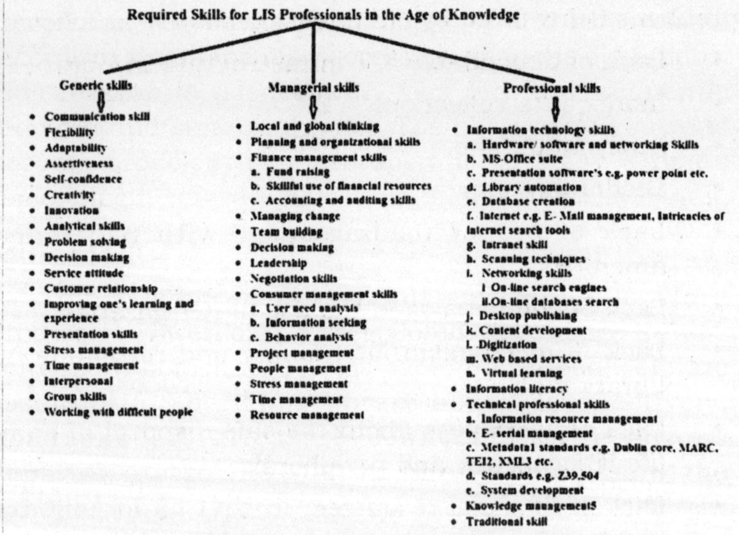

CHAPTER OUTCOME

ICT has brought many new avenues for LIS professionals to increase their own capabilities in organising and retrieving information in the 21st century. All the same it has given challenges to the profession in a different way. It should be kept in mind that professional and social acceptances of the profession depend upon the skills, attitudes and behaviours of the professionals. Due to the changes in the working environment of libraries, the LIS professionals are facing challenges day by day. Not only in the internal activities of the libraries but the demands of the user's expectations are also changing relating to information and communication technologies. The users' expectations always seem to exceed library's capacity in terms of documents, infrastructure facilities, finance, staff etc. So, the LIS professionals have to choose whether LIS professionals will manage and control the events that impact their workforce and produce stress or to allow stress to manage them.

3

Information Skills

Keywords : *Information Skills, 21st century Skills, ICT*

INTRODUCTION

Traditionally, librarianship has always been about facilitating acquisition of information. But, that presumed that librarians were the experts in the acquisition, evaluation and dissemination of information. Now that the 21st Century Skills movement is taking hold in user education, these Digital Natives will be taught "Information Literacy. "Accessing information efficiently and effectively, evaluating information critically and competently and using information accurately and creatively for the issue or problem at hand."

What learning is needed for the 21st century? These three themes – education and society, education and learning science, and education and learning tools – are all converging to form a new educational framework – one built around the acquisition of 21st century knowledge and skills. Skills such as critical thinking, communication, collaboration, and creativity will become even more important to organizations in the future. Success in today's society requires information literacy, a spirit of self-reliance, and a strong ability to collaborate, communicate effectively, and solve problems. Combining strengths in traditional learning with robust investment in modern communication infrastructures, libraries and museums are well-equipped to build the skills need in the 21st century.

21ST CENTURY SKILLS FRAMEWORK – ADAPTED FOR LIBRARIES

The need to enhance 21st century skills is a compelling national imperative. Built on a foundation of deep content mastery, these skills are the new workforce requirements for maintaining global competitiveness and ensuring each person's personal and professional success. Competencies like critical thinking, global awareness, and media literacy are no longer simply desirable—they are necessary. If 21st century skills are the new design specifications for national and individual success, our nation's libraries are well-positioned to respond to this need.

What sorts of skills are needed to support productive participation in this new 21st century workforce? The 21 century framework as the basis on which to customize this list of skills that is most relevant for libraries.

LEARNING AND INNOVATION SKILLS

- Critical Thinking and Problem Solving
- Creativity and Innovation
- Communication and Collaboration
- Visual Literacy
- Scientific and Numerical Literacy
- Cross-Disciplinary Thinking
- Basic Literacy

INFORMATION, MEDIA AND TECHNOLOGY SKILLS

- Information Literacy
- Media Literacy

- Information, Communications and Technology (ICT) Literacy

LIFE AND CAREER SKILLS

- Flexibility and Adaptability
- Initiative and Self-Direction
- Social and Cross-Cultural Skills
- Productivity and Accountability
- Leadership and Responsibility

21ST CENTURY SKILLS

- Global Awareness
- Financial, Economic, Business, and Entrepreneurial Literacy
- Civic Literacy
- Health Literacy
- Environmental Literacy

LEARNING AND INNOVATION SKILLS

Critical Thinking and Problem Solving

Reason Effectively

- Use various types of reasoning (e.g., inductive, deductive, etc.) as appropriate to the situation

Use Systems Thinking

- Analyze how parts of a whole interact with each other to produce overall outcomes in complex systems

Make Judgments and Decisions

- Effectively analyze and evaluate evidence, arguments, claims and Beliefs
- Analyze and evaluate major alternative points of view
- Synthesize and make connections between

information and arguments

- Interpret information and draw conclusions based on the best analysis
- Reflect critically on learning experiences and processes

Solve Problems

- Solve different kinds of non-familiar problems in both conventional and innovative way
- Identify and ask significant questions that clarify various points of view and lead to better solutions

Creativity and Innovation

Think Creatively

- Use a wide range of idea creation techniques (such as brainstorming)
- Create new and worthwhile ideas (both incremental and radical concepts)
- Elaborate, refine, analyze, and evaluate ideas in order to improve and maximize creative efforts
- Demonstrate imagination and curiosity

Work Creatively with Others

- Develop, implement, and communicate new ideas to others effectively
- Be open and responsive to new and diverse perspectives; incorporate group input and feedback into the work
- Demonstrate originality and inventiveness in work and understand the real world limits to adopting new ideas
- View failure as an opportunity to learn; understand that creativity and innovation is a long-term, cyclical process of small successes and frequent mistakes

Implement Innovations

- Act on creative ideas to make a tangible and useful contribution to the field in which the innovation will occur

Communication and Collaboration

Communicate Clearly

- Articulate thoughts and ideas effectively using oral, written, and field in which the innovation will occur nonverbal communication skills in a variety of forms and contexts
- Listen effectively to decipher meaning, including knowledge, values, attitudes, and intentions
- Use communication for a range of purposes (e.g., to inform, instruct, motivate, and persuade) and in diverse environments (including multi-lingual)
- Utilize multiple media and technologies, and know how to judge their effectiveness a priori as well as assess their impact

Collaborate with Others

- Demonstrate ability to work effectively and respectfully with diverse teams
- Exercise flexibility and willingness to be helpful in making necessary
- Assume shared responsibility for collaborative work, and value the individual contributions made by each team member

Visual Literacy

- Demonstrate the ability to interpret, recognize, appreciate, and Understand information presented through visible actions, objects and symbols, natural or man-made

Scientific and Numerical Literacy

- Demonstrate the ability to evaluate the quality of scientific and numerical information on the basis of its sources and the methods used to generate it
- Demonstrate the capacity to pose and evaluate scientific arguments based on evidence and to apply conclusions from such arguments appropriately
- Demonstrate ability to reason with numbers and other mathematical Concepts

Cross-Disciplinary Thinking

- Apply knowledge, attitudes, behaviours, and skills across disciplines in appropriate and effective way

Basic Literacy

- Demonstrate the ability to use language to read, write, listen, and speak

INFORMATION, MEDIA AND TECHNOLOGY SKILLS

Information Literacy

Access and Evaluate Information

- Access information efficiently (time) and effectively (sources)
- Evaluate information critically and competently

Use and Manage Information

- Use information accurately and creatively for the issue or problem at hand
- Manage the flow of information from a wide variety of sources
- Apply a fundamental understanding of the ethical/ legal issues surrounding the access and use of information

Media Literacy

Analyse Media

- Understand both how and why media messages are constructed and for what purposes
- Examine how individuals interpret messages differently, how values points of view are included or excluded, and how media can influence beliefs and behaviours
- Apply a fundamental understanding of the ethical/ legal issues surrounding the access and use of media

Create Media Products

- Understand and utilize the most appropriate media creation tools, characteristics, and conventions
- Understand and effectively utilize the most appropriate expressions and interpretations in diverse, multi-cultural environments

ICT Literacy

Apply Technology Effectively

- Use technology as a tool to research, organize, evaluate, and communicate information
- Use digital technologies (e.g., computers, PDAs, media players, GPS, etc.), communication/ networking tools, and social networks appropriately to access, manage, integrate, evaluate, and create information to successfully function in a knowledge economy
- Apply a fundamental understanding of the ethical/ legal issues surrounding the access and use of information technologies

LIFE AND CAREER SKILLS

Flexibility and Adaptability

Adapt to Change

- Adapt to varied roles, job responsibilities, schedules, and contexts
- Work effectively in a climate of ambiguity and changing priorities

Be Flexible

- Incorporate feedback effectively
- Deal positively with praise, setbacks, and criticism
- Understand, negotiate, and balance diverse views and beliefs to reach workable solutions, particularly in multi-cultural environments

Initiative and Self-Direction

Manage Goals and Time

- Set goals with tangible and intangible success criteria
- Balance tactical (short-term) and strategic (long-term) goals
- Utilize time and manage workload efficiently

Work Independently

- Monitor, define, prioritize, and complete tasks without direct oversight

Be Self-directed Learners

- Go beyond basic mastery of skills and/or curriculum to explore and expand one's own learning and opportunities to gain expertise
- Demonstrate initiative to advance skill levels towards a professional level

- Demonstrate commitment to learning as a lifelong process
- Reflect critically on past experiences in order to inform future progress

Social and Cross-Cultural Skills

Interact Effectively with Others

- Know when it is appropriate to listen and when to speak
- Conduct oneself in a respectable, professional manner

Work Effectively in Diverse Teams

- Respect cultural differences and work effectively with people from a range of social and cultural backgrounds
- Respond open-mindedly to different ideas and values
- Leverage social and cultural differences to create new ideas and increase both innovation and quality of work

Productivity and Accountability

Manage Projects

- Set and meet goals, even in the face of obstacles and competing pressures
- Prioritize, plan, and manage work to achieve the intended result

Produce Results

- Demonstrate additional attributes associated with producing high quality products including the abilities to:
  - Work positively and ethically
  - Manage time and projects effectively

- Multi-task
- Participate actively, as well as be reliable and punctual
- Present oneself professionally and with proper etiquette
- Collaborate and cooperate effectively with teams
- Respect and appreciate team diversity
- Be accountable for results

Leadership and Responsibility

Guide and Lead Others

- Use interpersonal and problem-solving skills to influence and guide others toward a goal
- Leverage strengths of others to accomplish a common goal
- Inspire others to reach their very best via example and selflessness
- Demonstrate integrity and ethical behaviour in using influence and power

Be Responsible to Others

- Act responsibly with the interests of the larger community in mind

21st CENTURY SKILLS

Global Awareness

- Use 21st century skills to understand and address global issues
- Learn from and work collaboratively with individuals representing diverse cultures, religions, and lifestyles in a spirit of mutual respect and open dialogue in personal, work, and community contexts
- Understand other nations and cultures

Financial, Economic, Business, and Entrepreneurial Literacy

- Demonstrate the ability to make appropriate personal economic choices
- Understand the role of the economy in society
- Apply entrepreneurial skills to enhance workplace productivity and career options

Civic Literacy

- Participate effectively in civic life through knowing how to stay informed and understanding governmental processes
- Exercise the rights and obligations of citizenship at local, state, national, and global levels
- Understand the local and global implications of civic decisions

Health Literacy

- Obtain, interpret, and understand basic health information and services and use such information and services in ways that enhance health
- Understand preventive physical and mental health measures, including proper diet, nutrition, exercise, risk avoidance, and stress reduction
- Use available information to make appropriate health-related decisions
- Establish and monitor personal and family health goals
- Understand national and international public health and safety issues

Environmental Literacy

- Demonstrate ecological knowledge and understanding of how natural systems work, as well as knowledge and understanding of how natural systems interface with social systems

- Demonstrate understanding of the relationship between beliefs, political systems, and environmental values of various cultures
- Demonstrate understanding of environmental issues caused as the result of human interaction with the environment, and knowledge related to alternative solutions to issues
- Demonstrate active and considered participation aimed at solving problems and resolving issues.

CHAPTER OUTCOME

Skill is an ability or proficiency in execution or performance, which is required for a person to plan and execute an action designed to achieve some goals or accomplish a particular task. A skilled person has the ability to perform any task successfully. He can face the challenges occurs in a particular profession because of the social, economic, education and technological changes. Thus in order to cope up with the ever-changing library and information science profession, the library professional must be a skilled professional. As the borderless library is fully a web-based digital library, so the library professional should be more acquainted with technological skill and so this skill should be enhanced among the working professionals. The LIS professionals have to face different kinds of tuff challenges; so there is the maximum need of the skill enhancement programmes for the library staff. Besides academic institutions, other organisations may also help in enhancing the skills of the library professionals. Along with the potential working skills, the library professionals should also have the positive attitude to work for the benefit of institutions for achieving its goals.

4

User Orientation

Key Words : *User Orientation, Traditional Services, Technological Services.*

INTRODUCTION

The Information access, storage and retrieval in a networked environment have become a great challenge for the library professionals. The development of networked information resources and services has significantly changed the methods and techniques of information access and delivery. The role of libraries has changed from 'information collection' to 'information generation'. The libraries are being designed to be more user-oriented and maximum number of services and resources are also being incorporated to meet the everlasting needs of their users. The changing paradigms in information explosion have also strengthened the co-operation among all libraries and users. Therefore user orientation is essential in all type libraries. Library Orientation is primarily concerned with ways of introducing the user to the general techniques of library usage, services available, the organisation layout and facilities of a particular library. Library orientation makes library users aware of the library and the services it offers. In traditional and technology based libraries proactive or reactive services provided through user orientation. User

Orientation works as a key for information hub. Traditional as well as technological services acts as important role for patron get satisfied.

LIBRARY ORIENTATION

According to the ***Collins Concise Dictionary***, the term "orient" means "to adjust or align (oneself or something else) according to surroundings or circumstances". The term "orientation" means "the adjustment or alignment of oneself or one's ideas to surroundings or circumstances. Also called: orientation course: a course, lecture, etc., introducing a new situation or environment"

USER ORIENTATION AND USER GUIDANCE

- Library orientation or user orientation has to do with introducing new library users to the library.
- User guidance is the actions whereby users are guided and directed towards the satisfaction of their reading or information needs.

FOCUS OF LIBRARY ORIENTATION

- Familiarize students with the library facility, resources and services.
- Acquaint students with basic database searching techniques.
- Introduce students to issues of academic integrity.

EFFECTIVENESS OF USER ORIENTATION

Libraries spending many lakhs to develop library resources and various facilities for modernization to promote the library services effectively. These facilities should be utilized in better way to enhance library usage effectively.

- Library orientation should be an integral part of the fresher's day when new comers welcoming.

- Library professional's role is very important to help the library users to pick their required information from the tons of tons information available.
- Library professionals should teach the users to basic literature searching skill and reduce their burden.
- Librarians should be proactive and teach the information skills, user of e-resources and various search engines.
- User interaction need to be conducted frequently, to the students & faculties and update them with the new additions and new innovative practices implemented in the library.
- Library services to be in pace with the needs of students, skilful librarians to be trained who can provide user orientation programs.

FRUITFUL ORIENTATION METHODS

- Brochures
- Presentation Method
- Demonstration Method
- Lecture Method
- Documentary on Library
- Help Desk at Welcoming Area
- Guided Tour
- Power Point Presentation
- Special Library Tour
- Email
- Library Website Video
- Virtual Tour

User Oriented Services

Traditional Library Services

- Reference and Research Services
- Current Awareness Service (CAS)
- Selective Dissemination of Information Service (SDI)
- Referral Service
- Special Services
- Reprographic service
- Inter Library Loan/Resource Sharing
- Bibliographic Service
- Library Alert Service
- External Membership Services
- Extended Hours of Library Services
- Industrial Institution Interacting Service
- Current Content Service
- Ask the Librarian

Technological Based Services

- Automated Library Service
- RFID Service
- Database Service
- Online Resource Sharing
- Web OPAC
- Reprints of Articles
- RSS
- Instant Messaging
- Weblog

Fig. 1. Traditional and Technology Based Services

USER ORIENTED TRADITIONAL LIBRARY SERVICES

Reference and Research Services

Reference Section is a backbone of any library. It is not the strength of library collection which makes any library big or small but it is way of providing information services. Large numbers of primary and secondary information sources are also available on the internet, which can be used in providing information to the users. Library staff supports the faculty and researchers in various ways like conducting extensive literature surveys, preparation of subject bibliographies on any given topic, reading lists, database searches, etc. Staffs also helps the students with information resources in doing their projects as part of the course work, conducting case studies, etc.

Current Awareness Service (CAS)

The Current Awareness Service provides the users with a list of latest documents and new issues of journals on specific subjects available in the library. Thus the user comes to know about the new collection of library. Library announces about the forthcoming conferences and also displays the subjects and areas of conferences. (Library Notice Board) display of photocopy copies of articles published by the scientists/staffs in various periodicals, being received in the library.

Selective Dissemination of Information Service (SDI)

Selective Dissemination of Information service is provided by Libraries for patrons. This service facilitates that the user is getting the latest information regarding our core subject by filling up the SDI form available in the library site and sending it to the library.

Referral Service

In Referral Service providing your patron with information about other institutional library resources meets the information need. At other times, you may need to refer a patron somewhere else to continue the search and get the information they want.

Reprographic service

On request, photocopy / ies of the document/s available in the library may be provided subject to copyright restrictions. The Libraries will determine the fee for this service from time to time.

Inter Library Loan/Resource Sharing

Due to increasing cost of the documents and non-availability of enough funds, libraries are unable to provide each and every material to its users. The powers of libraries have to be enhanced through resource sharing. The new concept of technological innovations such as networks will certainly bring about a tremendous change to build power to the libraries. Library has co-operative arrangements with other libraries to get documents. Faculty and researchers can avail this facility.

Bibliographic Service

Staffs are available in the library to suggest sources of information and to assist in locating the required material. The staff present at the Library main desk may be approached for any help in location of the required documents.

Library Alert Service

Library provides specific information services such as alert on upcoming day by day library progress, conferences, seminars, refresher courses, workshops details etc. to the academic community.

External Membership Services

Libraries are provided external services for external members from business/industrial and government setups as well as from the academics are granted membership under certain specified conditions.

Extended Hours of Library Services

Libraries are providing proactive services for patrons like 24 hour reading room facility, extended circulation facility etc. e.g. In VNIT, LIRC, Nagpur they provided same services out of normal working hours.

Industrial Institution Interacting Service

Libraries are provided services to various industrial patrons as per their need like Data books, Statistical year books, Almanacs, Atlases, Indian Standards, International Standards. Library also provide company profiles and annual reports of leading industries like, TELCO, TATA Steel, TISCO etc., have been organized under clipping and articles services.

Current Content Service

The Library circulates "Current Pages" of journals subscribed by other libraries like IIM's, ISI, etc., amongst the faculty members of the Institute and fulfils the articles request through procurement on resource sharing basis

Ask the Librarian

Users are encouraged to contact the Library staff via email if they have a query. Librarian will reply usually within 24 hours. If the question involves in-depth research assistance, the user is encouraged to speak to one of our library staff.

Other Activities

Library services are actively engaged in organizing Conferences, workshops, seminars & consulting activities. Library contains reports, photographs & newspaper clippings etc.

USER ORIENTED TECHNOLOGICAL BASED SERVICES

Automated Library Service

Automation makes the library system, resources, and services more attractive and interactive, helping libraries to meet their users' expectation. Libraries are one invaluable way to provide this education since each library is a hub of knowledge. This is one reason that automation is important for libraries-it is the way to effectively modernize their functions and services, which is in turn make them more efficient at responding to the needs of their users. Library automation is viewed as the total composite technologies needed to bring to the library user the necessary access and services to answer real-world information needs. The automation of library housekeeping functions, such as acquisition, cataloguing, circulation, serial control, stock verification, and article indexing using ILS, is an important parameter to evaluate library performance.

RFID Service

RFID (Radio Frequency Identification) is the latest

technology to be used in library theft detection systems. Unlike EM (Electro-Mechanical) and RF (Radio Frequency) systems, which have been used in libraries for decades, the RFID-based systems that libraries began to install in the late 1990s not only detect the unauthorized removal of library materials, but speed staff charge and discharge, simplify and speed patron self-charge and self-discharge, support electronic inventorying and shelf searching, and interface with materials handling systems. e.g. The NITs like VNIT, DNIT, Jallandar and NIT Surat have taken initiatives to implement RFID technology at their respective NITs for modernisation of library services.

Database Service

Users can search the CD-ROM databases themselves or request the librarian for a comprehensive search. The results can be verified and if necessary key word, search strategy etc can be altered till required results are obtained. Search negotiation is possible.

Technical Enquiry

Technical enquiry services includes enquiry of Databases, Directories, Handbooks, Indian Standards, International Standards, Conference and Seminar Proceedings, Reports, Yearbooks, Encyclopaedias, Science Direct databases, Online Articles, etc these type of information can be provided on demand.

Special Services

Special Library services provided for user like in IITs, NITs, IIMs, etc. Through INDEST Consortium, Repositories, NPTEL. e.g. If students not able to attend regular class room lectures he/she will can be made available on latter dates through DVDs, online lectures like NPTEL. NPTEL provides E-learning through online Web and Video courses in Engineering, Science and humanities streams. The mission of NPTEL is to enhance the quality of engineering education in the country by providing free online courseware. Therefore students can get information easily. This is more available right now VNIT provided this facility.

Online Resource Sharing

Online Resource Sharing Services offers several options for providing access to materials held in our collections or obtaining materials available from other libraries or sources. Rear book collection can be shared through online resource sharing in any form. Cloud Computing will help patrons for access online resources from anywhere, any time. Libraries can build digital library, content management system, and institutional repository, inter library loan system and integrated library system form locally managed to vendor hosted environment, of their own with the help of cloud computing technology. There are no geographical boundaries for patrons for accessing any resources. Cloud computing is to be done it vigorously for the same.

Web OPAC

Search Library Catalogue the entire Library collection including books, journals, etc. can be searched through the web enabled Online Public Access Catalogue (OPAC). Users can access the OPAC to find out the real-time availability of library materials from their own computer terminals. Faculty and students can reserve items, which are on loan. Faculty is also encouraged to send request for new acquisitions in the Library though the OPAC. Web OPAC is a web based searching platform, developed with advanced information technologies for dissemination of information to the users.

Reprints of Articles

Reprints of articles that are not available in the Library can be procured from other libraries on request. The Library has national and regional union catalogues of periodicals compiled by INSDOC for reference. Apart from this, the Library supplies articles from CD-ROM databases and forms our own library collection.

RSS

Academic libraries use the Really Simple Syndication service to inform their users of library news and developments in a way that resembles the "news service" that many libraries still have, often in collaboration with the RSS service: changes to the library's schedule, new acquisitions, library renovations, exhibitions, etc.

Instant Messaging

Library Help the patron enquiry answering service is trialling an online instant messaging service for answering enquiries. The service is aimed at library users with quick enquiries, and those users who may not be able to telephone us. Chat is available when the Library Research and Information Desk is open. Instant messaging using software such as AOL Instant Messenger (AIM), Yahoo! Messenger, MSN Messenger, and Google Talk.

Weblog

Weblogs are the subject of several papers regarding different aspects of their use by libraries and librarians and World Wide Web users. Library weblogs contribute to become known as "content creation" and the "participatory Web", since they are mainly used as a platform for delivering library news and not as an open discussion forum that library patrons use to interact with library personnel and other users. Library professional's activities can be shared or reported through weblog like LIS Link, LIS forum.

CHAPTER OUTCOME

The library can be called an information market and the library user is a consumer of information. Information is a vital resource for national development. Increasing realization of the role of information has resulted in the network of information systems to provide variety of information services and products. Today Library and Information centres are acquisition, organization and dissemination must be based on the hi-tech concept of marketing strategies to achieve more user satisfaction. It must endeavour to nurture culture of user services to enhance its image in the eyes of the users. 'Library User Orientation program' will educate or instruct the user about the library, library techniques, sources and services provided by the library in a more efficient and attractive way. User orientation programs play a vigorous role in communication between the library and its users. An ideal resource centre helps to give user friendly atmosphere with the development of new technologies. Modern Library orientation gives better image as a well organised and efficient place for patrons. Traditional services are also being provided through technology based services and can be provided through traditional services as per library infrastructure. So, both are complimentary to each other.

5

Digital Resources Management

Keywords : *Digital Resource Management, Electronic Resource Management, Knowledge, Management Skills.*

INTRODUCTION

Library patrons in today's environment expect access to electronic items as well as physical materials. In this fast digital age we all are know everything is available on one click. In fact, publishers are abandoning the traditional print model in favour of electronic formats that can be substantially less expensive for them to deliver. Physical and electronic versions of scholarly resources serve different purposes: the former may be preferred for embedded graphic objects, whereas electronic versions are easier to access, often in varying combinations of portable document format (PDF), hypertext mark-up language (HTML), MS Word, extensible mark-up language (XML), and text. To manage digital resources there are various management software's are available in the market some are free and some are chargeable.

As libraries build ever-larger collections of electronic resources, finding ways to manage them efficiently becomes a major challenge. The number of electronic journals, citation databases, and full-text aggregations held by most libraries has grown rapidly. Managing these electronic resources involves providing the library's user with convenient ways to find and access them and providing library staff with the tools to keep track of them. Libraries subscribe to electronic content in a number of different ways. Some publishers offer packages that include many electronic journals, some products may include electronic journals from many different publishers, and libraries acquire some electronic journals individually. Abstracting-and-indexing (A&I) products include citations to articles in journals from many different publishers. And since not everything is in electronic form, print resources cannot be neglected.

There are two fundamental aspects to managing electronic resources:

- Back-end Management Tools - Managing the digital resource details of back-end staff functions related to acquisition, payment, and licensing.
- Front-end Management - The front-end details of delivering the content to library users.

DIGITAL RESOURCE MANAGEMENT (DRM) / ELECTRONIC RESOURCE MANAGEMENT (ERM)

Digital or Electronic Resource management are one and the same things. Digital Resource Management is the practices and software systems used by libraries to keep track of important information about electronic information resources, especially internet-based resources such as electronic journals, databases, and electronic books. The development of DRM became necessary in the early 2000s. The idea of developing electronic resource management systems emerged in 2001-2002, growing out of research by Tim Jewell at the University of Washington. The Digital Library Federation and NISO began work in May 2002 to develop standards for DRM data. These standards were published in the

2004 as Electronic Resource Management: Report of the DLF ERM Initiative.

Presently library and information resources centres are mange e-resources as per their institutional requirements, some institutions themselves develop systems that deal with various aspects of e-resources management. There are various ways to manage e-resources like open source library software, content management software, and institutional repository software. The offering of some vendors consists of an electronic resource management system that forms an integral part of their integrated library system, whereas for others such as Ex Libris-the offering consists of a stand-alone module that works with a range of library systems and can also be packaged with other products from the same vendor. Figure1 shows some management software for digital resources.

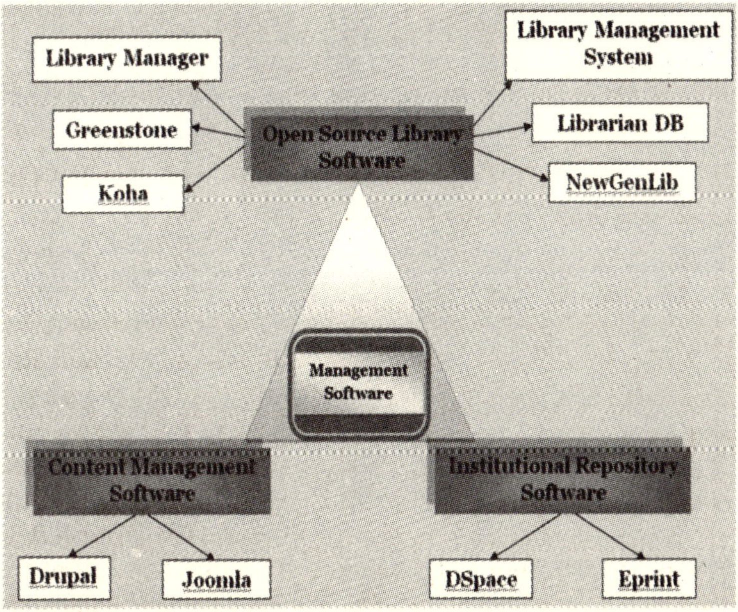

Fig. 1. Management Software for Digital Resources

NEEDS OF DRM ON PRIORITY BASIS

Digital Resource Management is the very important basic tool for librarians, but its impact also relates to end users. Digital management of e-resources serve as a starting point for user's interaction with e-resources. Such interaction would be built on the DRM system's integration with other library products, such as link to the server, Web-OPAC, institutional repositories, e-journals, e-books etc. Therefore there is no doubt that libraries need a system to manage their electronic resources. The table showing important needs for the DRM.

Table 1: Needs of DRM

Needs	Description Summary
Workflow management	Support across e-resources including resource tracking, reminders, status assignments, routing and redistribution of workflow and communication or notifications to stakeholders or patrons as necessary.
License management	Manage license details, agreements.
Statistics management	Obtain, gather and organize usage statistics. Auto uploads statistics.
Administrative Information	Store and make accessible administrative information such as institute ID or usernames and passwords.
Acquisitions Functionality	Provide acquisitions support for budget management, fund management, financial reporting, repository of cost data and invoicing.
Integration/interoperability with other systems	Interoperate across systems, to support auto feeds, data loads and auto updates.
Subscription management	Manage and maintain library subscriptions to electronic content (new, dropped, cancelled,

	transferred), vendor changes, maintenance of subscription history, and verification of continued access.
User display	Support a variety of user display options to the public including A-Z journal listing, database lists and article-level linking.
Vendor contact information	Store and provide access to vendor information including contact data and account numbers.
Support for collection evaluation	Align and report data as appropriate to support the evaluation of the collection and cost analysis.
Consolidate DRM information	Store and provide access to DRM-related data in one place.
Package management	Track titles within packages appropriate to institution
Holdings Management	Identify and maintain appropriate coverage and URLs per title; support holdings display in the catalogue.
Reporting	Provide query-based reporting on desired characteristics.
Usability	Provide clean, easy to use interface with consistent displays.

MAJOR FUNCTIONS OF DRM FOR PATRONS

All library activities are for only our precious patron. User satisfaction is the necessity of thc every library and resources centres. Our library user needs all type of collections like physical collection at local library, electronic resources, other libraries and individuals, internet resources and network files. Figure shows the major contribution for the gathering of all diffcrent type of material which is easily manages by the use of efficient digital management software.

ADVANTAGES OF DIGITAL RESOURCE MANAGEMENT

Every management systems are always beneficial to any institutions, so that hierarchy of the work flow are

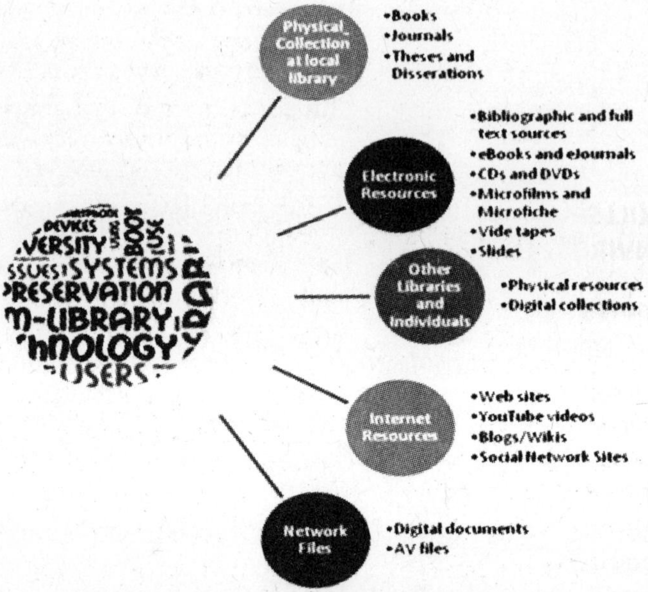

Fig. 2. Functions of ERM for Patron

maintained easily and effectively. By centralizing and assimilating all of the technical and administrative details for maintaining digital resources. DRM is the most Innovative comprehensive and flexible product of its kind. Following are the advantages of using digital or electronic resource management.

- Innovative DRM saves staff time
- Improves collection analysis
- DRM makes the most of scarce budgetary resources
- Easily accessible Web-OPAC
- DRM makes it easy for patrons to find the e-resources they need, elegantly presenting important information such as renewal dates, authentication, proxy data, and complete content descriptions
- Libraries can use Digital Resource Management as a stand-alone solution
- Libraries can enjoy the benefits of DRM's ability to

maintain resources, track licenses, and manage coverage data

- DRM is tailor-made to take advantage of Innovative Quick Start implementation program that includes hundreds of ready-to-use e-resource records

SKILLS / KNOWLEDGE REQUIRED FOR OPERATING DIGITAL ENVIRONMENT

Knowledge of Hardware

The hardware that is being acquired for digital library should be of latest configuration. The speed, storage printing, scanners, CPU, and other components accompanied with the system should be branded ones. The servers must be of reputed company. The node level machines can be configured separately as per the requirement. The library staff must have the preliminary knowledge of Hardware so that one is not befooled.

Knowledge of Software

The software market is such a vibrant that the library personnel should possess the exact information about operating, application, networking, security, technological and communication software. Even office automation, indexing, editing, Photoshop, etc software are also equally important.

Knowledge of Searching

The information searching is the most important phenomenon on network/internet. A novice needs to be trained for searching. There are different parameters like Boolean search, word proximity search, and other conditional searches need to be taught to users. The library personnel must update his/her knowledge regarding machine searching or networking searches.

Knack of Conversion

The information is available in different files but

users required in different format may be HTM, PDF or jpg any other ready to use format. Hence conversion of files to various formats must be learnt. Sometimes word file may be required for worksheet or power point, so the library staff must know this. The manoeuvring of the files for different purposes is required in digital environment. The complexity of files has increased so manoeuvrability is also demanded from the library staff. A single time entry/record and multiple times usage has become practice. This augur the competence of ICT savvy personnel and library staff cannot afford to remain aloof.

Desktop Operations

At node or PC level, one has to have internet connection, Microsoft Office, Photoshop and other related records to simultaneously access multifarious operations. The desktop is flooded with files that are frequently required and sent on the net. The library staffs have to become proficient in these operations. Many a time's remote login software like Team Viewer must be handy.

Editing Skills

Knowledge of all type of software like Word Processor, PowerPoint, Excel, CorelDraw, Image Editing software (Photoshop, Photos-cape, Photo pad), etc are essential for handling library activities effectively. Academic Libraries are connected with various departments so the staff of library must know the handling of all type of matters through these different software's. In this way the users of library get satisfied easily.

Knowledge of Modem Gadgets

Modem and other gadgets are very important for transformation of traditional to digital library. Modem, Wi-Fi, Bluetooth etc are very essential gadgets to manage the digital library. Therefore, the professional must know the operation of all type of above gadgets.

Printing Skills

As we know the library performs various kind of work with efficient delivery, there is a need of skilful personality. Multi-functioning operating printers are available in this digital age. Skilful person can easily manage documentation, distribution, production in the library. Library professional must aware about print, scan-copy and fax capabilities like in the form of one in all inclusive machines.

Copying Skills

LIS Professionals must possess effective copying skills and copying management because we created several document for our user's reference. For easy management save or print it out and take it for our patron, thus requiring the use of coping skills to adapt. Staff must aware the operation of different copying material like DVD, CDs, Pen drive etc. and also know about secondary storage device on the cloud like Google drive, android apps, Mobile apps, Cloud Space.

Knowledge of Configuration of Components

Knowledge of configuration of components is useful for establishing connectivity between node and server. Digitization needs the knowledge of all type of components hardware and software. Knowledge of configuration of components helps in customizing the product to meet the user needs. The product may consist of mechanical parts, services and software. Configuration of components is a major application area for digital implementation. LIS technocrats must have the efficient knowledge of handling all type of configuration based components.

Emerging Technology Skills

Now a day's technology enhancing so we call it as technological revolution. In this revolutionary age techno-savvy technocrats can only work efficiently and effectively.

LIS professional must develop the knowledge of new technology like cloud computing, web 2.0, data mining software and also aware about social networks like tweeter, face book, mobile apps which are fast and effective communication media.

Behavioural and Interpersonal Relationship Skills

The users of library and information science domain are now-a-days considered as valuable customers of various services made available to them. The consideration of customers is viewed as esteem opportunity for the staff of library and information unit. When this is acknowledged then, it is prerequisite that the staff or information personnel must have or possess certain skills to deal with customers. The skills could be different but for service organization behavioural skills are mandatory

Expression Skills

You may be effective knowledge of all these things but expression and presentation skills are not their so, you are not able to express your knowledge. Effective expression needs level of confidence, communication skill, voice etc.

Leadership Skills

Everyone knows the leadership more important is the idea of serving the people and the library professionals having the duty of serving the multileveled users. There is demand for library professionals having multidimensional aptitude in the areas of technical work, administrative work and also in providing user oriented services along with soft skills

Technological Service Skills

Now a day's various upcoming technological services are emerging in the LIS field. In this advanced age there is a need of technological services for efficiently and fast delivery of services for satisfied the user.

Knowledge Management Skills

Libraries are comes under social care region therefore to ensure that LIS professional must acquire, create, organize, share, use and build on the knowledge that is needed for their successful performance requires the right skills. These skills are needed by much of the workforce and organizations are now beginning to include competencies in knowledge and information management in their core competency lists. Staff must to know how to access e-books, e-journals and institutional repositories etc.

Minimum Technology Repair Skills

Library staff aware about repair of initial stage of spike buster, supply problem, Hard-disk or CPU loose connections, Printer USB port connection primary server problems, net connectivity, etc. so the library will smoothly running.

Remote Login Activities Skills

Library professionals must aware about remote login activities skills to sort out the problem regarding the library software and other things like connectivity etc. Now various remote login software's are available on line like Team Viewer, LogMeln, GoToMyPC etc.

Internet Surfing Skills

It is very important skill to find information on the internet and LIS staff must know comfortable use of any browser like Internet Explorer, Firefox etc. and know how to use key words to find images, shop online, research / find articles. In addition to that know how to use Google, Yahoo, Ask, MSN, etc. to search and research information on any type of matter. Generally in the society peoples know the fact that the LIS professional are expert for internet surfing or internet browsing. In this techno age internet browsing is the effective and efficient tool for fulfilling the requirement of patron.

Net Banking/Commercial Skills

Present scenario of library professional changes because emergence of latest technology therefore awareness about network banking, operation of credit card, e-marketing skill, e-business, etc are essential. Online procurement of Book purchase scheme may be implementing in recent days. Different operation of internet dealing must know by the library staff. In addition to the latest technology that the knowledge of tracing different type of captcha as show in diagram.

VIRTUALIZED MANAGEMENT SYSTEM

Now a day's latest technology of virtualized management system effectively work for efficient digital resource management in libraries and resource centre's. Virtualized management systems energy efficiently manages by virtualized cloud data centre's that reduces operational costs and provides required quality of library services. Utility of modern resources create growing demand for high performance computing infrastructures. This has led to the construction of large-scale computing data centre's consuming enormous amounts of digital e-resources. Large numbers of digital resources are allow to storage and manages by Virtualization technology. Virtualization technology allows one to create several virtual machines on a physical server and therefore, reduces amount of hardware in use and improves the utilization of digital resources. Among the benefits of virtualization are improved fault and performance isolation between applications sharing the same resource; the ability to relatively easy move from one physical host to another using live or off-line migration; and support for hardware and software heterogeneity.

Traditionally, an organization purchases its own computing resources and deals with maintenance and upgrade of the outdated hardware, resulting in additional expenses. The recently emerged Cloud computing paradigm leverages virtualization technology and provides the ability to provision resources on-demand on the pay-as-you-go basis. Organizations can outsource their computation needs to the Cloud, thereby eliminating the necessity to maintain own computing infrastructure. Cloud computing strongly supports NPTEL Lectures, online free as well as chargeable courses, lecture series, distance learning, audio visual conferencing etc. Virtualization plays important role for accessibility in 24×7 connectivity. Cloud computing naturally leads to energy-efficiency by providing the following characteristics:

- Economy of scale due to elimination of redundancies.
- Improved utilization of the resources.
- Scaling up and down – resource usage can be adjusted to current requirements.
- Efficient resource management by the Cloud provider.
- Providing quality of services environment

CHAPTER OUTCOME

Even in this new age of digital presence in libraries and proliferation of electronic resources in terms of production, acquisition and usage the management of e-resources remains a cumbersome process. The process involved in the management of e-resources has often overwhelmed the library personnel. In the library and resources centre activities are easily and effectively maintain by DRM. DRM fluently performing activities like trial access, selecting the specific resource from the gamut of other resources followed by acquisition of the specific resource into the library realm and then felicitating access to the users and then the follow-up of studying the usage of the resource for further continuation of those resources. In between these processes there is the cumbersome chore of going through the licensing agreements and keeping the records correct. All these processes are time consuming and involve a lot of work. These relentless arrays of work have made librarians to look for systems which can save their time and energy and provide efficient management of e-resources.

6

E-Library Management System for Content and Knowledge

Keywords : *E-Library Management System, Content Management System, Knowledge Management System.*

INTRODUCTION

In this revolutionary age accurate and punctual information management is very essential for pinpointed access and this outbreak information age having e-library management systems is the only tool for handling e-resources effectively. Successful library management is able to manage publishing, preservation, access and dissemination of information across the world energetically. E-library management help to manage electronic resources and highlighted the need for libraries to streamline their workflows and again to identify that next generation library management systems. E-library management based on knowledge (KMS) & content (CMS) management systems. Finally library management has become imperative as well as a survival issue for library and information professionals to master the e-resources. In recent past, new upcoming technologies have been substantially enabling and empowering the libraries and information centres for productive information management. E-library management system is a way used to manage the all housekeeping operations by the library. This helps to keep the record of whole transactions in the library. Delivery of effective proactive services possible through this management and it follows the user satisfaction. Management help in crucial maintenance of competitive advantages. Overall performance of librarian effectively and successfully works with the help of e-management systems. Librarian can easily manage all responsibilities of the LIS professional effectively. Revolutionizing way of an enterprise libraries and information resource centres through e-library management.

TYPES OF KNOWLEDGE

Broadly there are two types of knowledge

Tacit Knowledge

Tacit Knowledge is the information present in the idea form in the brain of human beings. It is very intangible in the sense unless it is put to use, no one can make use of this knowledge. The library possesses recorded or written form of knowledge in the form of documents and other non book material. Unless human being interacts with library or putdown his or her requirement in written form, we cannot cull out from entity. It is the form of knowledge when added with newer ideas and evolves new knowledge then only is known to others.

Explicit Knowledge

Explicit knowledge is not completely separate from tacit knowledge. Explicit knowledge is codified. It is stored in documents, databases, websites, emails, etc. It is knowledge that can be readily made available to others and transmitted or shared in the form of systematic and formal languages. Explicit knowledge comprises anything that can be codified, documented and archived. These include knowledge assets such as reports, memos, business plans, drawings, patents, trademarks, customer lists, methodologies, etc.

PILLARS OF KNOWLEDGE MANAGEMENT

- Management and Organization
- Infrastructure
- People and Culture
- Content Management Systems

ELEMENTS OF KNOWLEDGE MANAGEMENT

A complete knowledge management system must contain four elements

- Knowledge Creation and Capture
- Knowledge Sharing and Enrichment
- Information Storage and Retrieval
- Knowledge Dissemination

E-LIBRARY MANAGEMENT SYSTEM IN LIBRARY

"As Mahatma Gandhi has taught us, customers (users) are our God; we should serve them in the best possible way and without wasting their valuable time. This dictum leads us towards learning the needs of our users, learning the loop holes in our service sector, taking up feedbacks in all contact points, and to try to bridge the gap between demand and delivery."

The emergence of information in the well capable society has put forth the new challenges and responsibilities before the information centres and as we know the users are our God. Therefore to execute the demands of user or patrons an efficient e library management is the requirement of today's library and information centres. An efficient automated library system software help for manage successful e library management for handling basic housekeeping functions of a library and resource centres.

Fig. 1. E-Management System in Library

E library management system will help for manages the ordering of new upcoming products and coordinates the cataloguing activities related to e resources. Manages access tools, works with other departments to ensure software and hardware is updated to maintain correct links to licensed content, and resolves issues identified by staff and patrons. Works as a liaison with library groups and committees to evaluate and implement interface designs and changes.

CONTENT MANAGEMENT SYSTEM FOR E-LIBRARY

Content management systems (CMS) within libraries are becoming more and more important as mechanisms for content and services to be provided in the digital environment. CMS in resource centres and libraries are the discipline of collecting, organizing, categorizing and structuring content model by separating the content from the presentation and giving the content provider an easy to use interface for adding content. Libraries and information centres are allow for consistency in branding, look and feel, and the delivery of information.

Data + **Information** + **Content** + **Knowledge**

Data : Scattered, unrelated facts, writings, numbers, or symbols

Information : Selected, organized and analyzed data

Content : Pin pointed information in generalised parameter

Knowledge : Information combined with user's ability and experience that is used to solve a problem or to create new knowledge

Assembling and gathering of required data from different parts or location to form information and this information provide into generalised parameter is the management of content and this pin pointed information which usually asked by the people or being search by the people that called the content. This valuable content will form the knowledge. In this way accumulation of all such activities for e library with the use of latest upcoming new technology is the content management system for e library.

CMS for e library has discrete responsibilities for the management of all aspects of acquired electronic resources, providing support for collecting activities including the identification of potential new products and coordinating the library and information resource centres requirements. For managing resource centres and libraries selection of effective content management system is needed. CMS must possess the factors extensibility, reusability, understand ability and cost effectiveness. To overcome all problems during the management of e library system selection of appropriate CMS is the necessity and the figure shows the some popular CMS.

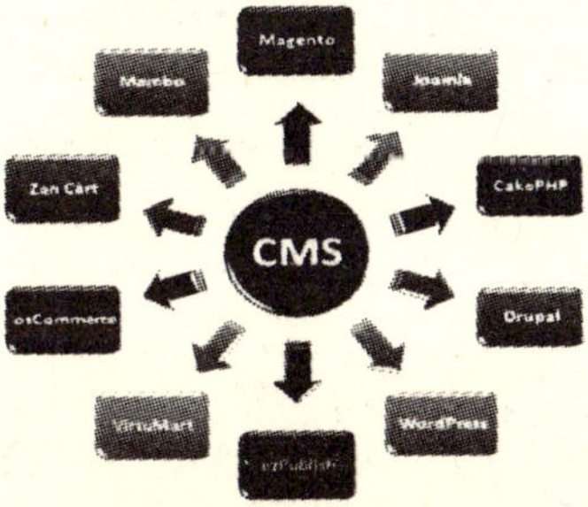

Fig. 2. Content Management Software's

E.g. If users / patron are not able to coming in the library or resource centres then library professional as per their requirement take the data from different files and then provide it to them. Again in addition to that we suppose to him for resource sharing through different location. Unearthing of this required information in the form of generalised parameter is called as content. Useful fact-findings resources provided at right time for the user / patron through networking communication which is useful for the users. It will definitely upgrade the usage of the resources in resources centres. Below figure shows content management system effectively works by proper maintenance.

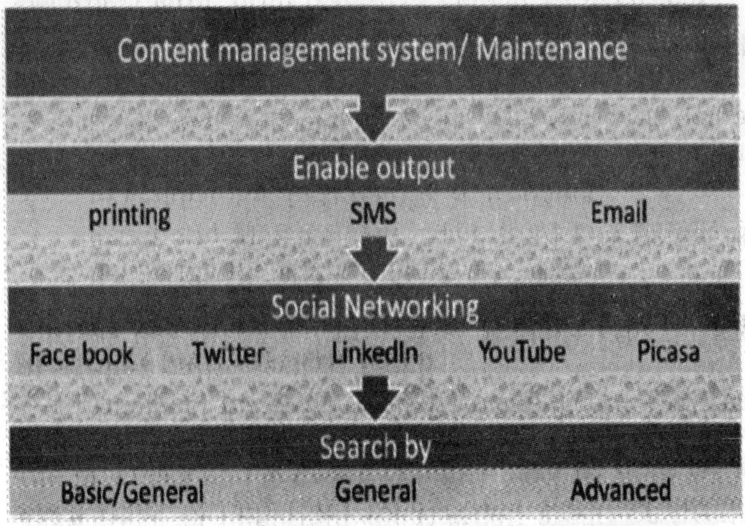

Fig. 3. Maintenance of Content Management Systems

Libraries and resource centres e-management efficiently work through providing required information in the form of generalised parameter without an interruption. Figure shows the e-content can be search by the patron / users through the different web browsers.

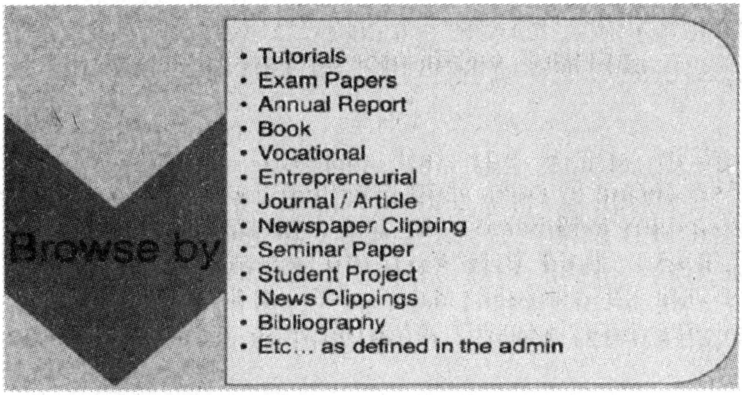

Fig. 4. Different accessible points

KNOWLEDGE MANAGEMENT SYSTEM FOR E-LIBRARY

The Information which is tested to the time frame is the knowledge. Knowledge management system serves as bridges between the user's information requirements and materials in the collection. The information knowledge management in libraries and information centres are the work of managing knowledge assets, such as knowledge products, technologies, organisations and markets and the processes that act upon these assets, such as developing knowledge, preserving knowledge, using knowledge and sharing knowledge. That means e knowledge management is the process of gathering, managing and sharing people knowledge capital throughout the libraries and resources centres.

Knowledge sharing throughout the organisation enhances existing libraries and resources centres processes, introduces more efficient and effective libraries proactive services. It is a discipline that promotes a collaborative and integrated approach to the creation, capture, libraries and information centres access and use of an enterprise's knowledge assets. Specific e knowledge management activities help focus on needs of users / patrons on acquiring, storing and utilizing knowledge for problem solving, dynamic leaning, strategic planning and decision making. It also prevents intellectual assets from decay, adds to firm intelligence and provides increased flexibility. In case of learning organisation libraries and information centres e knowledge management broadly categorized into three classes – Users, Process and Technology as shown in (Figure 5). The biggest challenge in KM is to ensure participation by the users / patron in the knowledge sharing, collaboration and re-use to achieve better results in their studies. Views of people about knowledge sharing are varied this requires changing mindsets and libraries and resources centres can take initiatives to change their mindsets and creating an atmosphere of trust. This is achieved through a combination of motivation / recognition and rewards, re-alignment of performance appraisal systems, and other measurement systems. In libraries and resources centre e knowledge management is a key to success to provide users / patron visibility.

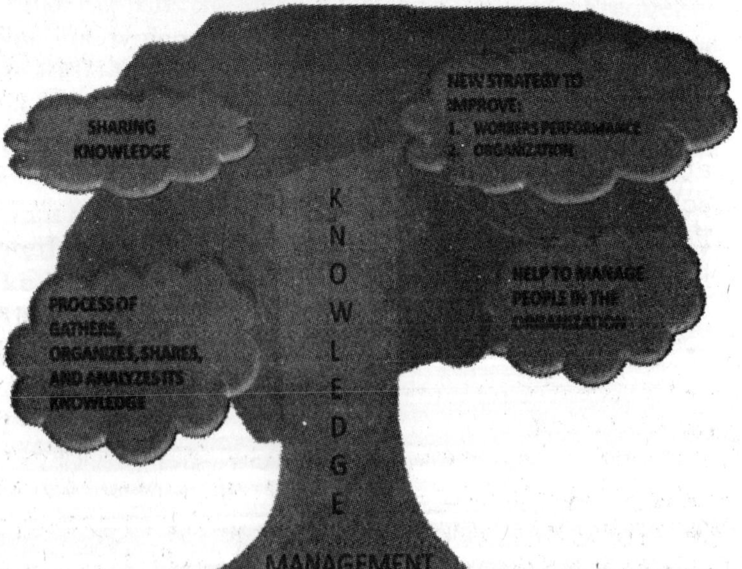

Fig. 5. Application of Knowledge Management

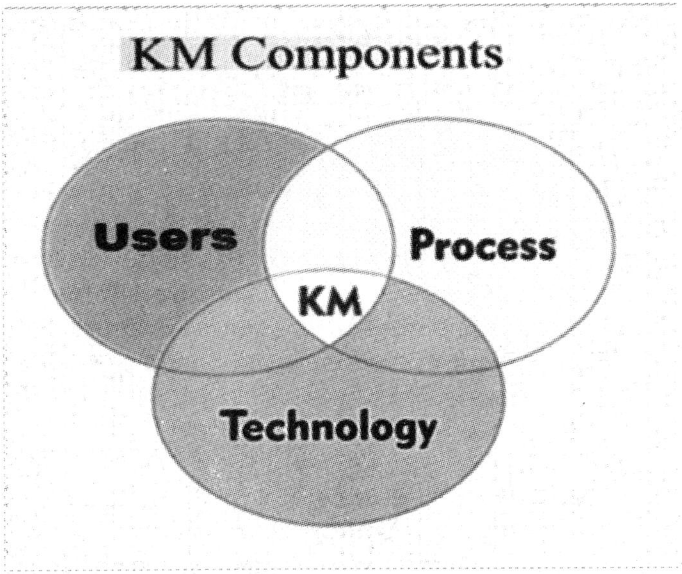

Fig. 6. Component of KM

RESPONSIBILITIES IN E-LIBRARY MANAGEMENT SYSTEMS

Manages the acquisition, processing and maintenance of electronic resources selected for libraries and resource centres for the purpose of providing scholarly and learning materials to the library users. Forges strong relationships with staff throughout the library and works to shape and improve access to electronic resources for library users.

- Manages licensing, order placement, activation, invoicing, renewal and cancellation of electronic databases and electronic books, working with over 100 major vendors of electronic library materials.
- Manages creation and maintenance of internal records in the Library integrated management system, and the Library's public information content management systems.
- Coordinates access-related problem resolution,

responding to patron reports and working with Library and vendor staff to resolve the identified issue. As appropriate, supplies patron with alternative options for access.

- Participates in the evaluation, configuration, and refinement of tools intended to provide access to collections via mechanisms of searching and browsing.
- Manages the configuration of e-resources, and maintains awareness of new and emerging capabilities of specific e-resources and opportunities for integration of e-resources with other research tools.
- Works closely with organisation and library technology units to conduct initial technical reviews regarding proxy, linking, and analyzing electronic resources to determine if software or plug-ins is needed for user access. Maintains proxy server access configurations.
- Works closely with Serial Resource Management staff to ensure that complex orders related to both print and electronic materials are properly coordinated.
- Supervises staff and works closely with other Technical Services managers to coordinate projects that exceed the capacity of the library unit.
- Provides support for license negotiation for university wide-resources, electronic books, and individual electronic journals.
- Supports large-scale contract negotiations with major international electronic resource vendors, providing data and contract analysis for Library administrators.

The Librarian and staff work closely with campus and other Library units to ensure e-resources are made widely available for use within our Fair Use rights as well as negotiated contract terms.

The Librarian is responsible for production and dissemination of statistics related to e-resource usage, running routine statistical reports, maintaining a directory of product-specific statistics links, and running ad-hoc reports as requested. Represents the library at professional conferences and meetings, and maintains professional networks and collaborative relationships with other libraries to both remain abreast of changes affecting electronic resources management and to assume an active leadership and advocacy role within the field.

CHAPTER OUTCOMES

The potential contribution of the library community is considerable but this will only be realised by adopting a much broader view of the service spectrum and by engaging more actively with KMS & CMS those responsible for delivering the better learning experience. In this digital era challenges of LIS professional increases and to overcome all these challenges effective & efficient, E-library management required. All responsibilities of librarian successfully uplift with the help of CMS & KMS.

7

Formulation and Testing of Hypothesis

Keywords : *Research, hypothesis, Formulation, testing of hypothesis, steps in testing hypothesis.*

INTRODUCTION

Social science research has a goal of further understanding a certain observable fact through a systematic, objective and comprehensive exploration of social phenomenon. Generally, any research must have a clearly stated problem that can be affirmed in terms of a hypothesis. This chapter discussion lighted the topic formulation and testing hypothesis in the research process. When research is conducted hypothesis formulation is one of the most preliminary steps. Hypothesis formulation helps in formulating research problem. Hypothesis formulation is not a necessary but an important step of research. A valid and reasonable research can be conducted without any hypothesis. Hypothesis can be one and it can be as many as possible.

Your will be expressing your hypothesis in 3 ways:

- As a one-sentence hypothesis
- As a research question

- As a title for your paper

DEFINITION

Kendra Cherry : A hypothesis is a tentative statement about the relationship between two or more variables. A hypothesis is a specific, testable prediction about what you expect to happen in your study.

Lundberg : A hypotheses is a tentative generalization the validity of which remains to be tested. In its most elementary stages the hypotheses may be any hunch, guess, imaginative idea an intuition whatsoever which becomes the basis of action or investigation.

TYPE OF RESEARCH HYPOTHESES

- Research Hypotheses
- Directional hypothesis
- Non-directional hypothesis
- Declarative hypothesis
- Logical Hypotheses
  - — Null Hypotheses
  - — Alternative Hypotheses
- Statistical Hypotheses

CHARACTERISTICS OF A WELL-FORMULATED RESEARCH HYPOTHESIS

Testable and Verifiable

Research basically tested by statistical analysis and, therefore it should be such that can be tested and analysed. After analysis the results can be obtained. Some hypothesis cannot be tested because they are too subjective and they are not suitable for research. Research needs objectivity and evidences without these two things any research is impossible to conduct. For example you may want to conduct a research on statement like "God exists" or God does not exist" but to prove the existence of God is a far different phenomenon and even you may formulate a hypothesis is but you cannot test it statistically, therefore, such hypothesis and research questions should be avoided.

Simple and Clear

The wording of the hypothesis should have to be simple and clear. Any complex ideas and wordings should be avoided. A simple hypothesis will make it easier for you to carry on throughout the research and will be easy for the reader to understand. In addition to the terminology and phrasing the hypothesis should have to be clear in your mind from every perspective. If there are any ambiguities or questions in your mind, resolve them at this stage; if they are not clear you will find it hard to conduct the study in later stages.

Relevant

The hypothesis should have to be relevant to the study that you are about to conduct. An irrelevant hypothesis will lead to an invalid research. Hypothesis is the possible answer to your research question if your presumption or your presumed answer is wrong and irrelevant your method to find its accuracy too will not result in any relevant conclusions. Check whether your hypothesis is related to the direction in which you have planned to take your research or not.

Importance of Research Hypothesis

Hypotheses are important as tools of research because they are derived from theory or lead to theory. The relationship expressed in the hypothesis tells the researcher how to conduct inquiry, what types of data need to be collected and how are the data to be analysed. For a new researcher it is important to have research hypothesis so as to be directional. Research hypothesis can be present in research and it may not be but if it is present it can have following diagrammatic benefits applicable to below example.

Let us study title of the Research study is "Study of User Oriented Library Services in NIT's in India" and have the following hypotheses statement

- The maximum user oriented services must have been implemented in the libraries of NITs in India.
- The technological based user oriented services might not have been judiciously implemented in many of the NITs.

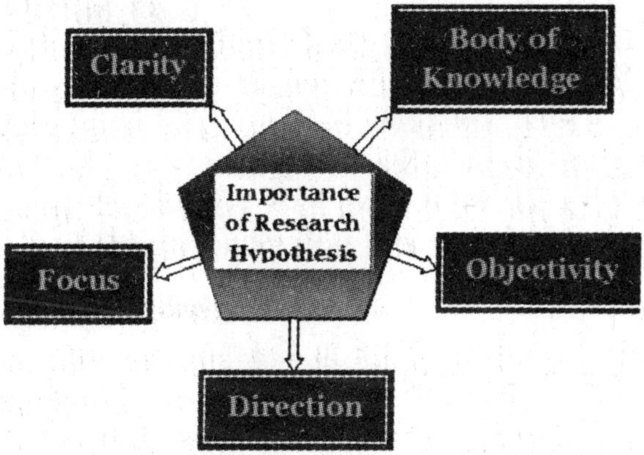

Fig. 1. Importance of Research Hypothesis

FORMULATION AND HYPOTHESES TESTING

Hypotheses are guesses or tentative generalizations, but these guesses are not merely accidents. Collection of factual information alone does not lead to successful formulation of hypotheses. Hypotheses are the products of considerable speculation and imaginative guess work. They are based partly on known facts and explanations, and partly conceptual. There are no precise rules for formulating hypotheses and deducing consequences from them that can be empirically verified.

MAJOR STEPS INVOLVED IN HYPOTHESES TESTING

The purpose of statistical inference is to draw

conclusions about a population on the basis of data obtained from a sample of that population. Hypothesis testing is the process used to evaluate the strength of evidence from the sample and provides a framework for making determinations related to the population, ie, it provides a method for understanding how reliably one can extrapolate observed findings in a sample under study to the larger population from which the sample was drawn. The investigator formulates a specific hypothesis, evaluates data from the sample, and uses these data to decide whether they support the specific hypothesis. Following are the major steps involved in the formulation and testing of hypotheses.

1. Set up type of hypotheses
2. Define the test procedure
3. Collect the data and calculate the test statistic
4. Decide whether to reject the hypotheses
5. Interpret the results in the context of the problem.

TESTING OF HYPOTHESES

When the purpose of research is to test a research hypothesis, it is termed as hypothesis-testing research. It can be of the experimental design or of the non-experimental design. Research in which the independent variable is manipulated is termed 'experimental hypothesis-testing research' and a research in which an independent variable is not manipulated is called 'non-experimental hypothesis-testing research'. Let us get acquainted with relevant terminologies used in hypothesis testing.

NULL HYPOTHESIS AND ALTERNATIVE HYPOTHESIS

In the context of statistical analysis, we often talk about null hypothesis and alternative hypothesis. If we are to compare method A with method B about its superiority and if we proceed on the assumption that both methods are equally good, then this assumption is termed as the null hypothesis. As against this, we may think that the method A is superior or the method B is inferior, we are then stating what is termed as alternative hypothesis. The null hypothesis is generally symbolized as H_0 and the alternative hypothesis as H_a. The null hypothesis and the alternative hypothesis are chosen before the sample is drawn. Generally, in hypothesis testing we proceed on the basis of null hypothesis, keeping the alternative hypothesis in view. Why so? The answer is that on the assumption that null hypothesis is true, one can assign the probabilities to different possible sample results, but this cannot be done if we proceed with the alternative hypothesis. Hence the use of null hypothesis (at times also known as statistical hypothesis) is quite frequent.

a) The level of significance

This is very important concept in the context of hypothesis testing. It is always some percentage (usually 5%) which should be chosen with great care, thought and reason. In case we take the significance level at 5 per cent, then this implies that H_0 will be rejected when the sampling result (i.e. observed evidence) has a less than 0.05 probability of occurring if H_0 is true. In other words, the 5 percent level of significance means that researcher is willing to take as much as a 5 percent risk of rejecting the null hypothesis when it (H_0) happens to be true. Thus the significance level is the maximum value of the probability of rejecting H_0 when it is true and is usually determined in advance before testing the hypothesis.

b) The criteria for rejecting

The criteria for rejecting the null hypothesis may differ. Sometimes the null hypothesis is rejected only when the quantity of the outcome is so large that the probability of its having occurred by mere chance is 1 time out of 100. We consider the probability of its having occurred by chance to be too little and we reject the chance theory of the null hypothesis and take the occurrence to be due to a genuine tendency. On other occasions, we may be bolder and reject the null hypothesis even when the quantity of the reported outcome is likely to occur by chance 5 times out of 100.Statistically the former is known as the rejection of the null hypothesis at 0.1 level of significance and the latter as the rejection at 0.5 level. It may be pointed out that if the researcher is able to reject the null hypothesis, he cannot directly uphold the declarative hypothesis. If an outcome is not held to be due to chance, it does not mean that it is due to the very cause and effect relationship asserted in the particular declarative statement. It may be due to something else which the researcher may have failed to control.

c) Decision rule or test of hypothesis

Given a hypothesis H_0 and an alternative hypothesis H_a we make a rule which is known as decision rule according to which we accept H_0 (i.e. reject H_a) or reject H_0 (ie. accept H_a). For instance, if H_0 is that a certain lot is good (there are very few defective items in it) against H_a that the lot is not good (there are too many defective items in it), then we must decide the number of items to be tested and the criterion for accepting or rejecting the hypothesis. We might test 10 times in the lot and plan our decision saying that if there are none or only 1 defective item among the 10, we will accept H_0 otherwise we will reject H_0 (or accept $H_{a)}$. This sort of basis is known as decision rule.

d) Two-tailed and One-tailed tests

In the context of hypothesis testing, these two terms are quite important and must be clearly understood. A two-tailed test rejects the null hypothesis if, say, the sample mean is significantly higher or lower than the hypothesized value of the mean of the population. Such a test is appropriate when the null hypothesis is some specified value and the alternative hypothesis is a value not equal to the specified value of the null hypothesis. In a two-tailed test, there are two rejection regions, one on each tail of the curve which can be illustrated as under:

If the significance level is 5 per cent and the two-tailed test is to be applied, the probability of the rejection area will be 0.05 (equally divided on both tails of the curve as 0.025) and that of the acceptance region will be 0.95. But there are situations when only one-tailed test is considered appropriate. A one-tailed test would be used when we are to test, say, whether the population mean is either lower than or higher than some hypothesized value. We should always remember that accepting H_0, on the basis of sample information does not constitute the proof that H_0, is true. We only mean that there is no statistical evidence to reject it. In addition to that several statistical testes are developed to test the hypothesis. There are variable tables to testify these test given in statistical books. For examples Z-test, Chi-Square test, t-test, F-test etc.

DIFFICULTIES IN FORMULATION HYPOTHESES

As already mentioned, a hypothesis is an assumption they may prove to be either correct or incorrect. It is possible to arrive at an incorrect conclusion about a hypothesis for a variety of reasons. According to Goode and Hatt, three main difficulties in formulating hypotheses are:

- Inability to phrase the hypothesis properly.
- Absence of clear theoretical framework or knowledge of theoretical framework.
- Lack of ability to utilise the theoretical framework logically.

The testing of a hypothesis becomes meaningless if any one of the aspects of your study-design, sampling procedure, method of data collection, analysis of data, statistical procedures applied or conclusions drawn is faulty or inappropriate. To avoiding the difficulties in hypotheses formulation all the steps in the research should be applying properly and carefully.

CHAPTER OUTCOME

A good hypothesis is a very useful aid to organizing the research effort. Hypotheses, though important, are not essential for a study. A perfectly valid study can be conducted without constructing a single hypothesis. Hypotheses are important for bringing clarity, specificity and focus to a research study. The greatest advantage is that they not only guide in goals of research but help in concentrating on the important aspects of the research topic by avoiding less significant issues.

A hypothesis is a speculative statement that is subjected to verification through a research study. In formulating a hypothesis it is important to ensure that it is simple, specific and conceptually clear; is able to be verified; is rooted in an existing body of knowledge; and able to be operational.

8

Library Security System

Keywords : *Radio Frequency Security System (RFID), Close Circuit Television (CCTV), 3M System.*

INTRODUCTION

Technologies always enforce the human beings in its way. Library having a big number of collection which include general books, periodicals, reference sources, compact discs, floppy disc, etc. Security system helps us to maintain our collection intact and available for users to check out. The beginning of automation of libraries and information centres in India started in middle of 1950's till 1980's. The concept of automation centre's on the use of computers for housekeeping operations and information services by individual libraries. There are certain factors responsible for the automation of the libraries. Information explosion increase User's demand, labour intensive nature of work, changing concepts of documents. There is a major threat libraries are facing that is missing materials. We have to plan a system that can reduce the missing items.

There are several methods of identification, but the most common is to store a serial number that identifies a person or object, and perhaps other information, on a microchip that is attached to an antenna. The libraries have to improve its circulation and inventory control, which helps to optimize the allocation of labour and financial resources. Self-service checkout and check-in is enjoying greater and greater acceptance at libraries around the world. Library security system provides a safe and secure facility for library resources for library patron. Nowadays most libraries are using cutting edge item level RFID technology, Video surveillance and closed-circuit television (CCTV), 3M detection system for securing their collection from theft threats.

NEED OF SECURITY SYSTEM IN LIBRARY

- No one wants to imagine that happen before with caution or not the wisdom of a collection agency and any other security problem affects the entire system. So we can protect the library's collection in safe mode.
- Our first purpose is to serve best service to the person who is using your library. By providing the materials he/her wants, we can fulfil their requirement as well as ours.
- When user come to take a particular book and it doesn't found in the library, it makes the users unsatisfied. Now the question is what happens to the missing material. Whether it is not kept in its place or might be it is stolen. So we need security system.
- In addition to printed materials, professional thief libraries and library patrons simply lose both audiovisual software and hardware.
- For these entire reasons library should have kept secured. Anti-theft detection tools can be used to safe our library's collection.

IMPLEMENTATIONS

Taking Precautions against theft

- In order to prevent theft protection should include

a good collection of security

- In devising a security system that is compatible with long-range library goals, library budget, service philosophy, staff and collection size, library managers should consider several questions

RADIO FREQUENCY SECURITY SYSTEM (RFID)

RFID is a method of remotely storing and retrieving data using devices called RFID tags. Take a close look at how RFID has the potential to seamlessly invade our daily lives. RFID enables greater automation of data collection process. This technology has been in use in libraries for book identification, for self checkout, for antitheft control, for inventory control, and for the sorting and conveying of library books and audiovisual materials. These applications can lead to significant saving in staff costs, enhance service, lower book theft and provide a constant update of media collections. The technical features of a modern RFID system are described to provide a guideline for the evaluation of different systems. RFID technology is a new promising technology that will spread in the near future to enter most of our everyday activities. It promises various benefits in management of circulation system, improved accuracy with speed, efficiency and full security of data sharing. This technology helped in activity the misplace resource with hand held scanner like structure from stack. The hours are at ease using this technology barring initial hick ups. This advance technology all routine work of library improving and it supports to staff in speed self charge and discharge, electronic inventorying, shelf searching and interface with materials handling systems.

COMPONENTS OF AN RFID SYSTEM

A Comprehensive RFID System has four Components:

- RFID Tags
- Readers or Sensors
- Antenna
- Server

RFID Tags

The heart of the system is RFID tag, which can be fixed inside a book's back cover or directly onto CDs and videos. This tag is equipped with a programmable chip on antenna. Each paper-thin tag contains an engraved antenna and a microchip with a capacity of at least 64 bits. There are three types of tags, 'read only', 'WORM' and 'read/write'. Tags are read only if the identification is encoded at the time of manufacture and not rewritable. WORM (Write Once Read Many) tags are programmed by the using organization, but without the ability to rewrite tem later. Read/write tags which are chosen by most libraries, can have information changed or added.

Readers or Sensors

RFID readers of receivers are composed of a radio frequency module, a control unit and antenna to interrogate electronic tags via radio frequency (RF) communication. The reader powers an antenna to generate an RF field. RFID exit gate sensors (readers) at exits are basically two types. One type reads the information on the tags going by and communicates that information to a server. The server, after checking the circulation database, turns on an alarm if the material is not properly checked out. Another type relies on a 'theft' byte in the tag that is turned on or off to show that the item has been charged or not, making it unnecessary to communicate with the circulation database.

Antenna

The antenna produces radio signals to activate the tag and read and write data to it. Antennas are the channels between the tag and the reader. This controls the system's data acquisitions and communication. The electromagnetic field produced by an antenna can be constantly present when multiple tags are expected continually. Antennas can be built into a doorframe to receive tag data from person's things passing through the door.

Server

The server is the heart of some comprehensive RFID systems. It is the communications gateway among the various components. It receives the information from the one or more of the readers and exchanges information with the circulation database. Its software includes the SIP/SIP2 (Session Initiation Protocol), APIs (Applications Programming Interface) NCIP (National Circulation Interchange Protocol) or SLNP necessary to interface it with the integrated library software but no library vendor has yet fully implemented NCIP approved by NISO. The server typically includes a transaction database so that reports can be produced.

ADVANTAGES OF RFID SYSTEMS

Rapid Check-Out/Check-In

The use of RFID reduces the amount of time required to perform circulation operations. The most significant time savings are attributable to the facts that information can be read from RFID tags much faster than from barcodes and that several items in a stack can be read at the same time. While initially unreliable, the anti-collision algorithm that allows an entire stack to be check-out or check-in now appears to be working well.

Simplified Patron Self Check-Out / Check-in

For patrons using self check out, there is a marked improvement because they do not have to carefully place materials within a designated template and they can check out several items at the same time.

Patron self check-in shifts that work from staff to patrons. Staffs are relieved further when readers are installed in book-drops.

High Reliability

The readers are highly reliable. RFID library systems claim an almost 100 percent detection rate using RFID tags. There is no false alarm than with older technologies once an RFID system is properly tuned. RFID systems encode the circulation status on the RFID tag. This is done by designating a bit as the "theft" (EAS) bit and turning it off at time of check-out and on at time of check-in. If the material that has not been properly check-out is taken past the exit sensors, an immediate alarm is triggered.

High-Speed Inventorying

A unique advantage of RFID systems is their ability to scan books on the shelves without tipping them out or removing them. A hand-held inventory reader can be moved rapidly across a shelf of books to read all of the unique identification information. Using wireless technology, it is possible not only to update the inventory, but also to identify items which are out of proper order.

Automated Materials Handling

Another application of RFID technology is automated materials handling. This includes conveyer and sorting systems that can move library materials and sort them by category into separate bins or onto separate carts. This significantly reduces the amount of staff time required to ready materials for re-shelving.

Long Tag Life

Finally, RFID tags last longer than barcodes because nothing comes into contact with them. Most RFID vendors claim a minimum of 100,000 transactions before a tag may need to be replaced.

DISADVANTAGES OF RFID SYSTEMS

High Cost

The major disadvantage because the technology does not require line-of sight. While the readers and gate sensors used to read the information typically cost around $ 2,000 to $ 3,000 each and the tags cost $.40 to $.75 each.

Accessibility to Compromise

It is possible to compromise an RFID system by wrapping the protected material in two to three layers of ordinary household foil to black the radio signal

Chances of Removal of Exposed Tags

RFID tags are typically affixed to the inside beck cover and are exposed for removal. This means that there would be problem when users become more familiar with the role of the tags.

Exit Gate Sensor (Reader) Problems

While the short-range readers used for circulation charge and discharge and inventorying appear to read the tags 100 percent of the time the performance of the exit gate sensors is more problematic.

User Privacy Concerns

Privacy concerns associated with item-level tagging is another significant barrier to library use of RFID tags. The problem with today's library RFID system is that the tags contain static information that can be relatively easily read by unauthorized tag readers. This allows for privacy issues described as 'tracking' and 'hot-listing'.

Reader Collision

Reader collision is signal from one reader can interface with the signal from another where coverage overlaps. One way to avoid the problem is to use a technique called time division multiple accesses.

Tag collision

Another problem readers have is reading a lot of chips in the same field. Tag clash occurs when more than one chip reflects back a signal at the same time confusing the reader.

Lack of Standard

The tags used by library RFID vendors are not compatible even when they conform to the same standards because the current standards only seek electronic compatibility between tags and readers.

ELECTROMAGNETIC SECURITY STRIPS

System used to apply 3M™ Tattle-Tape™ Security Strips to library print materials 3-5 times faster than manual application. Tattle-Tape Security Strips and 3M™ Detection Systems have been carefully designed to work effectively as an integrated system. 3M utilizes the highest quality raw materials combined with Statistical Process Control methods to control and improve manufacturing methods, yielding a specific strip that when used with the 3M™ Detection Systems results in a system which provides balance of detection and system reliability while minimizing unwanted alarms.

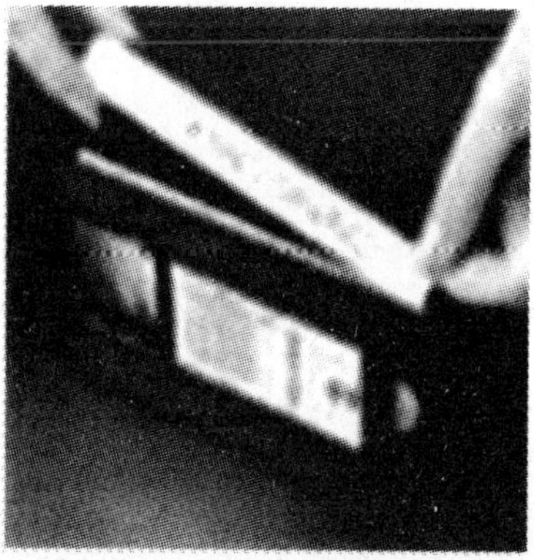

As a result of a proprietary testing method 3M can guarantee that every strip manufactured will perform to the necessary level required for detection by the 3M™ Detection Systems Substitute strips can be of unknown quality and consistency. 3M stands behind the performance of our 3M™ Detection Systems and Tattle-Tape Strips with a 100% Performance Guarantee.

Tattle-Tape

Tattle-Tape is a security system used in library books. The tape was designed in the 1970s by 3M. It consists of a magnetic metal strip embedded in a strip of thick, clear adhesive tape. This tape is usually affixed deep between the pages of a paperback book, or between the spine and binding for a hardcover book. If a person takes the book and attempts to leave the library premises, an alarm will sound as soon as the book passes through a special gate near the exit. As a result, in order to prevent this from happening, the books require desensitization by the librarian before being given to the library patron to take home. When the book is returned, it is re-sensitized.

ADVANTAGES OF 3M TATTLE TAPE

- 3M Tattle-Tape Security Strips and 3M Detection Systems have been carefully designed to work effectively as an integrated system.
- Substitute strips are of unknown quality and consistency. They perform in3M Detection Systems is also unknown, is often inconsistent and leads to performance issues and/or unwanted alarms.
- 3M utilizes the highest quality raw materials combined with Statistical Process Control methods to control and improve manufacturing methods yielding a specific strip that when used with the 3M Detection System results in a system which provides balance of detection and system reliability while

minimizing unwanted alarms.

- As a result of a proprietary testing method 3M can guarantee that every strip manufactured will perform to the necessary level required for detection by the 3M Detection System.
- It is easy to installation because there are no interconnecting parts in magnetic locks.

DISADVANTAGES OF 3M SYSTEMS

- Requires a constant power sources in order to be secured
- Can de-magnetize in the event of a power cut, disabling security
- Expensive in comparison to mechanical locks and requires additional hardware for safe operation

CLOSE CIRCUIT TELEVISION (CCTV)

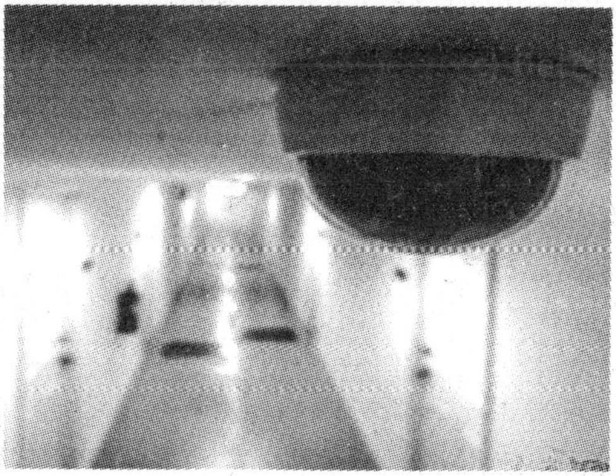

Close circuit television (CCTV) is defined as the use of video cameras to transmit video to a limited set of monitors. This type of system differs from broadcast television in that the signal is not openly transmitted, but is transmitted only to specific television monitors programmed or wired to receive a signal from those cameras. CCTV is often used for surveillance. Businesses, offices, schools, information centres and even residences may employ CCTV. The most common businesses and offices that utilize CCTV are banks, airports, casinos, military installations, schools, convenience stores, grocery stores and hospitals.

The latest development in the world of CCTV (October 2005) is in the use of wireless or USB digital still cameras that can take higher pixel resolution images of the camera scene either on a time lapse or motion detection basis. Canon's S2iS Powershot, Kodak's Easyshare One, and Nikon's P1 wireless camera are relatively low-cost digital stills cameras that can be used for CCTV purposes as well as for taking holiday photos. Images of the camera scene are captured and transferred automatically to a PC or laptop either via a USB cable, or wirelessly, and it takes only a couple of seconds for even large 1MB images to be downloaded from the camera. If the laptop or PC is accessible over the internet then images can be selected and uploaded to a remote server, and the camera window can be monitored live.

TYPES OF CCTV CAMERAS

It is very important to select the right camera for right application. Today's there are so many cameras are available in the market.

Bullet : A bullet CCTV camera is a wall-mount or ceiling-mounted unit that is typically designed for indoor use, but can also be fill some outdoor applications. The camera derives its name from its sleek, thin cylindrical shape. Many bullet cameras are also important as being waterproof. The camera is not typically designed to have pan/tilt/zoom control but instead to capture images from a fixed area. The unit is mounted pointing at a particular area.

Dome : A dome camera gets their name from the dome-shaped housing in which they sit. These housings are designed to make the cameras unobtrusive not covert or hidden. Typical applications are retail, where the camera is designed to be unobtrusive, but visible. These units serve as a dual purpose.

Covert/Desktop/Board Cameras : These tiny cameras are well suited for desktop use for Skype and other low-resolution teleconference applications.

ADVANTAGES OF CCTV CAMERA

- CCTV is the use of video cameras to transmit a signal to a specific place, on a limited set of monitors. It differs from broadcast television that the signal is not openly transmitted, though it may employ point to point (P2P), point to multipoint, or mesh wireless links.
- CCTV systems are designed to operate continuously. They can be as simplified or complicated as you wish
- Provide more security
- Easy to configure and easy to maintain
- Increase the security level in the financial area where the upper level people live
- It reduces crime

DISADVANTAGES OF CCTV CAMERA

- Invasion of privacy
- The data of the CCTV must be kept privately
- CCTV programme has to be updated frequently so as to prevent hackers to enter the system
- The quality of the video as the CCTV has to be the up to date system

CHAPTER OUTCOME

Nowadays Libraries and other government and private institutions have been plagued with security issues for a long time. But electronic security systems are very essential to smooth practicing the services and day to day activities watch. Electronic security systems are useful in all respective manners like book theft, user watching, misplacing the books, misbehaviour, etc. RFID, 3M Tattle Tape & CCTV all are having own importance, and working criteria are helpful to sort out the problems in the institution or any organization. These all security systems are useful in the library and will better ensure an effective security of library materials from theft, mutilation, or other forms of crimes.

9

Entrepreneurship and Intrapreneurship Elucidated

Keywords : *Intrapreneurship, entrepreneurial behaviour, collaboration, skills.*

INTRODUCTION

Entrepreneurs need to have a good understanding of their markets. They find out what customers want and modify their resources in line with user's requirements. Implementation of innovative and good ideas for improves quality of library services in libraries & resource centres. Entrepreneurship is the willingness to take risks and develop, organize and manage a business venture in a competitive global marketplace that is constantly evolving. Entrepreneurs are pioneers, innovators, leaders and inventors. In the present era the information needs of the users have been increased. Sometimes a library cannot afford all the information to the users. In that case library has necessary the cooperation between the other libraries and information centres for sharing the resources. The Library and information centres have sharing of resources in the parallel institutions and positive attitude.

Intrapreneurship is the act of behaving like an entrepreneur while working within a large organization. Entrepreneurship depends in Information communication technology (ICT). Without ICT, entrepreneurship cannot be possible. Entrepreneurship is an elusive concept. Entrepreneurship is difficult task to do but not an impossible. Entrepreneurship is concern economic source based on IT. Without creativity and hard work we are not suppose to be a good Entrepreneurs. In fact it is the most creative part. Entrepreneurship education is a lifelong process from child age to adult. Today's entrepreneurship gives us more opportunities including creativity, self confidence and over all greater sense in human being.

Intrapreneurship is the practice of entrepreneurship by employee within an organisation. An intrapreneurship is an individual employed by an organisation for remuneration which is based on the financial success of the unit. It is the term used to describe an integrated approach to innovation within an organisation to achieve goals. The pressure of the competition is generated from globalisation and technological changes. It is increasingly becoming used the term in a business world and other institution or Library and information centres to provide opportunities new ideas, innovate new service and products. Due to the dynamic nature of institution innovation, creativity and generate new ideas into a profitable venture operating within an institution. It is a rapid and cost effective innovation not for profitable. In the library world, opportunities for an integrated approach to innovation new ideas, knowledge and technology come from expected successes in Institution.

ENTREPRENEURSHIP AND INTRAPRENEURSHIP

Entrepreneurship and Intrapreneurship both are the willingness to take risks and develop, organize and manage a business venture in a competitive global marketplace that is constantly evolving. Development and modernization is the need of our society and the Libraries are playing important role in the development of the society in real manner. As we know the Intrapreneurship is the practice of entrepreneurship by employee within an organisation – is the practice of developing a new venture within an existing organization, to exploit a new opportunity and create economic value. Entrepreneurship and Intrapreneurship helps to risk of owning person and person employed by an organization respectively. Libraries or Resource Centres are the main core developmental element in the educational institutes and the educational institutes are creators of the future society therefore the it is very essential to develop libraries and resource centres with the new trends of entrepreneurs and intrapreneurs. Both entrepreneurs and intrapreneurs are motivated to make an impact on their work areas and deciding to become an entrepreneur by finding correct and balanced path.

Entrepreneurs and intrapreneurs must to puts the responsibilities clearly on employee shoulders. In the libraries and resources centres library professionals are accounting and providing services to patron with use of latest information technology and entrepreneurial manner.

THE CONCEPT

- A lot of people have ideas, but there are few who decide to do something about them now, Bushnell said. Not tomorrow. Not next week. But, today. The true entrepreneur is a doer, not a dreamer.
- Entrepreneurship is the willingness to take risks and develop, organize and manage a business venture in a competitive global marketplace that is constantly evolving. Entrepreneurs are pioneers, innovators, leaders and inventors.
- Intrapreneurship is the act of behaving like an

entrepreneur while working within a large organization.

- Intrapreneurship involves creating or discovering new ideas or opportunities for the purpose of creating value, where this activity involves creating a new and self-financing organisation within or under the auspices of an existing company. An intrapreneur is a person who practises intrapreneurship.

FACTORS THAT HELP COLLABORATION IN INTRAPRENEURSHIP

Need and Benefits

Participants of a collaborative effort need to convince themselves, their superiors and their staffs that more can be accomplished by working together and that greater benefit accrues to the user community by pooling resources in a formal structure. Benefits are not only economic; they are also related to the informational, educational, cultural and social needs of the clientele. For example, a individual libraries might need an integrated online system, a storage facility of library materials, to purchase an expensive microform set, or an online database. Participants see the possibility of pooling resources – intellectual, technical and financial – to make a purchase or develop a process with benefits to the user community.

Attitude

The persons included in collaboration must have constructive attitude that includes mutual respect and trust. Technical skill, knowledge and expertise are important and are generally regarded to be present in academic libraries; however, these attributes will mean little without a willingness to learn about the characteristics and culture of the other members of the collaboration: their operational techniques, traditional ways of doing things, approach to client relations, and their organisational structures.

Communication

Successful communication takes place at several levels, and in several directions. Developing the ability to understand and effective communication can help to connect with others, express what you really mean, navigate challenging situations and build better relationships at home and work place. When we do enhancing effective communication we need to manage the things like Stress, Emotional Awareness, Body Language, and Politeness etc.

Upwards in the Organisation

Any collaborative undertaking will require the support of immediate superiors, managers and the library's oversight or advisory body – board, council or committee. Because of the high profile and potential risk involved, library leadership should also seek the approval of the information officer of the organisation, the president, principal, or chancellor. A means of regular, brief and thorough communication with all of these is important. Occasional face-to-face meetings should supplement written reports at suitable intervals, depending on how rapidly the collaboration develops.

Within the Library

The people who are going to make the collaboration work, the library staff, must be brought into the discussion as early as possible. General communication might start with an all staff meeting with question period, followed up with regular divisional and departmental meetings. A newsletter reporting of developments and introducing participants is always appreciated by staff at all levels; staff members should also be encouraged to participate in this publication as well as the meetings. Continuous, meaningful communication to and from staff is a critical factor in the success of a collaboration.

Among Collaborating Partners

Regular meetings between the collaborating partners of the collaboration are very important. Strong personal links need to be established; membership on committees should have low turnover and infrequent substitutions. The communication styles among individuals and especially organisations differ and that a good communications strategy will reflect this. Depending on the size and complexity of the collaboration, a staff position for ensuring continuous communication should be considered. Communications about collaborative programs should be easily available to everyone.

With the User Community

Collaborating partners need to develop effective, formal and informal ways in which the library clientele can be informed of the advantages and benefits of the collaboration. Frequent announcements, visible evidence and concrete examples should be coordinated for release by all the partners for optimum effect.

Vision, mission, goals

The need of the collaboration is the expected results that each participant expects. These expectations form the collective vision of the collaboration. From these expectations the actions required to accomplish the vision are developed. The participants need to have the same expectations, which will lead to the development of a mission, objectives and to joint strategies. The expectations of the collaboration need to be clear to all participants expressed as both short and long-term goals.

Common goals will generate enthusiasm and a willingness to solve problems collectively.

Resources: Financial, Human and Leadership

Financial

The collaboration has an adequate and consistent source of new funding to support its programs. Participants will need to find funding from current operations. It is important that early collaborative ventures to short-term cost savings. Once the benefits of collaboration are proven, for successful projects it may be possible to secure financial support from the parent organisations.

Human

Collaborating will be expensive in the beginning, staff members will need to learn new skills and processes; additional or different equipment may be required. Library leaders need to be able to make resources available. Staff members who are willing and interested should be allowed to visit with their pears at collaborating libraries.

Leadership

Leaders initiating a collaborative venture need leadership, managerial and interpersonal skills. They also must have an easily recognised good process skill, a credible presence, and knowledge of library practices. Leaders will work collaboratively as a team. The support of this group must be visible, positive and frequent.

User Satisfaction

User satisfaction is the key element in the collaboration. User satisfaction and employee satisfaction are directly related to each other, seeing the satisfaction on user faces employees feel happy.

INTRAPRENEURSHIP TECHNOLOGICAL COLLABORATION

Collaboration is not a new idea, new opportunities for collaboration in 21st century. New technology has to reduce time and space for communication exploring new ideas in the area of collaboration. The latest technologies are used for collaboration to work together within and between organizations.

Many large organisations are developing enterprise collaborative strategies to allow their employees, users and partners to connect and interact. The effectiveness of a collaborative effort is driven by three critical factors: - Communication - Content Management - Workflow control.

Benefits of Technological Collaboration

Reduced Travel Costs

The use of collaboration technologies is undoubtedly reducing travel cost. The more accessible the technologies, greater will be the reduction in travel. The savings that can be reducing travel have more than paid for many implementations of Internet, web and video.

Team Work

Team work is the main focus point in technological collaboration. To manage and guiding the team time to time is the important to all persons involved in team. It is important for carrying out their work efficiently for smooth running of library. The people work as a team to collaborate they are basically pulling their knowledge as well as their resources and skills. The mixture collaboration and team work have to reach their goals the employees work on their own.

Actions done quickly

With a good online collaboration tool, there is no longer a need for arranging the meeting. Documents can be *uploaded* into the tool, and users can be automatically alert via email that documents have been uploaded. Users can be any comment the document and make any necessary changes and advise all team members that the document has been reviewed and is ready. This makes it much easier to keep a regular and organized work, with team members sharply contributing when necessary.

Quality Control

Quality is a customer satisfaction through product or by service. The customer in any library and information centre is the user/student/reader. Collaboration is a great way to make sure that mistakes are kept to a minimum and that good standard of quality is every part of the process. The team of collaborating will be more likely to make sure that the work is the best work as possible.

Communication

Communication is the main part of collaboration. Good communication requires understanding the people and self confidence with this one can achieve lot and solve problem.

RESOURCE SHARING IN INTRAPRENEURSHIP

Needs

The following factors create the need for resource sharing:

- An enormous growth of publication and explosion in knowledge.
- Increase in complex information demands of user and access to more library resources.
- Rising cost of published material and receding financial resources.
- To reduce unnecessary duplication of resources whatever possible.
- Increase demand for space.
- To increase the interaction and develop co-operation amongst professional.
- To bring up to date and alertness and make library resourceful of the user.

- To exchange the resources and publication for cooperation through accelerating speed of supply of information.
- Increase in the amount of information technology and fast technologies used processing, retrieving and disseminating the information changes which are powerful.

Importance

These are some important resource sharing:

- Facilitating joint preservation and archiving activities for print and digital materials.
- Collectively promoting, marketing and publicizing the library services.
- Initiating and supporting research projects of common interest.
- Sharing of information resources both traditional and digital of member libraries through network or document delivery services.
- Easy access to materials
- Enables co-operating institutions to extend limited resources
- Improve services to users
- Reduces the number of places which will need to go for services
- Improves working relationships between cooperating libraries,

TYPES OF LIBRARY RESOURCE FOR SHARING

Library and Information centre is the centre for source of information. There are various types of collection of books, journals, electronic resources and etc. Resource sharing is the integral part of modern library service. In the developed countries, no library services can be thought without sharing of resources.

With the development of science and technology and innovation of new techniques and devices, resource sharing has become easier due to the availability of databases, information network and online sharing facilities. Thus the resource sharing system helps one library to access to resources of other libraries. Used the intrapreneurship techniques sharing of library resources is a profitable opportunities to share the resources with other libraries. Some primary literature has been minimum charged for sharing to other libraries. There are various library resources for sharing. Some are explained

Books

A book is in a various collection. The sharing of resources is in a parallel institution i.e. IIT's to NIT's, in between medical colleges, science colleges, and etc. The rare books can share to other institutions in few days but the users can this book in more days they has been minimum charged for that book.

Reference Books

In the reference collection the books are valuable and rare books. Reference book or material in a library is one that may only be used in the library and not borrowed from the library. Many such books are reference works which are usually used only briefly or photocopied is allowed. Keeping them in the library assures that they will always be available for use on demand. Some reference books are valuable to permit borrowers to take them out by the authorities. If any user lost the issued reference book they will charged for that book. Most of the reference collection is used for sharing to other libraries.

Journals

Libraries can subscribe the journal package in print and online form. Most commercial journals are subscription based or allow pay per view access. Many institutions are to provide access to them for students, faculty and other persons. Access the e-journals sharing the information is very easy. E-journal is widely used and expensive journals give chance to earn by provision of access to users.

Abstracting/Indexing service

An abstracting service is a service that provide abstract of publication. An indexing service is a service that assigns descriptors and other kinds of access points to documents. The word indexing service is today mostly used for computer programs, but may also cover services providing back-of-the-book indexes, journal indexes, and related kinds of indexes. An indexing and abstracting service is a service that provides summarizing of documents and assigning of descriptors for referencing documents. It is also most useful service to sharing the information.

CD/DVD storage service

Some books are in electronic form. These materials are borrowed by the users. It is a easy way for sharing the information.

Theses/Dissertation

These materials are gifted material by the institution. UG/PG/Ph.D theses/dissertation is available in the library. It is useful to students, users, faculty and ph/d scholar. Some outside users can see these available materials by the permission of departmental head.

Newspapers / Magazines

Newspapers and magazines are available in the every library. It is also the important resource for sharing of information.

IMPORTANCE OF INTRAPRENEURSHIP TO ECONOMIC DEVELOPMENT IN LIBRARY

One of the most important concerns of managers is how to create new ideas in established organisations. Intrapreneurship or corporate entrepreneurship is considered as an important and valuable tool for institution. The term intrapreneurship has a massive marketing advantage. Allowing employees to introduce and implement new innovation within an organisation is a means of fostering economic growth. Few innovations have been derived from the most searches for innovation opportunities.

Areas of opportunity within an institution or information centre

- Unexpected occurrences
- Incongruities
- Process needs
- Industry and market changes

Additional sources of opportunities, which exist outside a company in its social and intellectual environment

- Demographic change
- Changes in perception
- New knowledge

Organisations employing intrapreneurial strategies have a competitive edge, which boosts economic development. The main reason for this is innovation. Ideas are at the heart of a business, organisations that ideas and innovation in their employees have a better chance of surviving, and thriving, in a competitive economy. The intrapreneurship technique is used in library and information centres for the development of economic growth. The Intrapreneurship has to be promoted widely as competitive factor resulting from the lifelong learning process. The importance of Intrapreneurship in Lifelong

Learning should be strengthening by further project both at the international and national level.

CHARACTERISTICS OF ENTREPRENEURSHIP IN LIBRARY

Innovation

Innovation means something new and something different to others. We have able to generate new ideas just like scientist, PHD student etc. They have thought future prosperity of new knowledge or new technology into social and economic wealth.

Interest

Interest plays very important role in entrepreneurial success. Without interest we do not achieve anything or we do not maintain your high position and our work ethics also. Your interest and performance decides that how good Entrepreneur you are!

Creativity

Without inspiration, if you can develop an idea and can do it with any helping hand, which means you are creator. All the people may not be a creative person but when they face problems arising in front of them then they will do it very easily and softly manner. This is the creativity for solve the problem and handle the position. Successful entrepreneurs face any problems and develop their business through creativity. They are (successful entrepreneurs) inspiration for other entrepreneurs.

Decision Making

For having any action one need to take a right decision and the results of that action depends on the skill of decision making. If we take good decision than the results through the action will be good and proper. Entrepreneur decision makes and decided the growth of the organisation/company.

Communication skills

It is important to have communication skills to convey your idea in a proper manner which satisfies the users. You must have the skill which can convince the customer. He should satisfy and by your explanation and behaviour.

Risk bearing

Entrepreneurship necessarily involves risk bearing since doing something new and different is always risky. Starting an entrepreneurship does not guarantee profit always. There is every possibility to incur losses also due to severe competition, change in customer performance. Skills required for entrepreneurship are as following

- Self confidence
- Flexibility
- Making the enterprise a success
- Problem solving
- Systematic planning
- Positive attitude
- Behavioural skills
- Self belief
- Optimistic

LIBRARY PRODUCT

E-resources

E-resources means electronic form of information just like internet based information, online journals, online database, electronic books and useful web link list. E-resources provide essential information in a short time to student, staff, and users. If we have detail information on any topic so we can found from E-resources.

E-Books

Published digital material is called E-Books. Conversion of the hard copy into soft copy is the digitization. Distribution of published E-Books is easier. From library point of view e-books are cost effective. Procurement of e resources are easy to manage and easy to maintain also. If we purchase e-book so we don't flow in these terms of shelving, binding, circulation, overdue notices and management of fines. Online availability, key word searching capability etc are the advantages of E-Books.

Few bigger organisations subscribe for expensive e-books which are not available to common people. But it can be done accessible to all with minimum changes along with the regular student and user of the e-books or e-materials. And common people can read them easily.

Online journals

E-journals are scholarly journals intellectual magazines that can be accessed in electronic form. The online journals have defined as a version of paper based journals. We are distributed in electronic form very easily. If you are subscribe online journals so we purchase bulk to packages and provide to access student, faculty and users. Now a day some online journals are purchase individually to original publisher. E-journal is widely used and expensive journals give chance to entrepreneurs to earn from the subscription by provision of access to users.

Photocopy products

Photocopy facility means Xeroxing facility/ Reprographic service. In this facility you are getting hard copy to hard copy. In library, photocopy facility should be available. Many users need the piece of information from the particular book, or material for furthers most student than photocopy of needful information will help them to have that information as well as rules of library to use books or material within library premises will also be followed. This again gives some earning to library.

Scanning products

This facility is not available in most of the library. Some libraries give us facility for hardcopy to soft copy and users handle easily. This is again is vital way to provide information in electronic medium. Scanning of various, documents, book and other material help users for further interest and studies, this is chargeable with minimum rate again give some earning to library.

CD/DVD right products

Library has some electronic storage which cannot be delivered but can be easily copy righted. This soft copy or copied material is available in electronic medium and can be used various times. This gives earning to the library.

Computer literacy

Today's is IT world, that's why IT education is very important to all of us without computer knowledge we don't stand to compete the world. Computer literacy means ability to operate computer and know about the how to use and work. Computer literacy is important skill for develop country. If you work as an employee in company so you must know the computer and all the system and also software ability. Today all the schools provided computer education including rural area. Now a day's most of the competitive exams online based it means computer based. So we can arrange computer literacy program for weekly or monthly and earn some charges. SITD (Society for Information Technology Development) is best example for all.

Eg. If we can arrange weekly computer class in our library so you can get improve your knowledge, develop your teaching skill and mentally satisfaction for social work.

CD/DVD Collection for Guest lecturers

This is the collection of guest lecturer in CD/DVD form. Anyone how are not attend the class so they are seen this CD in library. And users pay the minimum charges.

Eg. NPTEL-National programming technology enhanced learning. This is the collection of audio visual forms. That is collection of IIT Lecturers.

Book Bank scheme

Book-bank facility is makes availability of books for limited period on fixed deposit. The entries of issuing and receiving should be maintained through electronic way. After receiving the books for particular period a minimum amount should be kept within them self and remaining return to user. This gives earning to the library.

Library establishment

It is a best example of entrepreneurship in library. Library establishment is a type of business. This is done by only experienced persons. When you complete this work then they will give charges according to books quantity.

Library establishment work is difficult because all the things very are clear and minutely. This work just like, pass the library fund , place the book purchase, order to publisher/vender, receiving the books according to order copy, start the process all the books, feed the data in library software and last step is arrange the book for shelve.

Question bank in PDF form

The library collects the question bank in previous exams. And they give the student in PDF form. Question bank in PDF format is a good idea to the user. This should be accessible to all the users with minimum charges. This will help students to have all the previous exam question and library can earn with the minimum charges.

Abstracting and Full text products

This is the collection of abstract and full text database. When we purchase this product then we can use it in our library. And provide the users at minimum revenue.

Eg. Proquest is database for abstract and full text in electronic/ online. Proquest is just like encyclopaedia for abstract in theses, dissertations, library of congress database etc. It is very needful collection for all. Almost every conceivable subject is covered in the (PQDT) database. They are publishing more than 60,000 dissertations and theses each year. Unlimited downloads with unlimited simultaneous access of the complete content including the full text. That is package form.

BENEFITS OF THE LIBRARY PRODUCTS

Every time library is beneficial for users. This is best option for self study and collects the information more and more in various forms. There is an absolute change today than yesterday. Now we are collecting the information in many ways and we have variety of the information. And change in the product is giving information. Now, the users are very happy because library staff is providing special and specific information. This is important to users.

- E-resources do not need any transportation charges. It does not required paper and hence it saves trees therefore helps in preserving environment.
- You can also change the colour contrast, the lighting, and in some cases have the E-Resources read aloud to you. E-Resources can be read using an e-book reader or using an E-Resources application on computers, mobile phones or tablets.
- We can search information easily without turning pages one by one.

- People are more habitual of computer and internet in their life day to day. So it's very easy for them to read e-resources.
- We can store e-resources safely and carry any information very easily more than books.
- If anyone wish to read the material as a book then we can print the material and It's flexible to print how much you want to read and there is no need to carry whole book and hence easy to handle and inexpensive to.
- When you need certain information, you can get it immediately, by downloading product.
- E-resources can be very attractive for children and also adult because they are in audio-video and animations forms. Author is tried to convey the message.
- When the users use this product special benefit is they save the time. Now, many people say to that they have no time. Our life is very fast and that's why people have no time. By using this product, users can save the time. As we know the time is as important as money. This law is very important and biggest challenge to the librarian save the time of researchers and library staff. Librarian should always bear in mind that the time of users is very important and precious.
- Using this product, user will save the time and library earn for organisation.
- We have provided consolidate information for the student, staff and user.

INNOVATIVE ENTREPRENEURSHIP AND INTRAPRENEURSHIP IN LIBRARIES

Library entrepreneurs need to search purposefully for the sources of innovation, the changes and their symptoms that indicate opportunities for successful innovation. And they need to know and to apply the principles of successful innovation. Library Professional entrepreneurs must possess the following main and important skills for library and resources centres venture.

Ability to Plan

Entrepreneurs must be able to develop business plans to meet goals in a variety of areas, including finance, marketing, production, sales and personnel.

Communication Skills: Entrepreneurs should be able to explain, discuss, sell and market their goods or service.

Marketing Skills

Good marketing skills, which result in people wanting to buy goods or services, are critical to entrepreneurial success.

Interpersonal Skills

The ability to establish and maintain positive relationships with customers and clients, employees, financial lenders, investors, lawyers and accountants, among others, is crucial to the success of the entrepreneur's business venture.

Basic Management Skills

Even if entrepreneurs hire others to deal with the day-to-day tasks of the business, entrepreneurs need to know whether their company has the correct resources.

Leadership Skills

The ability to develop a vision for the company and to inspire employees to pursue it is imperative for success.

CHAPTER OUTCOME

Library and information professionals earned their

success through entrepreneurship and intrapreneruship as the position of their working conditions. The applications of ICT to libraries with entrepreneur's angle will be most welcoming proposition. The IT facilitates the routine in library. It offers error free transactions thus satisfying the users in general and library staff in particular. A few of the products and services based on ICT applications can be charged provided it is decided by the authorities. The product assures ready to use phenomenon and convenience in handling. The precise product can be obtained with the help of experienced library staff. The benefits or posterior use of these products are unquestionable. The products can be primary sources or secondary, print or online are very promising.

Successful collaboration requires the team work and team members understand the organisation and positive response from staff members is necessary for organisational change. Resource sharing is the main element in the library and information centres. It helps to get rare documents available at other libraries. Using the information technology processing, retrieving, and disseminating the information is very fast and changes which are powerful. Every library should be developed in the form of digital library. The challenges are to choose the right technology and will to implement it. Intrapreneruship is create a new ideas, innovate to new technologies used in a library and these technologies used for sharing of information.

The business culture in library will take some years to get established. But thinking has commenced on these lines. A few of the services or products of library are being charged but nominal. To use these products and services commercially for earning need brain storming sessions. The ball has started rolling in the direction of entrepreneurship. It will gain momentum with years to come. Entrepreneurship and intrapreneruship are effectively enforcing the library activity to modernise the services and to overcome the problems, LIS professionals must possesses the entrepreneurial skill which are very innovative and for getting the successful results.

10

Consortium Sensitization

Keywords : *ICT (Information Communication Technology), Library Consortia, Cooperation, Resource Sharing*

INTRODUCTION

In the present era of information technology, the information needs of the users have been increased. Sometimes a library cannot afford to satisfy all the information needs of users. The library is a global virtual library and is also called as network of electronic library. Information communication technology has improved the way of information is generated, created, assembled, combined, stored, retrieved, used and communicated. ICT is now enabling a level of cooperation that is much broader and deeper than even before. This has necessitated the need for effective linkages and cooperation between libraries and information centres for sharing of available resources and information through networking. The consortia for library can be considered as a major step towards library cooperation in sharing electronic resources. The consortium should take lead role in the development of a national strategy for information provision for research in higher education. The concept of library cooperation and resource sharing is as old as the libraries. At present, the more accepted system of resource sharing is called library consortia. The consortia can play important role in acquiring licenses and sharing electronic resources by acting as a platform for promoting activities and programmes and in the area of electronic resource sharing. Consortia approach is one of the many ways of maintaining cooperation and coordination among the libraries and in fact, it has emerged as the 'state of the art' in library cooperation in recent years. Library and information centres have sharing of resources in the parallel institutions and positive attitude.

The idea of consortium is not new. There were instances of several libraries coming together voluntarily for the mutual benefit of respective users just like cooperatives, it was the earliest stage of library cooperation. In the second stage, computerized networks come into trend for sharing of resources. Till this period, the library resources were mainly in traditional printed format. The networks created their bibliographical databases. The users of the participating libraries could get the required documents from other libraries through document delivery services. With the advent of e-resources, the concept of consortia has been introduced mainly for acquisition of e-journals. As the resources that are procured today through the consortium are mainly e-resources, it has become possible for the users to access and download the required materials without even going through the elaborate process of interlibrary lending. Though library consortia have been created with narrow purpose, these can be turned into efficient instruments for sharing all types of library resource.

CONCEPT OF LIBRARY CONSORTIA

Library consortia concepts came first time from academic libraries formed consortia for the primary purpose of sharing printed materials. Presently, academic libraries are having consortia to provide common access to electronic resources across the Internet, and they are forming these consortia on a state wide basis Library. This task is very difficult for a single library. However, by forming a consortium among libraries, it becomes possible to purchase information in reasonable and stabilized cost.

Historically, the common platform of library co-operation was the sharing the physical form of document through Inter Library loan, document delivery services, union catalogue, storage facilities, collection development and human resources at local, national and regional level. Another form of co-operation was based on inter library loan services where cooperating libraries agree to share their resources among the member libraries. This form of cooperation enabled libraries to borrow books, periodicals and other reading materials.

FEATURES OF LIBRARY CONSORTIA

These are the features of library consortia following below

- It provides each organizations and institutions with the capacity to share their resources without sacrificing the individuality of each member library
- The collections of the Consortium libraries enable each member library to support scholarly research for its users.
- Cooperative research and development in application of information communication and technology enhances service and realizes cost effectiveness.
- It is the cooperative task to reduce the cost of purchase consortia. As a result, end users can take benefits of more resources than would be available through one library.
- To advance library services are provided with an emphasis on access to new E- resources including databases and services offered through the internet.

- To expanding inter library searching at less cost is possible.
- Uncertainties in legal issues are handled with more confidence.

NEED OF CONSORTIUM

Access to resources is more important than the collection building. The consortium facilitates the libraries to get the benefit of wider access to electronic resources at low cost and at the best terms of licences. A consortium, with the collective strength of resources of various institutions available to it, is in a better position to resolve the problems of managing, organising and archiving the electronic resources.

Some of the major the need for consortium are

- With the exponential growth of knowledge, e-journal has made it more and more impossible for the individual library to purchase all the relevant information
- Academic and research users can now hope to have access to their learned journal articles in electronic form
- Better sharing of existing resources and jointly acquiring new resources at greater saving
- Recent trends and development in the area of ICT
- Reduction in the staff strength and cost savings for library budget would be useful

THE MAJOR ISSUES OF CONSORTIA APPROACH ARE

- Sources of funding to meet the subscription cost
- Identifying and negotiating the potential publishers/ vendors or aggregators to provide access under consortia purchase
- Legal issues involved in contracts and usage of material within the consortia

- Identification of libraries interested in participating and agreeing on common terms and conditions
- Identifying the necessary infrastructure for electronic access to resources
- Documentation and training to staff

ADVANTAGES OF CONSORTIA

Some of the important advantages of the library consortium are as following below

- A comprehensive collection is possible
- Avoid duplication of core collection specially for core journals
- Easy access to resource sharing on Internet by developing common resources database
- Consortia-based subscription to electronic resources provides access to wider number of electronic resources at substantially lower cost
- Reduce cost of information and time saving
- Improved resource sharing

CONSORTIA AT INTERNATIONAL AND NATIONAL LEVEL

International Level

Some of important consortia are

- Academic Libraries of Indiana
- Arizona University Libraries Consortium
- Boston Libraries Consortium
- Consortium of Academic Libraries in Manchester
- Co-operative action by Victorian academic libraries limited
- Missouri research consortia of libraries
- Ontario Library Consortium
- Pennsylvania academic library connection Initiative

National Level

Libraries in India are also facing problems such as increasing demands and high expectations from users, budget cuts, high costs of library materials especially electronic journals, and a rise in the amount of information resources. It is impossible for a single library to provide access to all materials to meet their user's needs. Library consortia have been initiated in India in order to overcome these problems, and efforts to form library consortia are still in their beginning. Some important consortia are

- INDEST consortium (Indian National Digital Library in Science and Technology)
- CSIR consortium (Council of Scientific and Industrial Research)
- UGC: INFONET (University Grant Commission-Information Network)
- FORSA consortium (Forum for Resource sharing in Astronomy and Astrophysics)
- HELINET (Health Sciences Library & Information Network)
- ICICI Knowledge Park (Industrial Credit and Investment Corporation of India)
- IIM's Library Consortia (The Indian Institute of Management)
- UGC-DAE Consortium for Scientific Research

Beside all these consortia one of the important consortia is INDEST for engineering students.

INDEST CONSORTIUM

Indian National Digital Library in Science and Technology is a consortium set up and funded by the Ministry of Human Resource Development (MHRD) in India. The ministry provides funds required for providing differential access to electronic resources subscribed to the members. It has its headquarters at IIT Delhi. The Ministry provides funds required for subscription to electronic resources for 62 centrally-funded Government institutions including IITs, IISc Bangalore, NITs, ISM, IIITs, IIMs, NITTTR's and few other institutions that are considered as core members of the Consortium. The benefit of consortia based subscription to electronic resources is not confined to its core members but is also extended to all educational institutions under its open-ended proposition. The membership is open to all other educational institutions under its self supported category. The access to the resources is being provided directly from the publisher's websites.

The INDEST-AICTE Consortium is the most energetic action taken so far in the country. It is the biggest Consortium in terms of number of member institutions in Asia. The Consortium attracts the best desirable price and terms of agreement from the publishers on the basis of strength of its present and expected member institutions.

Objectives

The INDEST-AICTE Consortium has the following objectives

- To extend the benefit of consortia-based subscription beyond the core members to other engineering and technological institutions
- To subscribe electronic resources for the members of the Consortium at highly discounted rates of subscription and at the best terms and conditions
- To impart training to the users and librarians in the member institutions on subscribed electronic resources with an aim to optimise the usage of subscribed electronic resources
- To increase scientific productivity of member institutions in terms of quality and quantity of publications

- To help new engineering institutes and colleges to make the right choice of e- resources
- To find more pathway of co-operation and interaction with other consortia

Membership

The INDEST-AICTE Consortium has the following three categories of Members

- Core Member Institutions
- Members with Financial Support from the AICTE
- Self-supported Engineering Colleges and Institutions

Services and Activities

The INDEST-AICTE is several services and activities that the Consortium performs to achieve optimal utilization of electronic resources subscribed by it. Some of the important services and activities of the Consortium are

E-Resource Purchasing

The INDEST-AICTE consortium is with a focus on providing wide access to electronic resources to support education and research in core subject areas of members. The Consortium is responsible for carrying out negotiations with publishers and aggregators of electronic resources for getting better deals. It also negotiates terms of licenses and agreements with the publishers.

Resource Sharing

A library is not possible to acquire all the documents demanded by the users due to either budgetary constraints or non availability of the documents for purchase. The sharing of information among the libraries is very important. If the documents requested by the user are available in other libraries, then request for loaning that document for some specified period can be made.

As INDEST-AICTE Consortium does not subscribe to all resources for all its members, the document delivery and inter-library loan is, crucial to the success of the Consortium. The service facilitates generation of automated inter-library loan requests directly by a user to one of the IITs, IISc and IIMs. While all requests for articles subscribed by the INDEST-AICTE Consortium are routed to IIT Delhi (Consortium Headquarters), requests for e-resources subscribed by individual IITs, IISc and IIMs are routed to the respective institution(s).

Training of Users and Library Staff

Training to the users and librarians in the member institutions on subscribed electronic resources with an aim to optimise the usage of subscribed electronic resources; The INDEST-AICTE Consortium holds extensive training programmes for the benefit of Library staff members from various institutions. All IITs, IISc, IIMs and NITs have also been assigned the task to conduct training programmes to users and library staffs.

E Resources INDEST-AICTE Consortium

Full Text Resources

- ABI/Inform Complete
- ACM Digital Library
- Annual Reviews (Through NME-ICT Project)
- ASCE Journals
- ASME Journals (+ A M R)
- ASTM Standards & Digital Library
- Capitaline
- CRIS INFAC Ind. Information
- EBSCO Databases
- Elsevier's Science Direct
- Emerald E-books (Business Mgmt & Economics Collection)

- Emerald Full-text
- Emerald Management Xtra
- Euromonitor (GMID)
- IEC Standards
- IEEE / IEE Electronic Library Online (IEL)
- INFORMS Pub Suite
- INSIGHT
- JSTOR (Through NME-ICT Project)
- McGraw-Hill's AccessEngineering (FKA DEL)
- Nature (27 titles Through NME-ICT Project)
- Optical Society of America(Optics Infobase)
- Springer Link
- Taylor & Francis (Through NME-ICT Project)

BIBLIOGRAPHIC RESOURCES

- INSPEC
- MathSciNet
- SciFinder Scholar
- SCOPUS Database
- Web of Science

CHAPTER OUTCOME

A consortium is an essential tool that increase collection and support cooperative technological development for libraries. Library consortia are considered as a merger between libraries, publishers and vendors.

Libraries in developing countries need to action with the problems that prevent a successful consortia effort for sharing electronic resources to other libraries. Consortia are better sharing of actual resources and jointly acquiring new resources at greater savings. Negotiate are always prevailing in consortia business.

11

Quality Management in VNIT Library and Information Resource Centre

Keywords : *Quality Management, Quality indicator, Library Services, LIRC, VNIT.*

INTRODUCTION

The term quality, according to various glossaries, means one of the following: fitness for purpose, fitness for use, conformity to requirements and absence of defects. The standard ISO 11620 defines quality of libraries as "totality of features and characteristics of a resources or services that bear on the library's ability to satisfy stated or implied needs". Over recent years one can observe an increasing interest and different approaches to quality in libraries and information services, especially in a management area. A common factor of several concepts and approaches to quality is the focus on user expectations and needs.

In the TQM context "The Quality of service is defined by the user's perception of both the quality of the resources and the service providing it" The quality of academic libraries is connected with services, product as well as staff, facilities, space. Academic libraries should fulfil their own strategic plans and also goals of the higher education system. They "like other service institutions have to show that they are using given resources for the right purpose and in the best way, that they are providing high quality services". In other words, they are being asked to demonstrate their worth, to justify their expenditure, and to adopt new practices that involve substantially improved and extended services to users.

WHAT IS QUALITY?

Quality is a vague concept, used in relation to various everyday things. But is it possible to say exactly what is meant when speaking about the quality of the Library and Information Science? Although quality is not an easy concept, the meaning of it can be agreed upon and there is an accepted way of describing What Quality is. IFLA has published Indicator of the quality for Academic Libraries they are:

- relevance in collection development
- degree of satisfaction
- hours open
- delay between order and availability on shelves
- percentage of requested itcms obtained

Academic Libraries all over the world display great variation in organizational, Financial and technical condition Quality is a relative term related to all these factors.

Why is Quality so Important?

For years, Quality has been important for industry. Quality is now seen also as one of the important means for public organizations, which are not competitive economically, but can compete with the quality of their services and products.

Quality aims at satisfying the users but Quality should also be improved in order to find key success factors, to ensure the better availability of resources etc.

Quality is like a two-sided coin

One side of the coin is the user with his or her expectations and the other side is the work done in the libraries for producing services and products of high quality. This work done is important, because it entails the promise for Quality. But are the expectations of the users as regards Quality and the promise given by the qualitative work process always met?

Work processes in managing information

The libraries always have taken care of the quality of the very central tasks. The Library and Information services use cataloguing guidelines to make uniform catalogues of book and journals and other material acquired. This had assured even quality of the catalogues. The catalogues are kept in order according to same rules. The shelf order is based on the classification system that each library users. So quality is controlled and assured by the guidelines prepared for these work processes. But this does not mean that the Total Quality of same Library and Information Services is managed well.

How to assure the Quality of all Functions?

Some system is needed for assuring quality. The system must cover all important functions and work processes of the organization. ISO has produced several standards for the development of the Quality System, meant to describe how Total Quality is managed. Quality Management is comprised of three steps:

1) Planning (What we want to do)
2) Controlled (What we are already doing)
3) Improvement (How to improve what we are doing)

QUALITY MANAGEMENT IN VNIT

Quality Management is also an important strategic tool for the Visvesvaraya National Institute of Technology. The library committee made a decision concerning the quality system at the VNIT, prepared the quality policy for the Institute and decided on the tool to be use in building the quality system of the VNIT. The application of the quality standards at all levels of the Institute has been under way of several years.

1. Institutional Level

Visvesvaraya National Institute of Technology (VNIT) is one of the 20 National Institutes of Technology Engineering Colleges established by the Indian Government. It currently imparts engineering and scientific education in 8 undergraduate, 11 graduate programmes and numerous other research programmes. Undergraduate programs lead to B.Tech. Degrees, while graduate students and postgraduate students earn M.Tech. and Ph.D. degrees respectively. VNIT also has an architecture school awarding the B.Arch. and M.Arch. Degrees. VNIT has also been given the added responsibility of mentoring NIT Mizoram for the academic year 2010-2011.

VNIT has been conferred with autonomy in financial and administrative matters to help achieve rapid development. An autonomous Board of Governors having representatives of the Central Government, State Government, AICTE, UGC, teaching faculty, industrialists and technologists manages the institute.

2. Departmental Level

The Institute has 14 departments. All the departments are recognized as Quality Improvement Program Centers by the Government of India. The laboratories in various departments have extensive research and testing facilities. The VLSI Design Lab was set up in 1997 under SMDP (Special Manpower Development Program) in the field of VLSI.

Departments

- Applied Chemistry Department
- Applied Mathematics Department
- Applied Mechanics Department
- Applied Physics Department
- Architecture & Planning Department
- Chemical Engineering Department
- Civil Engineering Department
- Computer Science and Engineering Department
- Electrical Engineering Department
- Electronics Engineering Department
- Humanities Department
- Mechanical Engineering Department
- Metallurgical and Materials Engineering Department
- Mining Engineering Department

A new department of Aeronautics Engineering is likely to be added in a few years.

Courses

These above departments of VNIT are organizing following courses. The institute offers 8 Undergraduate programmes in Engineering of four year duration, one Undergraduate programme in Architecture of five year duration and eleven Graduate programmes of two year duration. Ph.D. degrees are also awarded by the institute.

Undergraduate Architectural Programmes

- Bachelor of Architecture

Undergraduate Engineering Programmes

- Chemical Engineering

- Civil Engineering
- Computer Science & Engineering
- Electrical and Electronics Engineering
- Electronics and Communications Engineering
- Mechanical Engineering
- Metallurgical & Materials Engineering
- Mining Engineering

Post Graduate Engineering Programmes

Department	Program Offered
Applied Chemistry	M. Sc. Chemistry
Applied Mathematics	M. Sc. Mathematics
Applied Mechanics	M. Tech. In Structural Dynamics and Earthquake Engineering
	M. Tech. In Structural Engineering
Applied Physics	M. Sc. Physics
Architecture	M. Tech. In Urban Planning
Civil Engineering	M. Tech in Environmental Engineering
	M. Tech in Water Resources Engineering
	M. Tech in Construction Technology & Management
	M. Tech in Transportation Engineering
Computer Science Eng.	M. Tech in Computer Science Engineering
Electrical Engineering	M. Tech in Integrated Power System
	M. Tech in Power Electronics & Drives
Electronics Engineering	M. Tech in VLSI Design
	M. Tech in Communication System Engineering
Mechanical Engineering	M. Tech in Industrial Engineering
	M. Tech in Heat Power Engineering
	M. Tech in CAD-CAM

Metallurgical & Materials Engineering	M. Tech in Material Engineering
Mining Engineering	M. Tech. In Excavation Engineering

QUALITY MANAGEMENT FOR LIRC IN VNIT

The Library and Information Resource Centre (LIRC) in VNIT is 4 decades old having an independent three storied building. The collections of Books and Journals have been methodically developed through the years. It is always ensured that the collection is dynamic in nature by stacking separately ACTIVE and INACTIVE collection in tune with changes in syllabi. The Library and Information Resources Centre is automated and users LIBSYS Software. Students and faculty access library information through ON LINE PUBLIC ACCESS CATALOGUES indexed databases called EL-COMPENDEX PLUS. DISSERTATION ABSTRACTS INTERNATIONAL and SAE Technical Papers are on Campus-wide Network of 10/100 Mbps lines are available round the clock.

The Library and Information being personalized and human oriented services of any organization, need inter personal skilled human resources to man the services. This is one of the very judiciously utilized criteria when any new or innovation services are planned. Four decades are good span to get evaluated the very existence of any section or organization. Academically, the study has been done by number of students of Library and Information Science schools taking different aspects of LIRC unit. The LIRC has very strong collection in basic branches of engineering like, Electrical, Mechanical, Electronic, Architecture, Civil and Computer Science. All most all types of Hand books, Reference books, Standards, Society Journals and Almanacs are available for the faculty and the students. In addition to the existing library, a new digital library has also started functioning recently and has access to online journals and technology related websites. The complete campus is networked using fiber optic cables and also wi-fi connectivity provided to the students.

LIRC Objectives

- To support the learning community in their information needs by making available maximum possible information sources.
- To assist the clientele in tracing the documentary literature in the information unit to solve their problems.
- To help informally producing technical manpower for absorption in Indian industries and management.
- To harness their researching habits through procurement of appropriate & satisfying information needs of engineering students & researchers.
- To offer qualitative information, automated library and emerging services to its users other than college students on fee charge basis if decided.

LIRC Rules

Documents borrowed from the information unit are not transferable and borrowers are responsible for what they borrow. No plea will be heard from them and they must verify the documents in good condition before leaving the library.

- The documents from reference section are only meant for on site consultation and normally are not issued.
- The staff members of information unit at property counter are authorized to verify and examine everything that goes in or out of the unit.
- No outside student from any other engineering college is allowed. However, they are permitted in exceptional cases with proper authorization.

- The documents, which are lost by the borrower, need to be reported and replaced with recent edition of the same.
- All the documents to be taken on loan should be presented at the entrance gate together with gate-pass and only on proper authorization and verification he/she would be allowed to take away the documents.
- General etiquettes are expected from every member of information unit and clientele such as Singing, Loud Speaking. Shouting, Spitting, Sleeping, Smoking, etc. are strictly prohibited.

Enhancing Qualities of Staff

- Strong Ethical aspect.
- Integrity among the staff.
- Trust promotes full participation of all members.
- Training is very important for employers to be highly productive.
- Team work is also a key element and Quality Management.
- Good communication skills.
- Time management skills for user satisfaction.
- Acquiring new technological skills.
- Institute recommending staff for improving technical skills through special training programs. e. g. IITs, INFLIBNET, MHRD.

Collection of Library (Current Status - 2014)

VNIT Library has large collection and increasing annually. At present following status shows collection of books, journals, and other reading material.

Total 1,61,325 (Books, Journals, Standards & Non Book materials)

Collection of Books	**(Total Books – 1,33,687)**
General Books- 70264	E-Books - 4064
Book Bank- 27,950	Books From Students Aid Fund- 3,941
Social Welfare Book- 15,978	UGC / SAF Books- 4,331
Gratis Books – 4015	UGC Book Bank - 483
Addl. Intake 120 – 256	Book Bank Scheme for ST – 386
British Council Book Bank- 291	UG Project Report/PG/PhDs Thesis – 1,728
Periodicals	**(Total Periodicals & Bound Volumes –16,198)**
National Print – 52	International Print - 89
Bound Volumes- 13,754	E- Journals - 1557
Gratis Periodicals & Pamphlets- 73	
Standards	**(Total Indian & Foreign Standards -9,096)**
Indian Standards(Print)- 8,759	Society Standards- 337
Non-book Material	**(Total Non Book Material -1,837)**
CDs & Floppies- 1316	Audio Visual Material- 298
Audio / Video Material – 730	

QUALITY INDICATORS FOR ASSESSING LIBRARY SERVICES

AICTE has developed a set of objective indicators to facilitate assessment of the Library Services of VNIT. The VNIT Library is Central Library for all Departments. The Library has whole collections for academic and research purpose. In order to provides quality services in the library. Following are the parameters consider for quality in Library system.

Number of the days Library is kept open

In a year all 365 days library remain open excluding 5 days. It is very beneficial for users.

Working hours

In this parameters library has opened 8.30 a. m. to 9.30 p. m. So that the users or faculty members are use the library without disturbance to their academic schedules.

Library Advisory Committee

In this area library has a library advisory committee which includes the faculty members. The role of the committee and its function in developing library are well defined.

Manpower Development

In this parameter it is very necessary that the experience and qualifications of librarian as well as the library staff should be as per AICTE etc. They should have knowledge to provide information and services pinpointly, exhaustively and expeditiously and should encouraged in developing their professional skills by way of training programmes, attending meetings, seminars, workshops etc.

Infrastructure of Library

In this parameter the facilities available and required for library i. e. whether library have a independent building structure of the library, proper planning and organization of space, proper furniture, quantity and quality of reading chairs, tables, display racks, magazine racks etc.

ICT Infrastructure

In this parameter, it indicates the number of computers available in the library in order to provide electronic library service to the users. On-line databases and E-books would be easily access by the user and it upgrading the ICT infrastructure.

Budget

In this parameters the institutions has and

proportionate growth in the library budget. There should be separate budget provision for books, Journals and other resources and the ICT infrastructure as per the requirements of the institutions. The Ministry of Human Resource Development is providing fund for the same.

Registration

Students, faculty member and newly admitted students of the college have to register in library. Registration along with complete rules and regulations for the library user.

Cancellation of Registration / No Dues Certificate

No Dues Certificate has been provided through LIBSYS software.

Reference Service

A large number of Encyclopaedias, Handbooks and various reference sources are available in the Library. Reference staff is also available in the section to suggest sources of information and to assist in locating the required material.

Current Awareness Services for Journals

Current awareness services alert scholars, researchers, and Faculty Members to recently published literature in their fields of specialization. Journals are issue only for Faculty Staff for one day and also Xerox facility is available.

Selective Dissemination of Information Service

SDI service alert only for Researchers and scholars through library staff.

Referral Service

If the user need of the document are not available in VNIT Library. In this situation Library refer to other Library.

Journals/Periodicals Service

Journals being the primary source of information are essential to supplement the research activities and are required regularly. A number of foreign & Indian journals are being subscribed Full Text on-line to facilitate the on going research activities & to expand the areas of future research activities.

Library Catalogue (Web OPAC)

The library offers computerized catalogue search services through the Web OPAC. The bibliographic record consisting of more than 1,00,000 books available in the Library.

Special Collection for SC/ST Category (Social Welfare)

Selected text books are made available to issue 10 books for a period of one semester according to the rules framed for this purpose to the student belonging to SC/ST category.

Newspaper and Magazine Service

National and local newspapers are available in the library have been placed.

Xerox Service

Xerox copies of the library documents are made available mainly for academic purpose. The terms and conditions along with the rates for per page Xerox is also provided on the Library.

Expenditure during the last year

Sr. No.	Grants	Amount Allocation
1	General Books & Maps	70.00 Lac
2	E-Books TEQIP – II	60.00 Lac
3	Book Bank Books	15.00 Lac
4	Periodicals & News Papers	105.00 Lac

CHAPTER OUTCOME

During the Service Era, the quality of resources and services has become an unquestionable value for any organisation; the ability to move forward and adapt to the changing needs and expectations of users' governs the survival of the organizations.

The VNIT Library is to achieve high standards of excellence in generating & propagating knowledge in engineering. Library is committed to providing an education that combines rigorous academics with joy of discovery. Library contribute effectively to the national endeavour of producing quality human resource of world class standard by developing a education system, build an environment to create and propagate innovative technologies for the economic development of the nation.

12

Practical Application of Technology in VNIT: SWOT Analysis

Keywords : *SWOT Analysis, LIRC VNIT, Strengths, Weakness, Threats, Opportunities.*

INTRODUCTION

The management domain has given various techniques to be applied to different fields of knowledge or subject areas. The SWOT analysis is one of such techniques that will figure out the exact status of the section or institution. It offers the vision to the personnel involved about where you are and where you should have been. The candid application of this technique will spell out the current situation being enumerated faithfully. The frankness of this technique enlists definite position of all the four items involved in this. It not only assesses the exact status but also offer the things to be done for betterment while working.

The SWOT analysis means looking at your strengths and weaknesses and simultaneously grabs the opportunities and threats for their conversion to better prospects. This most proven technique will be applied to the library and information resources centre, Visvesvaraya National Institute of Technology, Nagpur to know its value and standing through decades. To begin with let us visualise the strengths of LIRC, VNIT, Nagpur.

Strengths

1. Facilitating Management Support
2. Separate Library building/complex.
3. Techno Savvy Chairman ET and LS
4. Committed Human Resources
5. No Lack of financial Support
6. Well Organised Library on functional Basis
7. Well defined Policies, Rules and Regulations
8. Enthusiastic Leadership
9. Uninterrupted Technological Support from the Institute
10. Conducive Ambience
11. ISO Accredited LIRC
12. 24X7 Reading Room Facility
13. Institute Status as National Importance

Weakness

1. Electric Furnishing in Library is not to desired quality
2. Automation with Office/Other Section could not happen
3. Vast Area of Building difficult to manage.
4. Sound/Echo disturbs peace environment.
5. Less number of Officer Cadre in Library.

Opportunities

1. Constant Aid from MHRD
2. Well Qualified and Trained Human Resources
3. BOAT Trainee Recruitment.
4. Contract Staff Recruitment.
5. Students Always on Tenterhooks
6. Facilities for E-resources Development
7. Enormous Building Area
8. Qualified Network Support
9. Oneness among Human Resources
10. Standardised working Practices

Threats

1. Comparison with IITs (Always)
2. Technological Obscelesence
3. No Permanent Staff for Library
4. Well trained staff are not absorbed
5. Officer Cadre is less in number.

STRENGTHS

Facilitating Management Support

The management of VNIT, Nagpur has played the role of facilitator for the Library and Information Resources Centre. Whether it be collection development, commencing new services, bettering library environment, increasing quota for the students or applications of emerging technologies in library, it has all the time upheld the idea of introduction of facilities for the students. The management has never turned their blind eye to the demands of the students and thus the facilities in the library are in its place. The human resources though on ad hoc basis were provided from time to time. There is no dearth of finance and it is being National institute with certain status that has been never compromised by the management.

Separate Library building/complex

The VNIT has separate complex for Library having 4 storied building. It has 150X80 ft halls four in numbers thus facilitating to accommodate huge collection of library. The entrance lobby is very big enough to spell out its grandeur. It houses Circulation counter having all the modern gadgets of ICT.

Techno Savvy Chairman ET and LS/Associate Dean

The Chairman of Library Committee always support for introducing new technologies in development of LIRC services. As they have prestigious knowledge of all new upcoming technologies, because of that they know the importance of application of new technologies. Presently LIRC VNIT has The Associate Dean of Library Committee Dr. S.G. Sapate and Previous Chairman Dr. A. S. Gandhi who is well known personality and he always involving with full devotion in all planning and development of new technologies as well as any library problems.

Committed Human Resources

We are already experiencing a shortage of qualified library staff available to rendering front-line and mid-level services in Library. For fulfilling above need of library there is a need of well qualified and trained staff. Provision of adequate staff is necessary for the proper and effective function of a VNIT library. VNIT library staff, in addition to their belief in service, brings a high level of education and motivation to their positions. They are committed to providing high quality library service to the campus & community as well.

No Lack of financial Support

For development of the Nation NIT's & IIT's plays a vital role, therefore Government provides fund through MHRD in huge amount. Again in addition Government provides national and international level fund under different research project like TEQIP, SMDP, MODROB, and CSEEPO etc. hence there is no dearth of fund. In present year 2012-13 150 lack funds received for all departmental books, e-books, journals, & e-journals.

Well Organised Library on functional Basis

LIRC's functions as per work sequence like Acquisition, Cataloguing, Technical Processing, and Circulation etc according to library Science norms of housekeeping operations. In LIRC all works are done as per code of conduct i.e. best procedures followed in Librarianship.

Well defined Policies, Rules and Regulations

NITs are very important institutions at national and international levels and strengthen the development of the nation. Hence well defined policies, rules and regulations are framed by the knowledgeable VIP's at national level. VNIT Nagpur has adopted well defined policies, rules and regulations as motivated to run such important institutions. Therefore the work of LIRC is running smoothly. However there is a scope to rectify the rules and regulations from the point of modern library users time to time by the competent authorities.

Enthusiastic Leadership

Great leaders excel in the art of communication and motivation, mutual respect, instilling confidence and enthusiasm, and showing credibility and integrity on a consistent basis. LIRC VNIT Librarian has looked at a number of characteristics that seem to go hand in hand with outstanding leadership. Excellence in leadership is acquired by staffs, which has a strong sense of vision, has passion and are able to get commitment of users need. LIRC staff team performs all activities to their full potential under the guidance of Librarian.

Uninterrupted Technological Support from the Institute

LIRC VNIT has well structured building with ample of uninterrupted technologies. All type of technological support enforces in library, due to that library provides all new technology based services like Web OPAC, Wi-Fi, kiosk, RFID etc. E-repository through Greenstone software is being introduced shortly for which the work is going on. All technological problems are solved on top priority basis by the concerns therefore; the interruptions if any are instantly removed.

Conducive Ambience

The library has inviting atmosphere that the clientele are being welcomed with smile on the face and they are being taken around the library explaining the various section and collection. The plan and the sign ages are very prominent in the entrance that helps any user to get guided without the help of any one. The housekeeping functions are done regularly and cleanliness is given top priority. The clientele will always like to visit the library frequently due to better ambience.

ISO Accredited LIRC

ISO is for quality management processes. According to ISO norms all functions of library are carried out. It also conforms to the Library manual. ISO has enforced some working procedures in the form of manual according to which they evaluate the enforcement in the organisations through easily installed Library management software LIBSYS that answer every query regarding in between processes. In VNIT, ISO norms are enforced and all works in the organisation are performed under rules of ISO. This exercise was done in the year 2009 and the LIRC was accredited as ISO Section of the Institute.

24X7 Reading Room Facility

Library remains open from 8.30 a. m. to 9.30 p. m. so that the users or faculty members can use the library at full capacity without disturbance to their academic schedules. Specifically 24X7 full time reading room facilities are provided by the VNIT library. Kiosk is helping in improved patron circulation services even when library facing staff shortage & after closing of library student can return and renewal of books through Kiosk.

Institute Status as National Importance

By virtue of having National institute of technology (NITs) are premier Institutes of Engineering and Technology in India and are new face of existing Regional Engineering Colleges (RECs). In the year 2002, the Govt. of India Ministry of Human Resource Development, decided to upgrade all the 17 existing Regional Engineering Colleges (RECs) as National Institutes of Technology (NITs), on the lines of the prestigious Indian Institutes of Technology (IITs). The NITs have the responsibility of providing high quality

Education in Engineering and Technology are to produce competent technical manpower for the country. There are presently 30 NITs in India. The NITs are deliberately scattered throughout the country with the idea of having one NIT in every major state of India to achieve balanced regional development. The NITs are rated just next to the Indian IITs in terms of quality of education, research and placements. Most of the NITs are autonomous technical university. The NITs offer B. Tech. program in various disciplines of Engineering and

Technology along with research programs leading to M. Tech., MSc. and Ph.D.

The VNIT Library collections of books and journals have been methodically developed through the years. It is always ensured that the collection is dynamic in nature by stacking separately active and inactive collection in tune with changes in syllabi. The library and information resources centre is automated and users LIBSYS software. Students and faculty access library information through online public access catalogue, INDEST databases technical Papers are on campus-wide network of 10/100 Mbps lines and are available round the clock. Library staffs are solving all queries of the user instantly like query under RTI, document delivery, all type of user query etc.

WEAKNESS

Electric Furnishing in Library is not to desired quality

Services of electricians are not rendered properly, there by resulting into inconvenience to the users. Concealed electric wiring is not properly working hence open casing wire system is adopted however the same is not properly done to match the requirement which needs modification and alteration for lights and fans points. At present the users and staff are facing difficulty due to above inconveniency.

Automation with Office/Other Section could not happen

At present LIBSYS software is used for all housekeeping operations excluding late fees collection which is separately done by other software. If the interlinking of both the software is done to make the all data available including that of late fees collection, the inconvenience of the staff and students can be avoided to a larger extent.

Vast Area of Building difficult to manage

Because of vast area in library and since various sections are scattered, manpower presently available become short to control the system in the library.

Sound/Echo disturbs peace environment

Sound/echo systems are not properly managed there by disturbing peace in environment. Simultaneously there are leakage problems also because of which appearance in various sections looks ugly affecting the structure also. It may result in spoiling the books due to moisture.

Less number of Officer Cadre in Library

The VNIT library is moderated and expanded in various aspects. To control such big library, more numbers of officer cadre persons are required. Various important posts are vacant. This drawback needs to be removed by providing essential officer cadre and more skilled persons adequately. Thus the efficiency of the library can be achieved in better way.

OPPORTUNITIES

Constant Aid from MHRD

For development of the Nation NIT's &IIT's plays a vital role, therefore Government provides fund through MHRD in huge amount. Again in addition Government provides national and international level fund under different research project like TEQIP, SMDP, MODROB, and CSEEPO etc. hence there is no dearth of fund. In present year 2012-13 150 lack funds received for all departmental books, e-books, journals, & e-journals.

Well Qualified and Trained Human Resource

To run such a big modern library, skilled and trained persons are required in addition to adequate staff. Hence we engage qualified persons on ad-hoc basis to whom we train and make them skilled for running library smoothly. But since these trained ad-hoc staff are working from 5-6 years their developed skill can always be banked upon by the management looking this as opportunity, it becomes difficult to manage the systems of library in absence of skilled and trained persons. Hence it will be fair on the part of organisation, if these trained and skilled ad-hoc staff persons are absorbed on permanent vacancies that are existing. To pick them as trained and skilled human resources, the authorities may accommodate in identified vacancies.

BOAT Trainee Recruitment

BOAT (*Board of Apprenticeship Training, Mumbai*) trainee's recruitment extends to provide helping hands in library working. Therefore the new comer acquaints preliminary working of library.

Contract Staff Recruitment

The contract staffs are recruited to fulfil the inadequacy of staff for permanent nature of work. Since the contract staff gets more terms in library working, they get trained and skilled for smooth working of library as a helping and co-ordinating to permanent staff.

Students Always on Tenterhooks

Due to the tremendous growth of technology day by day, students of the VNIT are always on tenterhooks creating questions of various natures, demanding new information; hence the staffs attending them has to be always informative and equipped with modern systems to suit their needs rendering better services.

Facilities for E-resources Development

We have been subscribing to the e-resources of Elsevier, Springer, John Wiley and ACS Books and journals. The NPIU Noida has given specific funds under TEQIP-II for these books and journals. Rs 89.00 Lakhs have been allocated for this purpose. This facility is available on the campus wide network in VNIT. This is IP specific i.e from outside it cannot be accessed.

Enormous Building Area

Enormous building area though it is difficult to manage in lack of manpower but it is fruitful to manage the library sections clearly. It is also beneficial from further expansion point of view in respect of developments in technologies, addition of books, space management for instruments required due to new technology.

Qualified Network Support

The network of good quality required for qualified connectivity with different important organisations and consortiums at national and international level is available in library.

Oneness among Human Resources

The library is a vast field keeping up-to-date knowledge of various fields under one roof helping gaining knowledge and facilitating interaction among various departments.

Standardised working Practices

The long span of our library working with vast experience has standardised working practices of our own and some standard working practices have been adopted form standard national and international institutions.

THREATS

Comparison with IITs (Always)

All the IIts are having huge financial resources as compared to NITs. It is always compared with IIt as the facilities and services are definitely more in IITs. This comparison poses threat to NITs existence. We are trying to match the facilities provided by them in the field of academics and other central campus facilities. But anything done less than the expectation will always be demanded.

Technological Obsolescence

Due to abrupt fast changes in technologies, it gets difficult to overcome various problems pertaining to technology in library services. Therefore one has to be careful in handling such situations co-ordinately, safely and smoothly in order to run the library successfully.

Insufficient Permanent Staff for Library

In lack of adequate permanent staff, proper watch in maintenance of important documents, equipments, books, handling staffs under them for various services is disturbed at a greater extent resulting into mismanagement of the library working. Hence it should be taken care of to keep sufficient permanent staff to fulfil the needs as per the standard norms. The LIRC VNIT Nagpur is facing this difficulty.

Well trained staff are not absorbed

As per the prevailing practice of discontinuing the trained and skilled staff on ad-hoc basis, the benefit of well trained and skilled persons is ignored in LIRC at VNIT Nagpur which creates trouble and disturbance for smooth harmonious and effective working of library. It may therefore be given utmost importance to absorb trained and skilled staff now available acquainted with the present working of modern library.

Officer Cadre is less in number

This idea gives hindrance to the progress of the library as no officer cadre human resources are available to share the load of single qualified person. The sooner these post are in place the better is for the future of the library. This uncertainty poses threats to otherwise well developed and organised LIRC, VNIT, Nagpur.

CHAPTER OUTCOME

The strengths of the LIRC are better than weakness identified. We will sort out the weaknesses to convert them into strengths. The visual opportunities will be recognised and the amelioration will be in progress. The threats are being identified and the same are being recognised to overcome.

13

Practical Application of Technology in VNIT: Implementation of RFID

Keywords : *RFID - Radio Frequency Identification, EAS - Electronic Article Surveillance.*

INTRODUCTION

The automation of libraries and information centres in India started in middle 1950's till 1980's the concept of automation was centred around the use of computers for housekeeping operations and information services by individual libraries. There are certain factors responsible for the automation of the libraries. Information explcsion increase User's demand, labour intensive nature of work, changing concepts of documents.

Application of modern management techniques reduced response time and need for resource sharing are important elements. With the tremendous capabilities of computer, libraries started using computers for the in-house operations. Emerging technologies that are relieve the personnel from time-consuming library operations; have always been of interest to libraries. When libraries of all kinds (public, academic, special) are facing budget crunches, considering new technologies as the potential alternatives for cost saving and hassle free management of library operations, is imperative, RFID (Radio Frequency Identification) system is such a promising alternative that aid in the efficient flow of library material. RFID is an innovative automated library system for automatic identification and tracking of library material. Currently RFID applications range from book tracking and stock management, to theft detection and automatic book sorting. Radio frequency identification (RFID) technology is a dynamic link between people, objects and processes and in the near future it plays a prime role in data collection, identification as well as analysis necessary for specific library operations. An automated library with the support of RFID technology would be a "self service station" that demands least intervention by the library personnel. Efforts are being made to introduce self-service "check-in" and "check out" that avoid long delay in the delivery of library material and also for achieving better efficiency in operations. RFID is used in libraries primarily to automate the book handling process including checkout, inventory control, check-in and anti-theft. When combined with Computer Assisted sorting equipment. RFID facilitates and speeds up even book sorting. Automating the library material handling process allows libraries to spend more time with the clientele, thus, increasing the 'user satisfaction'.

VNIT LIRC, NAGPUR

Visvesvaraya National Institute of Technology, Nagpur is one of the thirty National Institutes of Technology in the country. Earlier, the Institute was known as Visvesvaraya Regional College of Engineering (VRCE). It was established in the year 1960 under the scheme sponsored by Govt. of India and Govt. of Maharashtra. In 2002 VRCE become VNIT with Deemed University status from UGC and Central Government taking full financial & administrative responsibility. August 2007 VNIT becomes Institute of National Importance under the act of parliament.

The Library has been established in the 1960 when the state engineering college was in existence. The Library has also received recognition as one of the best libraries in central India due to REC status. VNIT Library serves its users with the best services and to fulfil the requirements of the users as well as the organisation. Since in this changing environment with the introduction of new technologies and the changing perception about the information and the information system it is seen that the library need to understand this change and work accordingly with the current situations and accept the current trends. As automation become a boon factor VNIT LIRC changed itself from a traditional library to the new modern library with the introduction of different technologies available for library automation. From 1994 onwards VNIT, LIRC is using LIBSYS software package for library activities. It made an infrastructure for LIBSYS software by using different networks like LAN and different points for user (OPAC) to consult the catalogue. After this it started with new technology i.e. Barcode technology in the year 2010 and now it has gone one step ahead with the implementation of Radio Frequency Identification (RFID). In VNIT LIRC implement this RFID technology with the initiative of Dr. S. S. Gokhale, Ex Director of VNIT Nagpur, Dr. R. M. Deshpande, Librarian VNIT LIRC Nagpur, Dr. A. G. Deshpande Library Ex Committee Chairman and his team executing this technology.

LIBRARY AUTOMATION

Library automation is nothing but the use of automatic and semiautomatic data processing machines to perform traditional activities such as acquisition, cataloguing, circulation. Library automation may be distinguished from related fields such as information retrieval, indexing, abstracting and automatic textual analysis. In library automation the first thing, which comes to our mind, is the technologies involved or which can be adopted to automate the libraries. As with a large research in development of new technologies some, which can be applied to libraries for easy working and for providing better services, are: Barcodes, Radio frequency identification etc.

VNIT LIRC Nagpur has purchased LIBSYS software to automate their library and also contract with company's maintenance service. A LIBSYS system is mainly client server model. This model is suitable for system that is smaller in size and less resource on the server side. This system is suitable especially within an organization. In 1993 LIRC Committee has come out with the recommendations of using LIBSYS Library Automation Package that was commercially available for one lac rupees. It has also procured the 12 Dump Terminals and Wipro Server as Hardware with necessary accessories and commenced the System on 14th August 1994. More than one lac records were made accessible through automation of usable collection. The LIBSYS used to generate all the vital statistics for reporting to management including OPAC. The OPAC is searching even the concept or minute keyword from title, abstract or other field. Daily backup is being taken, so that there is no loss of information. Since 1994 the Library Automation is practiced and maintained till date without any major break down. This is the greatest achievement made by VNIT LIRC in the field of Library Automation. Currently VNIT LIRC has upgraded their automated software with LIBSYS 7 for implementing RFID Technology.

TECHNOLOGIES FOR LIBRARY AUTOMATION

Library Automation is probably the main challenge that libraries have to face now. Libraries continued to be mildly interested in such machinery for most of in the 21st century. The general purpose computers that become widely available in 1960s changed all that and made it possible a second era of library automation systems. Presently various software are available for library automation some are free of cost like Greenstone, Koha etc.

VNIT LIRC Nagpur was automated in 1994 and day by day pursuing new technologies for further development. In the year 2010 implementing barcodes technology to all books, applying LIBSYS 7 updated version, introducing RFID Technology in the year 2011, and currently pushing digitization of records with use of Greenstone freely available software.

BARCODES

The basic structure of a barcode consists of a header, a manufacturer's identification number, item number and check digit. Barcodes is a fundamental technology for library automation and flow management. In application for the circulation of books, barcodes technology has been proven to be robust, reliable and efficient. Barcodes are noting but self-contained messages with information encoded in a series of black bars of varying breadths and white spaces between every two of them. Barcodes are used basically for circulation management of document. Barcode system is now being considered as an effective addition to support automation process. Barcode can eliminate human errors and are considered in terms of reliability of information ease, speed of operation and use. Barcode have distinct advantages over other techniques like manual data, magnetic stripes etc. Presently VNIT LIRC take all benefits of the same with special denotation of colours for different sections like for General, Book-Bank, Reference & Social Welfare barcode labels having black bars of varying breadths and white spaces between every two of them linings with base Red line, Green line, Blue line & Yellow line respectively.

RFID (RADIO FREQUENCY IDENTIFICATION)

RFID is a method of remotely storing and retrieving data using devices called RFID tags. Take a closer look at how RFID has the potential to seamlessly invade our daily lives. RFID enables greater automation of data collection process. This technology has been in use in libraries for book identification, for self checkout, for antitheft control, for inventory control, and for the sorting and conveying of library books and audiovisual materials. These applications can lead to significant saving in staff costs, enhance service, lower book theft and provide a constant update of media collections. The technical features of a modern RFID system are described to provide a guideline for the evaluation of different systems. RFID technology is a new promising technology that will spread in the near future to enter most of our everyday activities. It promises various benefits in management of circulation system, improved accuracy with speed, efficiency and full security of data sharing. This technology helped in activity the misplace resource with hand held scanner like structure from stack. The hours are at ease using this technology barring initial hick ups. Currently in VNIT, LIRC, Nagpur RFID Technology was implemented in the year 2011. Because of this advance technology all routine work of library improving & it supports to staff in speed self charge and discharge, electronic inventorying, shelf searching, and interface with materials handling systems.

RFID Hardware Software used in VNIT Library

Hardware Components	**Software Components**
Gates EAS Built in Electronic Control Unit	Library Automation LIBSYS 7
Scanners / LSmart Work Station	WEB OPAC and UNION OPAC
Kiosk	Client Software for Issue/ Return/Renewal
RFID Tags, Self Adhesive	
RFID Reader	
Wi-Fi Library inventory Reader from TAGSYS	

Gates EAS Built in Electronic Control Unit

The gate antennas act as a hardware which issue a warning signal and activate the alarm system if a book or file pasted with a label is leaving the premises or department without an authorized issue/ outward entry into software. Gates are easily mounted and are connected with warning light signals and also sound alarms to inform the security personnel that some mischief has taken place. These gates are used at the entry and exit points in the library.

Scanners / LSmart Work Station

LSmart is a suite of applications harnessing RFID technology for use in libraries. **LSmart** solutions based on RFID and EM technologies, taking automation and security in libraries to a new level. **LSmart** integrates RFID and EM hardware from world renowned manufacturers with LIBSYS using its more than two decades of experience in library automation. **LSmart** has proved to be strong on reliability, flexibility and ease-of-operations and combined with robust and quality hardware equipments. **LSmart**, having Security System through EAS gates as its core component, can be implemented in a phased manner enhancing operational efficiency at every stage. **LSmart** operated by library staff, it enables handling of books and other material having RFID Labels/ Tags.

Kiosk

Kiosk is a station for self service for charging and discharging by patrons without the help of staff. It works like ATM machine. Lots of benefits for patron like spend less time waiting in check-out lines by using self check in – check out & renewal systems. Self service enhances patron privacy. Kiosk is helping in improved patron services even when Libraries are facing staff shortage. After closing library student can return and renewal of books through Kiosk.

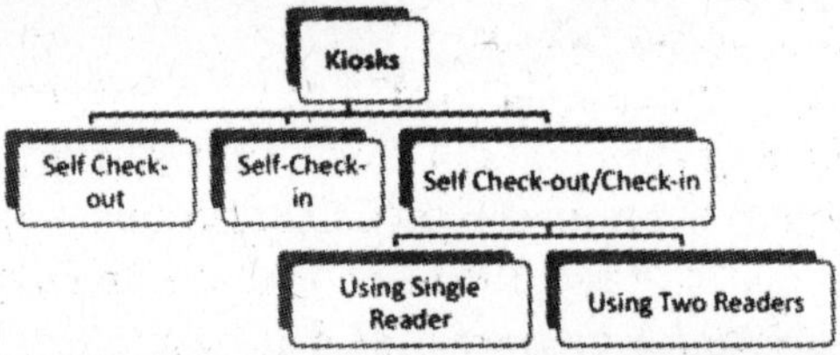

RFID Tags, Self Adhesive

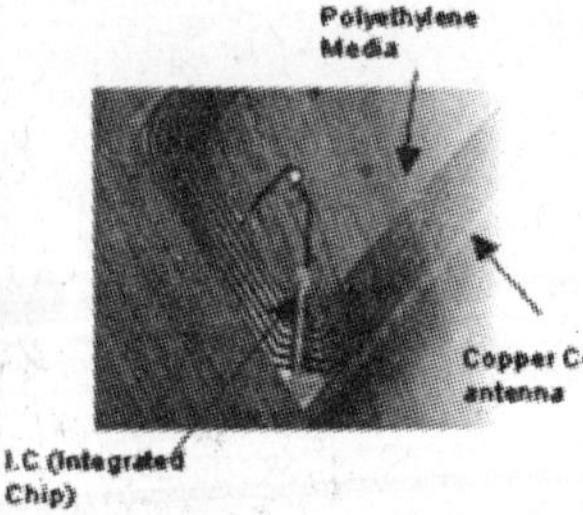

RFID Tags consisting of a microchip and an Antenna, these RFID tags are affixed on the library material for their identification by RFID readers. These self-adhesive labels come in various shapes and sizes (square, round and rectangle), have 1024 bits memory with built-in antitheft detection bit and are ISO 15693 and ISO 18000-3 compliant. For covering these tags we use VNIT logo as shown in figure.

RFID Reader

It comprises of a midrange reader. The equipment can easily be connected to a network or single workstation Pc or notebook and the application can begin functioning thereon. It also supports all RFID functions like anti collision feature allowing to identify multiple labels simultaneously, present in the reader field and full read/write capability. It is used at the issue/return counters at the library and also for label personalization. It is connected to a PC or computer terminal.

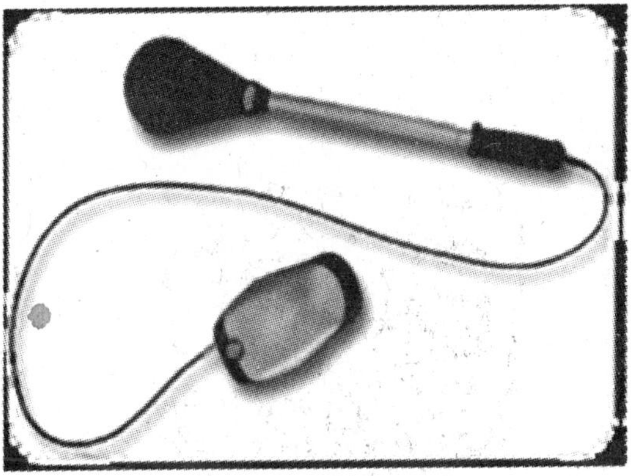

Wi-Fi Library inventory Reader from TAGSYS

This handheld Wi-Fi reader consists of a long lightweight handle with a flexible end-part that rotates to facilitate the identification of items on all shelves, especially hard-to-reach areas. It performs Stock-checking, Re-shelving, and also locates specific items by engaging minimal staff. It consists of a Wi-Fi Reader, Mini Laptop and LSmart-Client software.

Library Automation LIBSYS 7

It is a web based library software product from Libsys Ltd., Gurgaon, Haryana. It has the modules for acquisition, cataloguing, circulation, serials, article indexing, Web-OPAC, and reports. It supports international standard like MARC21 (USMARC + CANMARC), Unicode, SRU-SRW, Z39.50, NCIP-NISO, SICI-Barcode. If any library has the sufficient fund, then it can be treated as the most field-proven library system in a wide spectrum of libraries with unmatchable depth in functionality and features. Website: http://www.libsys.co.in/

WEB OPAC and UNION OPAC

The Library has installed new software, a web-based search platform, which brings the bibliographic database of the VNIT LIRC books. Members can go to their library accounts through Internet and can reserve/renew the books and can see their Library status as well as the status of the book.

For accessing Web OPAC, following links are use:

http://192.168.15.2:8080/jopacgwt/Gwt0PAC.html# TaskNum= 1&PageNum=1&WinState=Min&History Count=1

RFID BENEFITS IN VNIT LIBRARY

Stock management

Operations such as managing material on the shelves, identifying missing & miss shelved items and taking stocks regularly will be feasible.

Improved Patron Services

Spending minimal time on circulation operations

allows library staff to assist patrons Routine patron services are not disturbed even when libraries are facing staff shortages & budget cuts.

Flexibility and Modularity

Ability to add newer products and features as finances and customer needs dictate.

RFID Security

Library item identification & security is combined into a single tag, thereby eliminating the need to attach an additional security strip.

RFID BENEFITS IN VNIT LIBRARY STAFF

Less time needed for circulation operations

Implementing RFID will considerably reduce the amount of time required to issue, receive, transport, sort & shelve library materials.

Efficient Inventory management

Inventory management can be done using a handheld reader without closing the library and is at least 20 times faster compared to existing barcode based system.

Reducing Repetitive Stress Injuries (RSI)

RFID based system reduces repetitive scanning of individual items at the circulation desk during check in, check out and hence avoids RSI such as carpal tunnel syndrome.

ADVANTAGES OF RFID SYSTEMS

- Faster Circulation Transactions
- The perfect tracker
- Simplified self-charging/discharging
- Highly reliable

- High-speed inventorying
- Automated Identification of materials

DISADVANTAGES OF RFID SYSTEMS

- High cost
- Easy to deceive the technology
- Removal of tags
- Exit sensor problems
- Fear to invade Patron Privacy

CHAPTER OUTCOMES

The applications of RFID Technology have been viewed as an augmentation of LIBSYS based automation in LIRC, VNIT, Nagpur. The technology is helpful to staff, students, and academic committee who can handle the technology with the assistance of library staff once they are included in that operation. The main advantage of RFID is identification of reading resource in tons of documents. It has one handheld instrument to unearth the misplaced books in stacks. Major benefit of Kiosk is functioning outside working hours in library.

The technology is working smoothly at LIRC, VNIT form last 36 months. It has modern ambience to work in library that facilitates the freely process of library. At the back office level, it supports good back up facilities and easy tagging and labelling. The experiences of LIRC, VNIT are establishing the promise and bright future for this technology. The LIRC has taken lots of efforts, to train their staff for this technology. Implementation of RFID will provide a greater amount of efficiency and error free functioning.

14

Current Status of Libraries of NIT's in India

Keywords : *TEQIP, REC/NIT's in India, RFID Technology, INDEST Consortia, Library Automation, LIRC VNIT, Nagpur.*

INTRODUCTION

India is a huge country with a population of more than 1 billion. In India, by tradition, education and learning are highly valued. In fact, India has one of the largest higher education systems in the world, with regard to the number of institution. Education is a neccssity. It is the most effective instrument with which the people can acquire the knowledge, skills, and capability to develop wisdoms it is developing nation. The seeds for some of India's higher education institutions were planted in the latter half of the Twenty Century. National Institutes of Technology (NITs) are premier institutes of engineering and technology in India and are thc new faces of the earlier Regional Engineering Colleges (RECs).

In the year 2002, the Govt. of India's Ministry of Human Resource Development, decided to upgrade all the 17 existing Regional Engineering Colleges (RECs) as National Institutes of Technology (NITs), on the lines of the prestigious Indian Institutes of Technology (IITS). The

NITs have the responsibility of providing high quality education in engineering and technology to produce competent technical manpower for the country. Libraries being treasure house of knowledge and information are one invaluable way to provide informal education since each library is a hub of all academic activities.

- Every Regional Engineering Colleges (RECs) in India has witnessed growth its self in 5 decades. The idea of establishing RECs / NITs was provide the national integration in education system drawn from all states and vision territory in India. The central government has infused lots of funds for this novel Idea and all the states in India was allotted each Regional Engineering College for co-education of different cultured youths of India.
- The development of 5 decades not only seen the libraries being developed but all the central facilities on the campus such as Health Centre, Sports Activities, service items such as Bank, Post Office, Groceries etc. Earlier libraries were housed in main administrative building of college on ground floor or first floor with minimum of 100 students of seating capacity in each RECs / NITs. The Acquisition of reading resources was never allowed to get relegated. Hence, Reference Books, Journals, Text Books, Book Bank Books were judiciously acquired keeping in view the developing strength of students on campus. The comfort level of the students, staff and faculty was main focus while facilities in library used to get planned. There was an absolute coordination between the number of copies of reading resources and the currently of the syllabus for each year / semester. There used to be no dearth of copies of reading material.
- In the advent of computers and related technologies in last 2 decades have metamorphosed the libraries of each RECs/NITs in India. The Librarian of RECs/

NITs not only ensured that his customer growth is enhanced but the institute's growth is also simultaneously achieved. All the efforts to introduce computers in RECs/NITs libraries bore fruits of library automation that was herculean task as the retro conversion of library document into computer readable forms was the biggest challenge before library professions.

- The ICT Technology kept on developing newer and related technologies to get implemented in libraries of RECs/NITs. At every implementation of technology the staff of library was needed to get satisfied for that particular technology and they seen that the user are also using the services provided comfortably. The Digital Library, RFID and Institutional Repositories based on free wares like D-Space, E-print or Greenstone also got impetus in libraries of modern NITs.
- The virtual libraries where majority of e-form resources irrespective of its place of storage needs to be accessed on the networks that are specifically devised libraries for data mining and warehousing.

CURRENT STATUS

- Earlier in 1960s to develop cosmopolitan culture in higher education in Indian – RECs were commissioned.
- Each state in India was made responsible for each RECs in their state by 80:20 mode i. e. 80% Financial aid from centre and 20% financial aid from state with Administrative responsibility.
- In 2000 each REC was made developed University by UGC with 100% financial support like other traditional University.
- Finally, the MHRD has declared in 2002 each REC as NIT.

- In 2007, the Act of parliament was passed to upgrade each NIT to got status as Institute of National importance in India.
- The Library of each REC / NIT had received substantial share of grants from centre of excellence, project Grants, Digital Library Grants, TEQIP-I & now TEQIP-II Grants.
- There is great General Reference, Reference and Digital Resources of primary sources have been acquired through above grants by each library of REC / NIT in India. Around 200 Lacks of money in each category have been infused by Government of India to each REC/NITs in India.
- Every library has more than one lack reading resources.
- Well maintained Book Bank facilities for 250 students of weaker section.
- Every library subscribes more than 150 scientific journals in print form.
- Every library subscribes to 1708 e-Journals full text through INDEST.
- Every library has been fully automated and offer services based on them.
- Each NIT has separate more than 16000 mt^2 two or three storied library building
- A campus network has been established in each NITs to have access to full text e-Journals

FACTORS RESPONSIBLE FOR CURRENT STATUS OF LIBRARIES OF REC / NITS IN INDIA

India REC-UK Project

This project was launched in 1995-1999. Five years where in lot of reading resources were donated to identified 8 RECs in India. The books published in UK have been donated. The Human Resources were trained during various workshops & a trips to UK Huddlers fields in 1996 for Libraries of REC in India for special induction programme. The purpose of the project was to enhance to quality and relevance of the product of the REC system (the graduating engineers, training courses for engineers in service and capacity for tackling industrial R & D and consultancy.) This would enable the colleges to effectively support Industry responding to the changing market demands. India REC/NITs UK project was achieved in areas like Curriculum Development, Library Development, Educational Technology, MIS Development, Industrial Interaction, etc. REC/NITs Libraries upgraded in the form of books, journals, CD-ROMs and software worth Pound 380,000 provided under the UK Project.

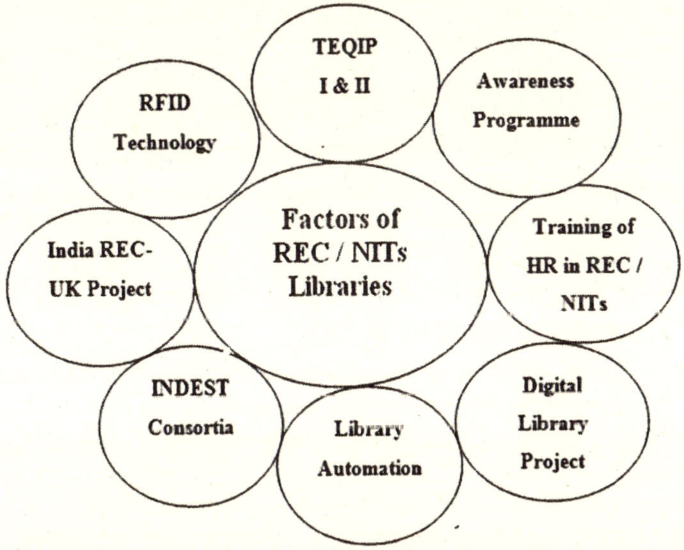

REC/NIT's Libraries under UK project help us to deliver high standard of Customer Service, it may be asked to behave courteously and reasonably towards the library staff and to other library users and to abide the library bylaws. The copy of which must be available in library either on demand or for inspection at any time.

TEQIP I & II

National Project Implementation Unit (NPIU) was established by Ministry of Human Resource Development, Government of India, in August 1990 for coordination, facilitation, monitoring and to provide guidance to the States / Institutions in all aspects of the projects. During 1991 to 2007, NPIU implemented three Technician Education Projects of Government of India assisted by World Bank, which helped to strengthen and upgrade the Technician Education System. World Bank took keen interest in systemic transformation of India's technical education system to make it globally competitive plan and shown its willingness to assist the Government of India to launch a Technical Education Improvement Programme (TEQIP) as a long term programme of 10-12 years and in 2 or 3 phases. The Project Agreement with World Bank was signed on February 04, 2003 for First cycle of First phase and on April 12, 2004 for second cycle of First phase in TEQIP I. In the First cycle of First phase, the six states (1) Haryana (2) Himachal Pradesh (3) Kerala (4) Madhya Pradesh (5) Maharashtra and (6) Uttar Pradesh were included. Tamilnadu has been selected in the Second cycle of First phase among the seven states (1)Andhra Pradesh (2) Gujarat (3) Jharkhand (4) Karnataka (5)Tamilnadu (6)Uttaranchal (7) West Bengal to participate in the programme. TEQIP (Phase-I) was implemented in 13 States and covered 127 Institutions including 18 Centrally Funded Institutions and 19 Polytechnics. It became effective in March 2003 and completed on 31st March, 2009.

TEQIP-II has been initiated around 200 engineering institutions are planned to be competitively elected to improve quality of Technical Education through institutional and systemic reforms. The second phase boosts efforts to prepare more post-graduate students to reduce the shortage of qualified faculty, and to produce more R&D in collaboration with industry. In VNIT, Nagpur currently we have access e-Journals & 576 e-books of John Wiley & 832 of Elsevier Science costing around 57 lacks. We are also planning to get some e-text books of Pearson Education and Tata McGraw Hill Publication. Emphasis is being given on the fundamental science like Physics, Chemistry & Mathematics for procurement of e-books in the respective field.

INDEST Consortia

The INDEST-AICTE Consortium holds extensive training programmes for the benefit of Library staff members from various institutions. Besides, all IITs, IISc, IIMs and NITs. INDEST Consortium has geared itself to provide consultancy services to its member, institutions, especially NITs in library computerization, digitization and in the development of computer and network infrastructure. The Ministry provides funds required for providing differential access to electronic resources for its core members through the Consortium Headquarters at the IIT Delhi.

In 2003, all NITs were made 2nd category institutional members of INDEST consortia in technical education in India where in 10-12 data bases Full text/ Images were made accessible to all NITs in India. Annual 1708 technical Journals were available in PDF format for down loading. All 20 institutions mentioned will get access to following electronic resources from May 2003 onwards:

- ASCE Journals
- ASME Journals
- ACM Digital Library
- IEL Online
- Pro-Quest
- ASTM Standards & Journals
- Science Direct (Elsevier's)
- Springer Link

- JCCC Portal
- Nature

Currently 23 National Institutes of Technology have joined this community of resource sharing consortium to which the benefits of JCCC@INDEST is extended as secondary members.

Library Automation

Automation makes the library system, resources, and services more attractive and interactive, helping libraries to meet their users' expectation. Libraries are one invaluable way to provide this education since each library is a hub of knowledge. This is one reason that automation is important for libraries-it is the way to effectively modernize their functions and services, which is in turn make them more efficient at responding to the needs of their users. Library automation is viewed as the total composite technologies needed to bring to the library user the necessary access and services to answer real-world information needs. The automation of library housekeeping functions, such as acquisition, cataloguing, circulation, serial control, stock verification, and article indexing using ILS, is an important parameter to evaluate library performance. The majority of the libraries are using LibSys, which is a professional integrated library software package from LibSys Corporation in India.

In way back 1993 where Dr. R. M. Deshpande was deputed to UK for information management (1991) to University of Ealing, he commissioned Library Automation in LIBSYS under UNIX in RECs. There were 05 Librarians who were deputed to UK under colombos plan on TCTP (of Government of India who after completion of training automated their respective libraries of RECS i. e. Trichy, Suratkal Bhopal, Warangal and Jaipur so library automation was introduced in RECs in middle 90s in five of 17 RECS in India.

Digital Library Project

Digital Libraries have received wide attention in the recent years allowing access to digital information from anywhere across the world. They have become widely accepted and even preferred information sources in areas of education, science and others. The rapid growth of Internet and the increasing interest in development of digital library related technologies and collections helped accelerate the digitization of printed documents in the past few years.

MHRD in 2003-2006 have granted 5 projects of IDLP (implementation of Digital Library Project) with 5 co-ordinater in each library of NITs in India e.s. Nagpur, Allahabad, Durgapur, Kurukshetra and calicat. All of these have done certain activities in 20 Lac project to each NITs. They acquired 20 Nodes in each NITs and accesses to INDEST databases was for the benefit of student, staff and faculty of NITs. The project ended in 2006 with different information services enabled in libraries of NITs in India. All REC/NITs have a Central Library equipped with technical books, literature, fiction, scientific journals, and other electronic material. Most have digitized their libraries. Some provide an intranet library facility. Every departmental library has high-speed connectivity. Electronic libraries allow students access to online journals and other periodicals through the INDEST consortium and NITs library web pages, like in VNIT Nagpur currently develop e-books and e-journal in the form of repository through freely available Green Stone Digital Library Software. In this way day by day all REC/NITs Libraries are pushes upgradable technology for fulfilling user's expectations.

Training of Human Resources in each REC/NITs

In order to serve the growing demand for trained quality technical manpower, the Government Of India started 14 RECs between 1959 and 1965 (NITs located at Allahabad, Bhopal, Calicut, Durgapur, Jamshedpur, Jaipur, Kurukshetra, Nagpur, Rourkela, Srinagar, Surathkal, Surat, Tiruchirappalli, and Warangal.

In the advent of various technology the leaders in REC/NITs have ensured that their human resource in library are get trained for where implementations of technology. This process was always ensured by library of REC/NITs in India. In this fast changing environment the library and information workers are required to possess enhanced managerial, professional and technical skills, adequate knowledge and right kind of experience. So, training the existing manpower or recruiting new professionals will become essential. They must possess flexibility of attitude, imagination and scientific bend of mind. Further, the libraries need to be upgraded along with the changing environment from its traditional to a digital environment. The REC/NITs libraries replaced by Internet café, knowledge kiosks etc. making way for other IT professionals. As a final word we would like to remind that immediate steps should be taken up for Human Resource Development keeping into view the changing digital environment. The library manpower is required to be trained in new technologies along with the traditional skills. In other words, the new technologies & the old / traditional skills are the two sides of the same coin. In VNIT LIRC, Nagpur possess trained, more efficient and progressive staff because of that they delivers all IT based user oriented services.

Awareness Programme for faculty and students for various technologies implemented

With recent advances in new and emerging education and information technologies, educators have transformed the way they teach and the way students learn, including how information is accessed, shared, synthesized, and communicated. Experimentation with and adoption of new technologies in learning environments has long been a staple of institutions of higher learning. The need for professional development activities to focus on increasing the awareness of the educate students.

The Librarian crusaders of REC/NITs in libraries in India were also complemented by their faculty and students for getting awareness developed by libraries for various services based on different technology in libraries. Periodical programmes were launched to current awareness for using technology. The cliental were satisfied to become aware for handling technologies.

Introduction of RFID Technology

RFID (Radio Frequency Identification) is the latest technology to be used in library theft detection systems. Unlike EM (Electro-Mechanical) and RF (Radio Frequency) systems, which have been used in libraries for decades, the RFID-based systems that libraries began to install in the late 1990s not only detect the unauthorized removal of library materials, but speed staff charge and discharge, simplify and speed patron self-charge and self-discharge, support electronic inventorying and shelf searching, and interface with materials handling systems. RFID is a combination of radio-frequency-based technology and microchip technology. The information contained on microchips in the tags affixed to library materials is read using radio frequency technology. A reader (aka sensor, scanner, or interrogator) looks for antennae on the tags and retrieves information from the microchips through them. It works as ATM machine, users use easily by its own without any help of staff. Therefore both user and staff save self time.

The NITs like VNIT, DNIT, Jallandar and NIT Surat have taken initiatives to implement RFID technology at their respective NITs for modernisation of library services. The hassle free circulation services that to beyond working hours was possible with RFID and with added advantage of unauthorised removal of resources from libraries. This technology helped in activity the misplace resource with hand held scanner like structure from stack. The hours are at ease using this technology barring initial hick ups. Currently in VNIT, LIRC, Nagpur RFID Technology was implemented in 2011. Because of this advance technology all routine work of library improving & it supports to staff in speed self charge and discharge, electronic inventorying, shelf searching, and interface with materials handling systems.

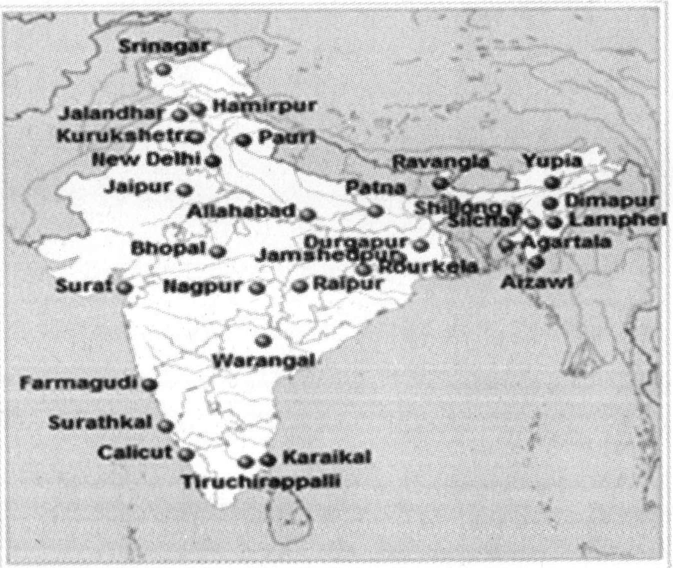

Location of the 30 NITs. Green indicates existing NITs and red indicates campuses in function effectively from 2010.

Figure 4 - Locations of the 30 NIT's

CHAPTER OUTCOME

Indian higher education system is prosperous by creating and promoting number of academic institutions. Libraries are backbone to educational institutions. They have been funded hugely for building infrastructure facilities which consist of resources, technology (automation), infrastructure (computer and network) manpower and services. Indeed, these are important facilities for an academic library system to serve faculty, students, and researchers to meet the optimal utilization of library resources and facilities largely. From the findings, it has been observed that all library facilities are highly and intermediately correlated with each other except the NI. Majority of NIT libraries have strong automation and services facilities at their end. Further, many NIT libraries have well equipped network infrastructure facilities, but lack of effective implementation and management at various levels are causing the libraries at immature stage of utilization these facilities among NITs. Therefore, the statistical inference of NI was unsatisfactorily correlated with other facilities. However, the NIT libraries are at developmental stage in implementing all facilities including NI. Besides, the academic libraries need supportive tools, techniques and perspectives in order to enrich their facilities to excel academic and scientific progress of the institute. Further studies are needed on user perspective to extract clear understating of using library facilities among the NITs in India.

15

Practical Application of Technology in VNIT : ROI a Progressive Outcome

Keywords : *Library Services, Library Activities, LIRC VNIT, Literacy Production, CCTV, RFID.*

INTRODUCTION

A Library has been treated as a Social Organisation for the Students, Faculty and Staff of any academic institution right from five decades. The organisation of various resources, setting, furniture, fixtures, products and services in library are viewed as services and non profit making entities. There was no element of looking at them from business point of view. When in earlier days that is almost five to six decades ago, the books, artefacts, photographs, reference books were very cheaply available. Many of the libraries got their books donated from various aristocrats and affluent families and people. The only Job of librarian in those days used to be acquiring the collection of books or reading material either through purchase or gratis, organise the collection, process them technically and put forth for services either through home reading or on site consultation. The bibliographies, card catalogues, subject list, recent addition, Xeroxing, lending to home reading and many other reactive services, were products and services in libraries of any academic institute. No thought like return on investment was percolated in the minds of the people or stakeholders of libraries in those days. Now, in the advent of technological changes, the minds, vision, angles have gone transformed into new thinking like return on investment.

In these days or last decade or so, the angle of vision for looking at library activities, products and services has changed. The management techniques, business fundamentals are being applied in library activities. This has altered with great impact to expect the returns on these activities, products and services. The advent of ICT has provided impetus to this thinking more and more learned elite are asking the questions on ROI. Though, no products are services in library have been tagged by price or cost but productivity of stakeholder is continuously being queried. It is not difficult or hard to arrive at return or out come and enhance the academic value of library activities. We need to change the angle of looking at all the processes, like acquisition, technical processing, periodical processing, E-books purchased and E- journals acquisition. In this ICT era it is very easy comparatively to assess the usage or log of activities that are available or continually created by system software as compared to traditional librarianship.

The usage statistics are very handy to calculate the return on investment and can be submitted instantaneously. The various ICT technologies like library automation, digital library, RFID Technology, Cloud computing enable automatically to generate various reports in whatever forms you need. The on line data can be captured through generated statistics for presenting to any person. The top management of any institute can be offered any type of statistics through manipulation. The return on investment of any elements can be given immediately. Thus is the power of ICT application. It has been boon to new era where the library is being viewed as business or enterprises and any activity, product or services can be tagged by money. The investment and return can be computed very effectively by the help of ICT application.

THE ACQUISITIONS OF READING MATERIAL

The academic libraries have been acquiring the reading material purely from investment angle. The library has to serve the generations of the students, faculty and staff of the institute. The library focus is very clear, to provide judicious number of Text Books that are included in syllabus for corresponding number of students. It has to acquire the reference books for piece of information, data, figures, statistics, etc. The procurement of scientific journals that provide primary source of information is focused on the subjects that are being taught.

This investment either in print or electronic form will definitely attract the users from ease point of view. The content pages of print version will tell the topics or articles of their interest where as in electronic version they have facility of searching at finger tips. The investment and its use are great that can be captured either manually or through machine generated statistics through automation. The great number of resources acquired can be put to effective use where the horizons of the stake holders will be widen in their academic pursuits. These can be computed manually or machine generated statistics.

The subject wise titles and volumes acquired of reading material either in print or electronic forms and its use statistics will offer the precise return on investment. Getting graduate or postgraduate or doctoral degree from any institute by using the reading material from library justifies the investment done in library.

At LIRC, VNIT the requirement of reading material for the students has always been kept in mind when order is placed. The priority for books in book bank is also extended to demand and corresponding number of students belonging to weaker section. Thus fulfilling satisfied users for whom the investment is done by the institute.

THE ORGANISATION OF LIBRARY

The library has numerous functions to perform while organising and planning the areas of reading spaces, areas of stacks, separate reading enclave, faculty cubicles, acquiring reading materials, furnishings and fixtures, services and skilled human resources. The major aspect the library has to focus is technically processing and stacking the reading material for its effective use by its stake holders.

Nowadays, the library can be organised with books and journals traditionally. But in the advent of ICT and its applications, the library has no choice to remain aloof from applications of ICT. The library has to have techno savvy human resources so that modern practices of information handling can be taken up immediately. The various functions such as acquisition, circulation, serials management and technical processing, indexing, OPACs, Web OPACs are always viewed from better investment point of view. In case, the library is focused and organised with proper planning and implemented ICT applications is bound to fetch the desired returns.

While organising the library, users focus has never been compromised e.g. the space between the rows of the stacks is 4 ft so that even when books are browsed by standing the users get comfort. The managers of LIRC are aware of the facts of comfort zones of their clientele thus the hustle bustle of the users in library pays good returns.

PLANNING THE SERVICES

Except the very old libraries where the reading used

to be done on the premises, the medieval and modern ones have lot of services to offer to its clientele. Alternatively, it can be said that user oriented services received top most priority while planning of services is conceived. A lot of brain storming is required for this activity in library. The ICT applications and emerging technologies assisted in planning better services for their enlightened customers.

The library services are devised on accumulation of reading materials in various forms and format, irrespective print or e-form or online access and place of residence. All the services revolve round the reactive and proactive phenomenon. The human resources in LIRC are on their tenterhooks to provide best possible services to its users. There are about 15-17 different services traditional or ICT based are provided to VNIT clientele. The users are very satisfied by the services as many of them are without human intervention. They are operated automatically and hassle free. The rules are very distinct with minimum problems.

The services are very excellent measure of investment in library and the satisfied users are good returns to be evaluated.

TECHNICAL PROCESSING

The technical processing of reading materials is done with standard practices set in through yesteryears. The new technological development such as automated processing Barcode and RFID technology labels and to enable each document getting circulated based on above technology is implemented in Library.

The keyword or word or Boolean with traditional author, title, subject searches have been made operational in LIRC since 1993. The OPAC and WEBOPAC were made operational in 2000. For binding and torn books are continuously separated from active collection. The enable the focused books are kept on the stacks that are conspicuously retrieved for reading purposes.

To bring the active books on forefront from huge collection of 1.20 lakhs is a good example of return on investment. The visibility of new books out of old collection facilitates more and more circulation and use of documents. The counter of usage statistics of technically processed documents offers extraordinary returns.

PRODUCTS GENERATED BY LIRC

A very few products of library is generated but are being effectively used. "VNIT LIRC AT A GLANCE", List of Elsevier books and journals, Department wise list of books and documents purchased in a financial year, Annual Report, are to mention the products. Presently, they are being internally marketed for the purpose. These products can be put for external market, if permitted by the authorities and revenue can be generated.

A portal to access the on campus e-resources with the help of Green Stone software is developed by one of the Library staff. This is being hosted on VNIT Website under "Library and Information Resources Centre". The content of this portal are, 2887 E-books, 697 online Elsevier journals of 5 subject collection, NPTEL resources, WEB OPAC of LIRC and other resources. This is an electronic product but it can be marketed to needy users outside the campus by tagging money to it.

VARIOUS FACILITIES DEVELOPED/ CREATED

A very specious reading room accommodating 250 students at a time is created at LIRC that works 24X7. A computer centre enabling to access the net related activities for students is housed in LIRC.

The 20 OPACs M/Cs for accessing library information have been deployed on each floor of Library. They can access on line journals and down load them in secondary media.

A self performing password guarded Circulating activities through KIOSK is created in entrance enclave of library. This enables the circulation done beyond business hours of library.

The whole library is under electronic Surveillance by installing 50 CCTV cameras where every activity of users is recorded. Any miscreant can be spotted through this mechanism.

The ambience of library is very inviting. The continuous cleaning, mopping, through housekeeping, welcoming human resources, guiding sin ages, hassle free process, elevator for physically challenged users, Suggestions BOX, are few of the entities done for inviting and welcoming the users in library.

This will definitely attract the non visitors and will increase the use of library investment giving maximum returns on facilities developed or created.

LAYOUT OF STACKS, FURNITURE FIXTURES CIRCULATION, PROPERTY ROOM

The quality stacks, furniture and fixtures where no compromise is done have been procured for use in 175X80 ft halls on each floor. The positions where to place has been methodically thought as per need and requirement of the students. The 12 mm glass top tables offers corporate look and cannot be mutilated by users. Spacious Standing Newspapers arrangement, 4 ft browsing space between stacks, window side reading arrangement, proper illumination offers inviting atmosphere thus giving corporate and easy to use look.

The property enclave has 2 CCTV cameras to monitor student's activities. Any missing or stealing is recorded for a month to help justice given to victim. The circulation counter has accommodated nodes, barcode hand held scanners and RFID Antenna, UPS, etc to offer hassle free activities.

A giant look of library with huge building complex speaks the investment idea and plans for posterity from the authorities. The external grandeur of Information complex gives fair idea of the internal activities being done from return on investment angle.

APPLICATION OF ICT AND GENERATION OF STATISTICS

The LIRC, VNIT Nagpur has been the forerunners for applications of ICT in their information activities. In way back 1993, the library automation including Barcode technology was conceived and made operational. The automated library and information services were not only started in LIRC but also on the campus too.

Then came digital library activities by getting sanction the project of IDLP from 2003 to 2005 costing Rs 20.00 lakhs where in vigorous activities pertaining to electronic library were undertaken.

The third one RFID technology was commenced in 2010. Every document in LIRC was tagged with chip and through electronic gate the property got secured. The Information KIOSK was placed at conspicuous corner where in the users can transact outside working hours of Library. A signature free activity through modern gadget was made operational and the system is reasonably stabilised from 2010.

The investment in the above three technology has established a reasonably hassle free ambience in library. The returns on this investment are number of visitors increased, misplacement of documents eradicated, peaceful environment, and error and hassle free transaction with library.

LOG OF ACTIVITIES IN LIBRARY

The applications of all above technologies has assisted the library to get generated the vital routine statistics while functioning on line. No separate programmes are needed to set in for this.

The LIBSYS 7 automation offers all the routinely required statistics. A daily transaction of circulation is automatically recorded as the library has decided to function online. Midway queries and reports in any module like acquisition, technical processing, and serials control and circulation can be answered conveniently. A management required stats such as slow and fast moving tiles, non visiting members, who have borrowed what and when it is expected back, statistics on stock I, II, III, history of who has taken which documents throughout the tenure can also be culled out.

Through digital library applications the log of usage can be conveniently culled out. Who has searched what, who has down loaded what, number of successful hits, history of query formulation, etc can be conveniently known.

The RFID unearth misplacement in the stacks through handheld inventory device by putting Accession number plus controlled and secured document stock. The transaction of the documents has been integrated with LIBSYS automation where in 'N' number of documents can be issued or returned in one go. The unauthorised operations done by miscreants in library can be detected at electronic gate. The major advantage of RFID technology is 24X7 transactions. The reading room facilities are also 24X7 in library.

The log of operations and availability of statistics at finger tips of the documents justifies the return on the investment done in library.

LITERARY PRODUCTION OF FACULTY/STUDENTS

The usage of library by clientele both students and faculty motivate them to have literary products of their own in the form of presentations, article in journals, book writing, chapters in book, research activities. This is the best return the library accrues through investing in information sources.

The students getting accreditation of degrees based on their studies in library, getting knowledge through years is a good return on investment. The alumni activities the yester year's students performs to their Alma matter is a good sign of return and acknowledgment displayed to the library they have used during their students age.

PLACEMENT OF THE STUDENTS IN INDUSTRIES

The students appear for campus selection activities during 4 years and get good openings in industries only due to excellent library facilities they get for lifelong learning. Around 70-75 % students get job opportunity during their education life. The library contributes to their information and knowledge base from where they become successful.

The placement of students can be viewed as good returns the library contributes to the life of the students. The investment done in the form of information resources in library and they are getting used in the development of knowledge of the students and ultimately getting good job at the end of studentship can be attributed as excellent returns on library investments.

PRODUCT AND SERVICES WITH MONETARY RETURNS

When the term ROI is discussed, it necessitates relating the activities to monetary terms. The investment that is usually done what monetary gain it has made is always questioned.

In Information and library environment, the products that are literary in nature and the services that are organised for the clientele, are meant for development of information and knowledge. But as on today no money is being earned as business in academic field.

The document enhances the personality, educational standard, culture and interpersonal relationship. The overall learned image and stature are developed. To tag this with money requires lot of brain storming sessions among the educated pundits and if decided the library can tag money to its product and services.

CALCULATION OF RETURN ON INVESTMENT AT LIRC

The necessary processes and activities delineated above in LIRC can be substantiated from return point of view. Every year huge funds on reading material, provision of facilities, applications of emerging technologies are infused as an investment. The asset value of library that has been calculated for insurance purposes is around Rs 10.00 Corers in 50 years. If we look from return point of view of this investment then we get the data of 10,000 graduates, 6,000 postgraduates and 2000 doctorates. The knowledge gained by these learned products has definitely given rich dividends on the investment done.

In academic field, the return on investment is intangible. The library activities are for the posterity of generation to come. It can be computed only on achievements and knowledge acquired by the stake holders. It is lifelong learning activities and can be put to use at any time by the learned product. The contributions to literary products can be one of the measures of return on investment but again it need to be tested on time frame. The time alone will assess the success of learned products through the investment done at LIRC.

The alumni activities done by yester year students (Learned products) help the Alma matter, is a pay back of investment. Nowadays, lot of competitive, sharing the experiences with students on campus, industry expertise and assistance in financing modern equipments for department, are the welcome gestures expressed by learned products. This can be visualised as excellent return on the investment.

CHAPTER OUTCOME

In this chapter, it has been discussed lot at various

points the concept of ROI. The library at VNIT has started its activities in the betterment of students and faculty knowledge base. As on today, they are social service activities. But tomorrow, if authorities decide to earn money out of the library activities, the library is in all readiness to perform. It has got vision and preparedness for new conceptualisation. There is always a caution, the moment the activities of library are tagged with money, the users will become demanding. In that situation it will be difficult to manage as the resources availability in library always remains a question mark due to lot of constraints in functioning of library.

The attitude of users for library to look from business point of view has not been established. It may take years to fix this but not that it is impossible. The change needs to be percolated slowly and effectively then the desired results can be achieved.

16
Applications of Cloud Computing with Special Reference to NITs

Keywords : *Cloud Computing, Cloud Based Services, NIT's.*

INTRODUCTION

The term "Cloud Computing" refers to any computing capability that is delivered as a service over the Internet. While there is no authoritatively accredited definition of the concept, one of the most frequently used definitions is the one given by Gartner, who describe cloud computing as a style of computing where massively scalable IT-related capabilities are provided as a service across the Internet to multiple external customers. For NIT's level cloud computing will help the integration of all institutes in a painless easy manner. Institutes will be able to share their data like admission process, hostel position, departmental activities, research work progress, student's achievement as well as activities, library e-resources sharing, video conferencing, distance learning etc. through cloud computing. The dependency of external agencies for different software in different department matters will be reduced considerably. Scalability of cloud computing will also help in saving money. Institute will also become greener by embracing the cloud. Server utilization, which will increase considerably, along with multi-tenancy, will help reduce carbon emission annually.

The institutional and LIRC functions of all the NITs will help-full for jumping in the cloud. No doubt these functions are increasing the efficiency of the institute and libraries services. Cloud based services will be producing new age for our today's engineers. They will invent new world for the betterment of lifelong learning. Implementation of cloud model plans to further enhance its ICT infrastructure by leveraging cloud virtualization for its entire fraternity of NITs.

BACKGROUND OF NITS IN INDIA

India is a huge country with a population of more than 1 billion. In India, by tradition, education and learning are highly valued. In fact, India has one of the largest higher education systems in the world, with regard to the number of institution. Education is a necessity. It is the most effective instrument with which the people can acquire the knowledge, skills, and capability to develop wisdoms it is developing nation. The seeds for some of India's higher education institutions were planted in the latter half of the Twenty Century. National Institutes of Technology (NITs) are premier institutes of engineering and technology in India and are the new faces of the earlier Regional Engineering Colleges (RECs).

In the year 2002, the Govt. of India's Ministry of Human Resource Development, decided to upgrade all the 17 existing Regional Engineering Colleges (RECs) as National Institutes of Technology (NITs), on the lines of the prestigious Indian Institutes of Technology (IITs). The NITs have the responsibility of providing high quality education in engineering and technology to produce competent technical manpower for the country. Libraries being treasure house of knowledge and information are one invaluable way to provide informal education since each library is a hub of all academic activities.

All the 30 NIT's now offer degree courses of Bachelors, Master and Doctorate levels in various branches of Engineering and Technology. The entire non recurring expenditure and expenditure for post graduate courses during the REC times were borne by the central government. On the other hand the entire recurring expenditure on undergraduate courses was shared equally by the central and state government. NITs have a Central Library equipped with technical books, literature, fiction, scientific journals, and other electronic material. Most have digitized their libraries. Some provide an intranet library facility. Every departmental library has high-speed connectivity. Electronic libraries allow students access to online journals and other periodicals through the AICTE-INDEST consortium, an initiative by the Ministry of Human Resource Development. Students also have access to IEEE documents and journals. While some have video conferencing facilities, others are upgrading under the World Bank funded TEQIP scheme.

FUNCTIONS OF INSTITUTIONS FOR PORTING ON CLOUD COMPUTING

Cloud Computing has become more popular now because it is realistically attainable by the all type of patron. This newly introducing technology has been put in place to improve efficiency of betterment in the services performed by the Institutes. All NITs having IT based infrastructure with huge collection of e-resources. At Institutional level cloud computing functions in the following ways:

- Established policies rules and regulations
- Availability of Highly qualified Techno savvy staff
- Consolidation of all the Institute and LIRC Resources.

- Adequate financial support for NITs
- TEQIP-II Project Functional
- Modern technological environment with 45 and 75 mbps internet connection lines.
- Huge collection of e-resources
- Well developed infrastructure for accessing cloud

FUNCTIONS OF RESOURCE CENTRE FOR PORTING ON CLOUD COMPUTING

Well developed infrastructures of all NIT's resource centres are ready to uplift the cloud based model. Application of Cloud Computing will improve the efficiency of the library services for reaches the user needs. Following are the present function delivered by resource centre of NIT's.

- Standard Practices at each LIRC
- Established Policies, Rules and Regulations
- Enriched awareness filled Human Resources
- Facilitating Management Support
- Adequate Financial Support
- TEQIP Funding
- Judicious & Resourceful Holding of basic branches and its access to E-resources
- Uninterrupted Technological Support from Institute
- Connectivity to INDEST-AICTE Consortium
- Qualified Network support
- Automated Libraries
- Functional RFID Implementation at few places
- Library Digitization Progress

JUSTIFICATION FOR NIT'S FOR MOVING ON TO CLOUD

The NIT's that are scattered geographically throughout India and having well developed access mechanism of electronic resources, should come together for single access resources mechanism. All the resources are available on different servers in all NIT's. But through cloud computing hiring the resources will be well organised and access will be disciplined through single window search.

The search formulations prepared for searching need not be applied for 30 different places that are how the situation. One single intelligent search mechanism will search and retrieve the resources showing placed at 30 places. The porting of NIT resources to cloud environment will avoid unavailability of resources due to non-functional servers at any of NIT's. The data or information collected at cloud can be diligently accessed 24 X 7. The cloud agency takes care of data security, availability and maintaining servers up for 24 X 7.

The convincing point for moving on to cloud by each NIT is cost sharing all resources at one point, assured access connectivity by cloud players. Many of the NIT's have resources in electronic form and wish to share with each other for their development. There will be no additional cost of acquiring the resource when it is available with other NIT and can be shared through cloud mechanism. The NIT consortia are in offing. The NIT Warangal has takes initiatives to share the Elsevier Journals of various subject collections. The NIT consortia can take up bringing the reality of cloud based services with single NIT Cloud.

CLOUD BASED SERVICES

By providing a cloud-based virtual desktop environmental services, students can study and access development coursework while effectively utilizing their time by connecting to the NIT's data centre at any time or place, instead of only being able to work at the information processing laboratory on the institutional campus. Distributed resources of all the NITs, in case, clubbed together will enable the single window access mechanism through cloud computing. Cloud computing includes three major delivery models for the cloud based services

PLATFORM AS A SERVICE (PAAS)

Platform as a service is a type of services meant for cloud developers, means to develop a platform to build up, install and control SaaS applications. This platform usually includes databases; software glue with its infrastructure and services is internet accessible by institutional user. Cloud-computing platforms are emerging from a number of organizations like OCLC (WorldShare Platform), ExLibris (Alma), Serials Solution, Library Thing, Hathi Trust, SirisDynix, Summon, DuraCloud, Google App Engine. Microsoft Azure services, CloudFoundry, Amazon Web Service, and Enterprise KOHA have since demonstrated the usefulness of cloud computing in hosting NIT's workflow on to a common platform.

SOFTWARE AS A SERVICE (SAAS)

Software as a service a software distribution form in which applications are hosted by services supplier and ended to clientele over the internet. Clientele purchase the facility to access and utilize an application or service which is packed in the cloud. SaaS is usually available on demand and via the internet and can thus be configured remotely. SaaS service providers offer special selections of software running on their infrastructure. SaaS is also known as software on demand. Thus, this service is highly cost-effective and location independent. When all NIT's collaboration implementing cloud based software as a service they automatically get benefit to institute and students also regarding the cost. The applications are accessible from various client devices through a thin client interface such as web browser (e. g. Web-based email).

INFRASTRUCTURE AS A SERVICE (IAAS)

Cloud computing offers virtualized systems to access to computer hardware resources such as networks and storage. IaaS, Infrastructure as a service, defined by the variety of services to supply, i.e. servers, storage and network hardware. IaaS provides virtual machines and other related hardware and software systems through a service-based application programming interface (API). The gathering of NIT's are having capability provided to the all institute scattered geographically all over the India is to provision processing, storage, networks, and other fundamental computing resources where the institute can easily manage or control the underlying cloud infrastructure & control over operating systems; storage, deployed applications, and possibly limited control of select networking components. E.g. like Education ERP.net, Microsoft Flexiscale, Amazon S3, Cloudstatus, GoGrid, and Oracle Coherence are offering IaaS.

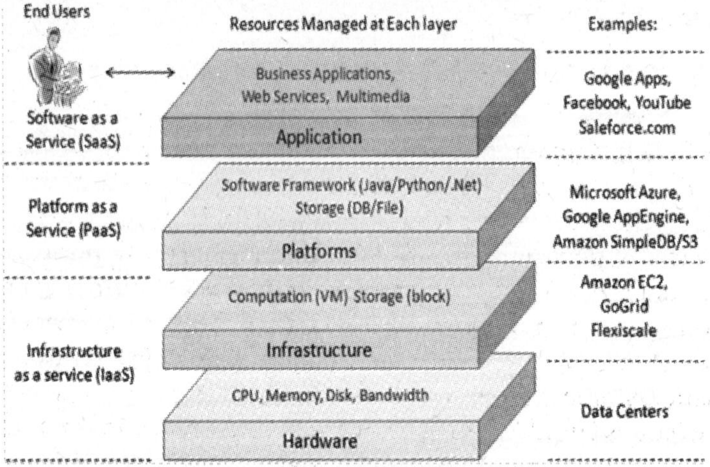

Fig. 1. Cloud Computing Service Delivery Model for gathering of NIT's

FEASIBILITY AND IMPLEMENTATION

For attempting future challenges & decision face by institutes it is necessity of determining feasibility of the adoption of cloud computing in the NIT's. The feasibility of cloud based architecture can adopt to solve financial and technical challenges in the Institutes. When cloud computing promising innovative uses to serve institutional and students need as well then it is feasible for institutes. Implementation & Feasibility of cloud computing promises a radical shift in the provisioning of computing resource within the institutes.

It is necessary to have a pilot study for feasibility and implementation done at any cloud savvy NIT. Depending upon the infrastructure any NIT can be chosen to have this study before moving on to cloud platform. The study will direct the NIT for coming together for cloud computing. Initially, they may have lot of reservations for these CC activities that is why the feasibility study needs to be undertaken. Many computing experts may discard the very idea of cloud computing but to convince them for this platform, we expect this study will assist them in right direction.

CONSENSUS OF NITS RESOURCE CENTRES FOR CC

As all of us know, now a days' cloud computing is an emerging technology. For tagged cloud computing as standardization, virtualization and all advancement model consensus of opinion is the necessity. Coming together, is the major issue for implementing this newer paradigm of cloud computing. There is an art in building this consensus, as different NIT's with unique requirements need to come together to make this a success. The key is communication and consistency starting from collection of requirement to delivery of services.

Despite of having tremendous infrastructure with each NIT, it is necessary to come together and identify the unique resources that can be ported on cloud for the benefit of others. Those resources can be either intuitional related or library related. The idea for moving on to cloud platform by each NIT is, to access the varied and significant resources that need to be shared by every NIT. For this there is absolute need to have consensus among the NITs. The NIT consortia that are in offing can be a good platform for this cloud computing activities. The consensus for cloud computing will be advantageous in saving the future infrastructure and cost reduction in acquiring and maintaining various servers and nodes that can be hired at reasonable cost. It will promise the green computing environment at every campus of NIT.

ADVANTAGES OF CLOUD COMPUTING TO NIT COMMUNITY

Easy Management

The maintenance of the infrastructure, be it hardware or software is simplified, thus, less headaches for the NITs Community team. Also applications that are quite storage extensive are more easier to use in the cloud environment compared to the same when used by the organization by its own. Also at the user level, what you mostly need is a simple web browser with internet connectivity.

Flexibility and Innovation

Many people's love to use the cloud computing because of the great benefit of flexibility, users can access stored data anywhere in the world, but the thing is you need a computer/laptop/smart phone/Android/ Blackberry and other applicable devices with internet connections. NIT's staff and users can access the data and files outside the office and library at any time. Cloud computing provides flexibility in implementing changes and new technologies without high risk and cost. OPAC and the mobile web application hosted in the cloud, the resources devoted to each will shrink and expand as traffic raises and drops. Further creating and configuring new virtual server instances is fast and easy in the cloud.

Disaster Management

In case of disasters, an offsite backup is always helpful. Keeping crucial data backed up using cloud storage services is the need of the hour for all IT infrastructural based NIT's. Also cloud storage services not only keep your data off site, but they also ensure that they have systems in place for disaster recovery.

Green Computing

Harmful emissions due to extensive use of systems in NIT's, electronic waste generated as the time passes and energy consumption is the main disadvantage of the present day computing systems. This can be reduced to some extent by using cloud computing services. This leads to environment preserving. Also the e-waste is generated to minimum extent.

Lower Cost Reduction and Increased Efficiency

One of the most significant features of cloud storage is cost effectiveness, as a library needs to pay only for the cloud space that its data actually requires and does not need to pay for storage overhead in advance. There is also no need or cost for file storage equipment, server setup and maintenance, staff time, power usage and backup. A cloud provider can offer an infinite amount of resources to many users. Because of reduced cost and time, institutes can focus efforts elsewhere and be more efficient. Cloud computing offers price savings due to economies 0 scale and the fact that you are only paying for the resources you actually use. Like water and electricity, a computing cloud is a communally-shared resource that you lease on a metered basis, paying for as little as you need, when you need it. When all NIT's gathered for implementing cloud computing, a cloud platform can reduce costs by 80% or more, because non-core code is already engineered same time they can increased efficiency in all departmental work with accuracy. E.g. like even simple applications like email can be set up and mostly free through applications like Google Apps.

Lower risks

All NIT's working platform are similar in manner so, cloud platform can reduce risks by as much, because common functions are already tested, sometimes over a period of years.

Faster time-to-market innovation

Cloud platforms dramatically reduce time-to-market, because they serve as a launch pad for software engineering efforts. With the use of cloud computing innovators production can be produced by NIT's.

Higher profit margins

Department wise requirement of software developers and system integration firms can deliver more for substantially less, thus higher margins on fixed price contracts, automatically NIT's are achieve profit margins

Higher security and interoperability

NIST (National Institute of Standard and Technology) indicates that the cloud suffers from major security issues, largely because vendors are implementing disparate and unproven security models. But for NIT's Cloud platforms provide a common, proven security model. If cloud software uses the platform, then it is inherently secure.

Reliability

While internet connectivity and the provider itself being subject to outages is a scary fact of the nature of cloud computing, there is still more reliability in comparison to in-house systems because of the economies of scale. The vendor is more able to give 24/7 technical support and highly trained experienced staff to support the infrastructure at its best condition, and the benefits will reach all their clients. Compare this to each NIT's having a team of on-site IT people with varied skill set.

High Secured Infrastructure

High security is the today's need for all NIT's. Cloud computing may affect libraries and other departments of the NIT's, as well as IT infrastructure of the foundation of the library system and Institution. It is known that IT unit within a library and institutional departments always takes on heavy duties and hold high responsibilities for an entire NIT's. Usually, a library allocates a large amount of its budget to build up its secured infrastructure, such as computing abilities, networking equipment and storage, however IT resources are not effectively used among the integrated library system (ILS) and various digital initiatives. Instead of relying on in-house IT infrastructure, some libraries have begun using high secured cloud infrastructure for their IT services among the all NIT's collaboration.

Fast Service (Always up time)

Cloud computing service providers are having cloud infrastructure, so server always in up-time. This results you no destruct ions in resource centre. Depending upon the NIT's students educational needs have to choose plans for fast access service.

More Storage Capacity

No need to worry about the lot of data and files to store, this provides more data to save the files in server. Here depending upon the data and usage you can choose the plan, available in different modes. Everything is online, store the entire data in cloud and can access at any time, ant where in browser.

Simplicity of Integration

Cloud computing may play an important role in

transforming the integrated library system(ILS) that provides core services for a library and is comprised of an online public access catalogue, a cataloguing module, a serials control module and reporting module.

CHAPTER OUTCOME

To develop cloud based economy and industry becoming increasingly competitive; NIT's institute strives to cultivate highly talented individuals who will flourish under such an environment. To fulfil this goal the institute has undertaken a number of initiatives, including strengthening its student support, expanding its academic curriculum, beginning with pre admission education, promoting its career support services and enhancing its campus facilities. As part of these efforts, and in order to offer high quality education resources that can be conveniently accessed, National Institute of Technology can be shortly developed a cloud based virtual desktop environment for its all NIT's campus.

There is an absolute necessity for NITs to switch over the cloud computing environment, though they have excellent infrastructure developed. But the common resources either institute oriented or LIRC developed, need a common platform for accessing the information through single window. Single search retrieving information irrespective of its forms and format and location, would be reality through cloud platform. The sharing of much information to student's activities on the campus, placement records, syllabus content, faculty academic excellence, emerging information services, specific information source etc will be required nowadays by students, faculty and staff of NITs.

17
Information Literacy

Keywords : *Information Communication Technology, Information Literacy, LIS Professionals, Library Services.*

INTRODUCTION

In this digital age explosion of information and knowledge and advancement in technology, every day comes with new idea and new developed technology. Information is doubling every three to five years and technology is providing increased access to previously restricted or unknown information source, user face both difficult challenges and unlimited opportunities. Therefore to achieve the success everyone must aware to the ICT literacy. When LIS professional are familiar with the advancement then there is not arising any problem providing the library services and understanding the user's problems. Information and Communication Technologies (ICT) over the last few years have transformed and continue to transform the way in which we communicate. Within a relatively short period of time, the Internet has grown to the point where it is now possible to access information on almost every conceivable subject with just a few clicks of a button. However, this new availability of information raises many issues for the Librarians, Information Managers and Library Users. Finally the skills are needed for understanding working responsibilities and smooth functioning of services to satisfy the user requirements.

Developments in the ICT have made profound changes in each and every field. These developments are also known as computer/information/communication/ Internet/multimedia revolution, binary age, information age, information society, information superhighway, and digital age. The changes are evident all over the world, and its effects being felt in every walk of life and in every field of knowledge. Information Communication Technology (ICT) is a combination of computer and telecommunication techniques which makes possible new systems and products to help people at work in education and at home. Information communication technology is the application of a wide variety of electronic technologies to the information handling activities.

THE CONCEPT

Information Literacy is a new art that extends from knowing how to use computers and access information to critical reflection on the nature of information itself, its technical infrastructure, and its social, cultural and even philosophical context and impact (Shapiro & Hughes, 1996).

Information Literacy is the ability to: locate, use, present and evaluate information effectively and efficiently for a given purpose or need.

Several definitions are created by scientists and thinkers but for library professional related to library science appropriate wording adopted by the American Library Association (ALA), 1998 'To be information literate, a person must be able to recognize when information is needed and have the ability to locate, evaluate, and use effectively the needed information. The information literate individuals are those who have learned how to learn'. They know how to learn because they know how knowledge is organized, know how to find information, and know how to use information in such a way that others can learn from them.

DEVELOPING THE LIBRARY STANDARDS

Information literacy is a core instructional pedagogy in higher education. The Association of College and Research Libraries, the primary professional organization for academic librarians, first described information literacy in 1989. Numerous disciplinary and accrediting associations have also incorporated the Information Literacy Standards for Higher Education and/or information literacy language into their documents. All our librarian-provided research instruction is based on these five standards

- Can the student identify the information need?
- Can the student find the information needed?
- Can the student evaluate the information retrieved?
- Can the student synthesize to create a new information product?
- Does the student behave with an awareness of the ethical and legal issues regarding information use?

These five standards are very useful to satisfy the users, when these standards follow by all LIS professionals definitely the revolution occur in the field of library. After all housekeeping operation of the libraries are doing for the patron. Therefore the ICT literacy among the LIS professionals is the topmost priority. We all are aware about the traditional literacy programmes like Read, Write, Calculate and knowing the related things etc. Computer Literacy programme includes PC Operation, Spread Sheet, Word Processor, Presentation, Email etc. and the Information Literacy programme involve Computer Literacy, Information Finding, Information Understanding, Information Value Creation, Collaboration and Communication with additional quality of ability to solve problems takes advantage of information technology and networks. Social development required these ICT literate personality for modernising the library ambience and innovation in the library services.

NEED OF ICT BASED INFORMATION LITERACY PROGRAMME

Information literacy is more than just teaching students how to use the library. The goal of information literacy is to develop 21st century information and technology competencies and the skills for lifelong learning. Information literate students are able to find, evaluate and use information effectively to solve problems and make decisions. Learn more about how the librarians can support your student and collaborate with you to improve the research skills of your students. Information overloads needs the ICT based services and products, the library professionals need to enhance their level of ICT literacy. Some are the ways to organise the ICT based Literacy Programmes

- Workshops
- Tutorials
- Brainstorming Sessions
- Techniques, tools, methods
- Different ICT based literacy programmes
- ICT based policies
- Principles
- Pilot Projects
- Models

INFORMATION LITERACY STANDARDS AND INDICATORS

In 1998 American Association of School Librarians and Association for Educational Communications and Technology prepared a document titled 'Information literacy standards for student learning: standards and indicators', which is widely accepted worldwide as a set of information literacy standards that can be imparted to produce information literate citizen. The each standard has some indicators that show kinds of competency and parameters to accomplish that standard. As far nine standards are identified which have three broad spectrums, such as information literacy standards, independent learning standards and social responsibility standards. Although these standards and indicators are initially developed for students, these can be equally applicable to the common citizens as well as technical libraries users. The information literacy standards and respective indicators are shown in the Table indicates that information literates are also independent learners, and information literates who contribute positively to the community use information ethically and responsibly.

Information Literacy Standards and Indicators

Standards	**Indicators**
Information Literacy Standards	
1. The person who is information literate accesses information efficiently and effectively.	1. Recognizes the need for information. 2. Recognizes that accurate and comprehensive information is the basis for intelligent decision-making. 3. Formulates questions based on information needs. 4. Identifies a variety of potential sources of information. 5. Develops and uses successful strategies for locating information.
2. The person who is information literate evaluates information critically and competently.	1. Determines accuracy, relevance, and comprehensiveness. 2. Distinguishes among fact, point of view, and opinion. 3. Identifies inaccurate and misleading information.

	4. Selects information appropriate to the problem or question at hand.
3. The person who is information literate uses information accurately and creatively.	1. Organizes information for practical application. 2. Integrates new information into one's own knowledge. 3. Applies information in critical thinking and problem solving. 4. Produces and communicates information and ideas in appropriate formats.
Independent Learning Standards	
4. The person who is an independent learner is information literate and pursues information related to personal interests.	1. Seeks information related to various dimensions of personal well-being, such as career interests, community involvement, health matters, and recreational pursuits. 2. Designs, develops, and evaluates information products and solutions related to personal interests.
5. The person who is an independent learner is information literate and appreciates literature and other creative expressions of information.	1. Is a competent and self-motivated reader. 2. Derives meaning from information presented creatively in a variety of formats. 3. Develops creative products in a variety of formats.
6. The person who is an independent learner is information literate and strives for excellence in information seeking and knowledge generation.	1. Assesses the quality of the process and products of personal information seeking. 2. Devises strategies for revising, improving, and updating self-generated knowledge.

Components of ICT Literacy

Proficiency	Definition
Define	ICT tools to identify and appropriately represent an information need
Access	Collecting and/or retrieving information in digital environments
Manage	Using ICT tools to apply an existing organizational or classification scheme for information
Integrate	Interpreting and representing information, such as by using ICT tools to synthesize, summarize, compare and contrast information from multiple sources
Evaluate	Judging the degree to which information satisfies the needs of the task in ICT environments, including determining authority, bias and timeliness of materials
Create	Adapting, applying, designing or inventing information in ICT environments
Communicate	Communicating information properly in its context (audience, media) in ICT environments

ELECTRONIC INFORMATION LITERACY

The more electronic resources libraries acquire and make available to users, the grater the demand for instruction in how to access and use those resources effectively and efficiently. Information literacy includes information technology skill, such as use of computers, software applications, and information retrieval tools, but it is a broader area of competence that encompasses the content, analysis and communication of information.

CHANGING TECHNOLOGY LANDSCAPE

Technology is highly dynamic and changing at a

very fast pace. Rapid advance in ICT is constantly changing so fast that it is becoming increasingly difficult for LIS professional to keep track and pace with the emerging technologies. There were also various types of electronic sources through which LIS professionals improving their competencies for their effective utilization of high quality information services to the user community.

- E-Books
- E-Journals
- Portal
- Vortals
- Subject Gateways
- Knowledge Centres
- Document Delivery Service
- Electronic Selective Dissemination of Information

E-Books

Electronics book or e-books are books in file format in the computer, which can be read with specific software. It is interesting to read with animation, sound etc. they are fast, cheaper, searchable and can print, make a copy etc. Some of the software used for e-books reading is Acrobat e-book reader/ glass book reader, Microsoft reader, Net library e-books reader etc. E-books available on the web sites are downloaded either free of cost or paying a fee.

E- Journals

Electronic journals are a fast-developing feature of electronic publishing. E-journal can be defined as any journal exiting in an electronic format that embraces all periodicals available electronically as well as in paper copy, including the text of periodicals accessible through online networks. Many e-journals are available on internet or different field, particularly for the field of library science for the benefit information users as for example LIBRES (Library and Information Research Electronic Journals), MC (The Journal of Academic Media Librarianship) and Electronic Journal of Communication etc.

Portal

The demands of the contemporary society has become highly selective and expect customized information be it either about products or services, Reaching out to such demands successfully has become possible through mechanisms namely 'Portals'.

Michael Looney and Peter Lyman define them as "Portal gather a variety of useful information resources into a single, 'one-stop' web page, helping the user to avoid being overwhelmed by info-glut or feeling lost on the web". Portal is the frame work of higher education as a site having the following characteristic:

- Gateway that provides a single point of entry to information and tools
- Targeted used group
- Easy to use
- Accessible from anywhere anytime

Vortal

Vortal is short for voice portal. Vertical industry portal is a portal web site that provides information and resources for a particular industry. Vortals are the internet's way of catering to customer's focused environment preferences. Vortal typically provide news, research and statistics, discussions, newsletters, online tools and many other services that educate user about a specific industry.

As the web becomes a standard tool for business, vortal will join and may be replace general sites like AOL and YAHOO as a common gateway to the internet. On the web a vertical portal (sometimes called as Vortal) is a web site that provides a gateway or portal to information related to a particular industry such as health care Insurance.

Subject Gateways

Subject gateways are familiar features of the world information landscape and fulfil a useful role in directing Internet users to quality information. Gateway information is e-journal, datasets, e-books, educational institutions, and homepages. The establishing of the gateways as a process of identification, filtering, description, classification and indexing before they added to a database which is freely available via www the most essential element of a subject gateway is a catalogue, or directory of internet sources, Subject gateways are online services and sites that prove searchable and brow-sable catalogues of internet based resources.

Knowledge Centres

The Knowledge Centre, through which the centres already provides a vast database of explicit, cutting-edge knowledge from all over the world, plans to grow into an interactive knowledge incubator, organiser and producer over the years, Users of the Knowledge Centre can access the vast library, Gyansarovar, as well as value added services through the online databases, digitised brochures. Pre-programming and post-programming material, additional readings related to the training and development programmes conducted at the college library or knowledge centre. Other resources offered include a vast array of articles from relevant journals, case studies and documentation on best practices.

Document Delivery Service

INFLIBNET has already initiated a pilot project under which six libraries have been identified to serve as document delivery centres using their own resource base. The services of three UGC information centres in this respect will also be utilized. INFLIBNET also act as a document delivery centre to acquire and deliver the required document INFLIBNET play the role of catalyst in promoting co-operative collection development rationalization of periodical collection, reciprocal borrowing and promote other viable methods which facilitate maximization of resources.

Electronic Selective Dissemination of Information

By maintaining 'user profile' and 'document profile' one can provide E-SDI service to its users. The list of latest addition to the library, journal articles of user's interest can be scanned and sent as an attachment. Also articles of interest downloaded from www can also be saved later on sent to the user or pasted on the bulletin board of the library page, it save the time required to surf the net.

CHAPTER OUTCOME

LIS professionals in Information Literacy have to play important role. In the era of information communication technology, information knowledge, information storage and retrieval has become unbelievable. Globalization of new technology and increase in quality of information are all sources of information like various types of e-document, media and internet. LIS professional have to play a significant role to promote information literacy in society. There exists a gap between librarians and the user's information needs. To bridge the gap they need to educate and re-educate themselves to acquire new skills, new knowledge and competencies for a new role and they need to cultivate the concept of lifelong learning of information literacy skills. LIS professionals need to play an important role in education process by making people aware of need and motivating the use of e-technology a new knowledge and new ability.

18

Ideas of Dr. S. R. Ranganathan in the Light of Digital Era

Keywords: *Dr. S. R. Ranganathan, laws, digital era, library services, e-resources, digital library, reference service, search formulation.*

INTRODUCTION

In the era of information explosion, the tremendous amount of information is being generated and transmitted from every corner of the world. Information is the key to democracy. We all are very much well acquainted that information are rapidly explored. So it is our duty to manage that information systematically and properly with the help of digital technology. Libraries and information centres put lot of effort and energy into designing information services and products and distributing them to satisfy their users. Dr. S. R. Ranganathan is the greatest thinker in the field of library and information science and his overall contribution lead to present digital era. His precious contribution is five laws of library science, colon classification (Library classification scheme), classified catalogue code, indexing, chain indexing, abstracting, and documentation and its facets. Dr. S. R. Ranganathan views are seen as representing the past libraries and it is against this background that we need to go back to his principles.

In this technological age the role of librarians and the importance of libraries are even now based on the basic principles of library science described by Dr. S. R. Ranganathan in his five laws of library science. At the age of Dr. S. R. Ranganathan his way of looking at future libraries five laws of library science strategy exactly applicable in this digital era. Successful organic relationship between Dr. S. R. Ranganathan age to digital age for search formulation or pinpointed information search is possible through these five laws. Not only five laws but also all the ideas regarding library science are ultimately reaches fast and easy retrieval of information for the patron. To fulfil the challenges in digital era reference service play a vital role for library professionals. Views of Dr. S. R. Ranganathan for reference service are very effective in today's libraries. According to him multiple cross reference entries, cross reference index entries, ready reference service and long range reference service are useful in all each and every moment, ancient to present environment for retrieving information of the needs of patron. Allots of search engines are available and procurement of needed information is very difficult task for library professionals. When we search information for particular term we get at-random information and for retrieving pinpointed information from the garbage appropriate search formulation is the necessity. As per Dr. S. R. Ranganathan's views for search formulation the terminology like alternative terms, synonyms, antonyms, homonyms, identifier, indexing terms, descriptive terms, descriptors these all helps for retrieving right information to the right user at the right time. It is a measure greatness of Dr. S. R. Ranganathan of his way of looking at libraries can influence our strategies for today's digital library services.

INFORMATION PROCESSING AND DISSEMINATION SERVICES

Information Processing and dissemination is a proactive information service designed to educate and inform focused groups of users on social, economic and educational issues, problems, and opportunities of interest to them. It requires systematic planning, collection, organization, and storage of information for its delivery to the target audience using different media and communication means. Let us now discuss the importance of information Processing and dissemination before moving on to a user's information needs.

Information processing and dissemination services in resource centre/libraries are the proper term for glorifying patron expectation. It is not the only symptom of the digital era libraries are coping with but with no doubt it is a huge challenge, for libraries. It gives the library the opportunity and the duty to research itself and define new roles, more fitted to this changing environment and its users. Libraries and its librarian have a lot to offer. Their expertise within the field of information including retrieval skills, metadata, information and knowledge management or even the familiarity of using criteria in order to judge reliability and accuracy of information is an important professional tools. It is rare qualities and valuable ones at the current information environment.

PREAMBLE OF DR. S. R. RANGANATHAN

Shiyali Ramamrita Ranganathan's life span 9th August 1892 to 27th September 1972, he was a mathematician and librarian from India. His most notable contributions to the field were his five laws of library science and the development of the first major analytic-synthetic classification system, the colon classification. He is considered to be the father of library science, documentation and Information science in India and is widely known throughout the rest of the world for his fundamental thinking in the field. His birthday is observed every year as the National Library Day in India. He was a university librarian and professor of library science at Benares Hindu University (1945–47) and professor of library science at the University of Delhi (1947–55). The last appointment made him director of the first Indian school of librarianship to offer higher degrees. He was president of the Indian Library Association from 1944 to 1953. In 1957 he was elected an honorary member of the International Federation for Information and Documentation (FID) and was made a vice president for life of the Library Association of Great Britain. He had great capacity for work and was renowned for his abstemious life-style. Due to his standard life-style he received a number of high honors like, in the year 1948, he received an honorary doctorate of literature from the University of Delhi, 1970, he received the Margaret Mann Citation in Cataloguing and Classification of the American Library Association, After his death, the FID, in 1976 established the Dr. S. R. Ranganathan award in his memory, etc.

MAJOR CONTRIBUTION OF DR. S. R. RANGANATHAN IN LIS

Five laws of library science

Dr. S. R. Ranganathan's contributions to library science were in the Five Laws of Library Science (1931) was widely accepted as a definitive statement of the ideal of library service. He also drafted plans for an national and several state library systems, founded and edited several journals, and was active in numerous professional associations.

Colon Classification

Colon Classification is the system of library organisation developed by Dr. S. R. Ranganathan in

(1933). It is general rather than specific in nature, and it can create complex or new categories through the use of facets, or colons. In it, there are 108 main classes and 10 generalized classes, which are represented by a mixed notation of Arabic numerals and Roman and Greek letters. Each main class comprises five fundamental facets, or groups: personality, matter, energy, space and time.

Classified Catalogue Code

Classified Catalogue Code in (1934), just a year after The Colon Classification came out Dr. S. R. Ranganathan published another important work, the Classified Catalogue Code. Dr. S. R. Ranganathan maintained, however, that a catalogue should consist of two components one part should be classified by subject, reflecting the library's classification system, with class number entries. The other should be a dictionary catalogue, including author, title, series, and similar identifiers, as well as alphabetized subject entries. The function of a catalogue is to itemize works so they can be found by author, title, series, and so forth. It must also allow readers to review the selection of works on a given subject.

Chain Indexing

Chain Indexing to determine subject entries for the dictionary catalogue, Dr. S. R. Ranganathan devised an ingeniously Simple method called chain indexing. This method simply uses each facet of a subject, together with its immediately preceding facets, as an index entry. Thus, all important aspects of the subject, from the most general to the most specific, are automatically covered. Chain indexing can be adapted to other classification systems as well.

Five Laws of Library Science (1931)
Colon Classification (1933)
Classified Catalogue Code (1934)
Prolegomena to Library Classification (1937)
Theory of the Library Catalogue (1938)
Elements of Library Classification (1945)
Classification and International Documentation (1948)
Philosophy of Library Classification (1950)

Classification and Communication (1951)
Headings and Canons (1955)
Reference Service, 2nd ed. (1961)
Documentation and Its Facets (1963)

Prolegomena to Library Classification (1967)
Documentation: Genesis and Development (1973)
New Education and School Library (1973)

Fig. 1. Dr. S. R. Ranganathan Contributions

HOW DR. S. R. RANGANATHAN'S LAW IDEAS GLORIFYING DIGITAL ERA

Regular change is the continuous process in every stage of development, but every change should be developed with the support of basic principles. Technology has drastically changed the way librarians define themselves and the way they think about their profession and the institutions they serve. The librarian in the digital world now acts as a guardian of information, as a consultant to the users, an information broker and also a continuous learner. The platform of Internet and WWW has helped to change the ways of accessing and locating information and thereby change the functions of an librarian and library in the modern information society. The role of librarians and the importance of libraries in this digital era are even now based on the basic principles of library science described by Dr S.R Ranganathan in his Five Laws of Library Science.

In the digital era it might be useful replace the term "book" with the term "sources of information and knowledge" and the term "reader" with the term "user" like that Dr. S. R. Ranganathan original laws are applicable to digital environment. Dr. S. R. Ranganathan laws are meant to be elemental, in order to capture essential meaning and to convey a deep understanding of libraries. As libraries innovation and creativity is needed for pro-activism. Success in such initiative is a road in which the libraries can turn Dr. S. R. Ranganathan's vision into the evolutionary reality.

Dr. S. R. Ranganathan Five Laws to Digital Era Five Laws

Dr. S. R. Ranganathan Five Laws	Digital Era Five Laws
Books are for use	Digital resources are for use
Every person his or her book	Every user his/her Digital resource
Every book its reader	Every Digital resource its user
Save the time of the reader	Save the time of the user
The library is a growing organism	The Digital resource is a growing organism

Books are for use ⟹ Digital resources are for use

The first law constitutes the basis for the library services. Dr. S. R. Ranganathan observed that books were often chained to prevent their removal and that the emphasis was on storage and preservation rather than use. According to him preservation and storage are important, but he noticed that the purposes of such activities are also promoting the use of them. This law of library science supports that the library should have well educated and well qualified staff so that they can provide better service to the users. Library staff should not forget the noble cause of service, which secured them the scholarship, training, emoluments and status. They should see that the books are put to maximum use by readers. The collection should be kept up-to-date and balanced. Librarian should be cheerful and lovable. He should act as friend, philosopher and guide to his readers.

This new revised version of Dr. S. R. Ranganathan law ideas gives us the grounding for library profession in this digital era. This law focuses on the selective use of information. For proper use of information there should be proper storage and dissemination of information. "Right information, to Right user at the Right time" is the duty of each and every professional in library and information science. Digital era libraries are well automated, fully equipped with recent technology and very much advance in nature which should be support for proper storage and dissemination of information to right reader. The Web was designed to meet the human need to share information resources, knowledge, and experience. Digital era professionals want interact to patron with their web sites and pages, click on them, read them, print them if they need to, and have fun. This law implies that the digital resources are for using and learning information for use through ICT technology. Government of this digital era has also taken initiatives to serve the information to its citizens in the form of e-government projects. ICT has play important role through the internet which can avail information globally. This law is very important because information serves no purpose if it is not utilized and at least available for patron to attempt to learn. The role of the digital resources like e-journals, e-books, repositories are to serve the individual, community and service, and to maximize social utility in the communication process. The library and information professionals have to perform the role of information navigator, knowledge manager, information evaluator etc. Libraries/Resources centres all are serving organisations which having duty of fulfilling readers need at any cost and every professional must faith in this law for this, professionals always prevent obstacles in the way of readers, like restriction in digital access password, membership etc. This law dictates that development of systems that accommodate the use of digital resources. For instance, updating and regular indexing of digital resources as well as user orientation to justify the use of digital operations. If Dr. S. R. Ranganathan were alive today he would applaud the open access movement on the grounds that "books are for use".

Every person his or her book □□□ Every user his/her Digital resource

The first law was from the side of books, whereas the second law is from the side of users of the books i.e the law belongs to user oriented way. This law guides the library or information professionals to take care of information users, so that they can access information without any obstacle. Here is a necessity of user survey, user study and user education. The library staff has a great role of play in the success of the second law. The staff should try to attract the users to the library and expose them to the collection. This can be done in different ways-by publicity, by extension activities, by display within the library, etc. This law suggests that every member of the community should be able to obtain materials needed. Dr. S. R. Ranganathan felt that all individuals from all social environments were entitled to library service, and that the basis of library use was education, to which all were entitled. These entitlements were not without some important obligations for both libraries/librarians and library patrons. Librarians should have excellent first-hand knowledge of the people to be served. Collections should meet the special interests of the community, and libraries should promote and advertise their services extensively to attract a wide range of readers.

Presently no information centre or library is self sufficient to serve all types of information to a particular patron because of information explosion, budget crunches in the library and raising cost of the digital resources. But through the networking and the consortium approach of the e-journals e-books, help to meet the needs of patrons. This law has many implications for the digital era and law reveals the fundamental need for balance between making digital resources and the basic right of all users to have access to the digital resources they need anywhere in the world. Digital resources must contain appropriate material to the needs of all its users. Librarian must know their users well if they are to provide them with the materials they need for their research or that they wish to read. Every librarian has a responsibility to instruct and guide users in the process of search for web documents they need for enjoyment, education or research. Clearly, it is the duty of Librarian to know the user, to know the web resources, to actively help in the finding and retrieving by every user of his or her digital resource, and to help search engines in the process of indexing web sites and digital resources. Librarian must acknowledge that users of web sites, themselves included, use and value different means of communications in the pursuit of knowledge, information and entertainment. Every patron has a right to information so; digital resource designer should do their best to meet reader's needs. And every cyberian/librarian must value of all means for preserving and communicating the records and achievements of the human mind and heart.

Every book its reader □□□□ Every Digital resource its user.

Third law is information oriented. Dr. S. R. Ranganathan observed that the library could devise many methods to ensure that each book finds it appropriate reader. One method involved the basic rules for access to the collection, most notably the need for open shelving. Open access provides an opportunity for the reader to go around the stack at his will and pleasure. It gives an opportunity to the reader to lay his hand on any book he wants. Every piece of information should be serving to users. Thus information professionals have to organize the information in such a manner that maximum information is used by user correctly and properly.

In modern situation information professional have to accept the information technology to organize and manage the information. In today's digital age most of the university and institutions libraries in India are digitized. Now e-books, e-journals, and other e-resources have taken place into the libraries instead of the print collections. Automated technical process of the library collection such as cataloguing, indexing and abstracting etc. helps user in the context of the third law of library and information science. Patron searches the web sites, or gains access to the web's services; there are certain web resources that will meet his or her needs. It is librarian job to ensure that the connection between the user and the digital resources is made and that connection is as practical, easy and speedy as possible. Appropriate arrangement of documents in a web site is also an important means of achieving this objective of the third law. According to Dr. S. R. Ranganathan views digital resource exists for every user and that resource should be well described and indexed in the search engines, indexes, displayed in an attractive manner on the site and made readily available to users. This law leads naturally to such practices as open access rather than closed files, a coherent site arrangement, an adequate site map and a search engine for each site. It should be easy for users to search for information from any page on a site. Every page should include a search box or at least a link to a search page.

Save the time of the reader Save the time of the reader

Everybody knows the importance of the time because ones it passed it never come again. Dr. S. R. Ranganathan glorifying the ideas how we save the time of the reader. This law highlighted on, how fast information can be delivered to its users that is recognition that part of the excellence of library service is its ability to meet the needs of the library user efficiently. Dr. S. R. Ranganathan recommended the use of appropriate library service methods to improve library management. He observed that centralizing the library collection in one location provided distinct advantages. He also noted that excellent staff would not only include those who possess strong reference skills, but also strong technical skills in cataloguing, cross-referencing, ordering, accessioning, and the circulation of materials. Library time saver factors are devices, open access, shelf arrangement, classification, stack room guides, catalogue, bibliography, reference work, charging and discharging, location of library etc.

As we know the time is as important as money. This law is very important and biggest challenge to the librarian save the time of researchers and library staff. Librarian should always bear in mind that the time of users is very important and precious. Digital collection must be designed and arranged in an inviting, obvious and clear way so as not to waste the time of users and they search for digital resources they need. There are other ways to satisfy this law. Saving the time of the user means providing efficient, thorough access to digital resources, it means satisfied users. In order to save the time of the user, digital resources are need to effectively and efficiently design systems that will enable the users to find what they are looking for quickly and accurately, as well as to explore the vast amount of collection of information available that could potentially be useful. This fourth law emphasizes efficient service to the users, which implies a well design and easy-to-understand any resource. ICT has helped user in getting their required information into their laptop, palmtop and desktops. Today's the concept "Library without wall" has come into the picture. Through broadband connection information professionals serve the information to its patrons with in a fraction of second. Day by day internet is speedy and reaching to every patron irrespective of the place and time.

The library is a growing organism — The Digital resource is a growing Organism

The fifth law enunciates a fundamental principle that should govern the planning and organization of libraries. It is an accepted fact that growing organism alone will survive. Library as an institution has all the attributes of a growing organism. This law focused more on the need for internal change than on changes in the environment itself. Dr. S. R. Ranganathan observe that library organizations must accommodate growth in staff, the physical collection, and patron use. This involved allowing for growth in the physical building, reading areas, shelving, and in space for the catalogue. The main part of library are book, readers and staff both of three are require proper and balance growth among the three constituents which indicates the health of the library. As per growth it needs proper spacing for library building because it always affected growth in stacks, books and space for reading room. Therefore we plan library building that can meet all our future needs.

In the present electronic/digital age, resources are available in electronic forms, such CD-ROM, DVD, VCD, Optical Disks. Due to availability in electronic format of the resources, space problem of the library gets no sense and smaller place can acquire billions of collection. The main problem of the library is availability of inadequate funds. In that case resource sharing and networking between libraries and information centres are very much essential. To short out the library budget problem, consortium approach has come to the picture making libraries agreeing to share the resources under common platform. According to Dr. S. R. Ranganathan fifth law idea, spontaneity in digital resources rises continuously. As we know day by day billions of digital resources available on internet so, it difficult for searching pin pointed information for the patron. Librarian can play important role in weeding through the dross and establishing annotated lists of links that patrons can feel confident about using. Therefore we need to keep our own skill levels moving forward. Then an only we are enforcing Dr. S. R. Ranganathan fifth law in this digital age. Every one keeping in view the importance of e-form resources but print form also has an importance because it is all time easily handle anywhere with their own reading habits.

PLACE OF REFERENCE SERVICES IN DR. S. R. RANGANATHAN TO DIGITAL ERA

Dr. S. R. Ranganathan approached librarianship theoretically. Reference service is that phase of library work which is directly concerned with assistance to readers in securing information and in using resources of the library in study and research. He sought to establish fundamental principles from which effective library practices could be systematically derived. Dr. S. R. Ranganathan defines reference service as personal service to each reader in helping him to find the documents answering his interest at the moment pin-pointedly, exhaustively and expeditiously. Both definitions convey that reference service means process of establishing contact between a reader and his documents in a personal way. His ideas of a more in depth and detailed reference services while in library school. He coined it, "long range reference service" and distinguished it from ready reference service. He believed reference service is the "trialogue among reader, librarian and catalogue" and established that reference service plays most important work and serves as the hub of all library practices. Digital age reference services are changing to meet patron's needs and expectations but it based on basic principle of Dr. S. R. Ranganathan reference service principles. As we know above how five laws are applicable in this digital era again these laws are lighted reference services also. Reference services are very helpful in the sorting digital age challenges. Digital reference service is only an advancement of the same traditional services which is emerging as natural solution to meet the user's information needs in the changing technological environment. Internet is an indispensable valuable source of information and efficient information delivery medium offers a platform for a wide range of existing and future reference services. Some of the prevalent forms of digital reference services available through internet are E-mail based reference services, ask a librarian, ask a question, ask an expert, online pathfinder (e.g. http://www.pathfindersonline.org.)

DR. S. R. RANGANATHAN'S TO DIGITAL ERA SEARCH FORMULATION

In this digital scenario there is lot of importance for search formulation. Dr. S. R. Ranganathan has lot of leverage on the searching aspect like indexing, abstracting, catchy and appropriate key words and the search is being made on that, then only you can retrieve pinpointed information, otherwise very difficult to have retrieved the information. Ranganathan's five laws which are reversible as stated above followed in digital age. For example when you searching any terms in Google search engine or any search engine lots of website are opened with in few seconds, but you cannot retrieve proper information which you want. Therefore the way of selecting prefer terms and section of correct path of searching is the requirement for getting the appropriate information.

Overall Dr. S. R. Ranganathan findings like colon classification (Library classification scheme), classified catalogue code, indexing, chain indexing, abstracting, and documentation and its facets, etc are use for searching formulation. Multiple cross reference entries, cross reference index entries, and cataloguing rules etc. all are ultimately for the easy searching of library books and documents. Like this lots of ideas put up by Dr. S. R. Ranganathan for searching only. Same work is getting utilised in the digital era in the form of various search formulation. Terminology like alternative terms, synonyms, antonyms, homonyms, identifier, indexing terms, descriptive terms, descriptors these all amounts to different categories of searching terms. These all are describing as key words. Different identifier or different indexers will have its own preferred terms for searching.

Fig. 3. Word with Different Terminology

e. g. The word "design" has a lot of preferred terms is display in the figure 2. So that you need to search in exactly which terminology you want like plan, pattern, innovation, study, etc. that means same concepts are being represented by different words or terminology. If these terms are not use for search formulation you cannot retrieve appropriate information or your search is not on correct path. Therefore Dr. S. R. Ranganathan ideas for searching perfectly enlighten in this digital age for retrieving information from the garbage. As per Dr. S. R. Ranganathan in pattern recognition and information retrieval, recall means that an algorithm returned most of the relevant results, while precision means that an algorithm returned substantially more relevant result than irrelevant. That means if you don't have proper indexing terms then recall rate is more and you may not have precision ratio.

CHAPTER OUTCOME

It is the greatness of Dr. S. R. Ranganathan that so many years after his death, we strongly realised that his way of looking at libraries or information centres are influence by his important library strategies for information centre or libraries. Overall digital age lighted by the views of Ranganathan's, his inspiration in respect of the priority he gave to the service to the reader. Dr. S. R. Ranganathan age search formulation techniques are effectively working in this age also. The waves of Dr. S. R. Ranganathan are dynamically enforcing to this digital age for facing today's challenges. Our God is our user when we satisfy our user then an only we get satisfied. If we do not have search the proper terms we cannot retrieve proper information so we need proper search formulation techniques. Dr. S. R. Ranganathan has a foresight for all these digital era for search formulation to be made now a day's what we are doing with different terminology like alternative terms, synonyms, antonyms, homonyms, identifier, indexing terms, descriptive terms, descriptors, key words these all amounts to different categories of searching terms. It has got lot of importance and significance in digital era. Unless the concepts are being properly indexed or identified by the preferred terms or search terms, nothing can be retrieved. All ideas of Dr. S. R. Ranganathan like five laws of library science, colon classification, classified catalogue code, chain indexing, abstracting etc. are fully enforcing in digital era for searching formulation.

19

Copyright and Digitization

Keywords : *Copyright Law, Copyright Act, Digitization, Optical Character Recognition.*

INTRODUCTION

The copy right and digitization, both these concepts are more or less are being functional in the field of LIS since very long year. The later may be a decade and half old but copy right has been in vogue long time in connection with printed matter and now applicable to digitised sources. In ancient form, it is a safe guard to unlawful production of literary product of an individual or institute or corporate entity. Basically it deals with allowing copyright of its portion purely for academic purpose and not for commercial purpose with permission of copyrighted authorities. It also envisages depositing one copy to three places. Viz. National library Calcutta, Delhi Public Library, and Asiatic Society Library, Bombay. The purpose of this deposit is to facilitated production of National Bibliography of Library Product. The copyright phenomenon will be described further in more details.

The second one most recent digitization is process of conversion of printed material into electronic form and facilitating it to search and retrieve most efficiently with effective formulations. In the digital world when we try to use the readymade material of digitized form and channelize the access to our clientele with available internet infrastructure. The last priority is given to digitization process where in significant and archival materials are given priority. The process involves lot of paraphernalia like copying through scanner, OCRING i.e. Optical Character Recognition, Indexing and stirring the digitized sources for posterior use. This will also be explained in details further.

In LIS field these concepts are very much important as the stakeholders had to be prevented from doing unlawful activities and avoid duplication of e-resources that are already digitised. The most pertinent would be to scared whether they are already been done by others and simply lay hands on these resources and make it available to our esteemed clientele immediately.

COPYRIGHT LAW

Copyright is a form of protection provided by the laws, enacted by government to the authors of "original works of authorship", including literary, dramatic, musical, artistic, and certain other intellectual works. This protection is available to both published and unpublished works. Protection provided by the law to an individual or entity for original works produced by that author. Copyright law protects the authors of original works.

According to the *World Trade Organization*, "intellectual property rights are the rights given to persons over the creations of their minds. They usually give the creator an exclusive right over the use of his/her creation for a certain period of time. (2003) One of the main types of intellectual property is copyright, which protects material such as music, films, software, multimedia, and literary material. "Copyright gives the creators a wide range of material, such as literature, art, music, sound recordings, films and broadcasts, economic rights enabling them to control use of their material in a number of ways, such as by making copies, issuing copies to the public, performing in public, broadcasting and use on-line. It also gives moral rights to be identified as the creator of certain kinds of material, and to object to distortion or mutilation of it."

Today almost every nation has a copyright law in place and is mostly standardized to some extent through international and regional agreements such as the Berne Convention and the European copyright directives. Historically copyright is a capitalistic conception. The practice was developed in the Italian City states. This practice gradually spread to other countries of Western Europe. In the reign of Elizabeth-I, a series of patents to encourage foreign inventor to import their inventions and work them in England and also to help domestic producers were made. Originally copyright grew out of the same system as royal patent brands, which gave the authors and the printers the executive rights to publish books and other materials. The purpose was too providing Government to increase its revenue and control over publication content. The system was in use by Italian City states namely Venice. Later England, France and other Western countries adopted this. Intellectual property refers to property created with the use of intellect or creation of mind. The h i t of man's brains can with utmost propriety be called his property. Such creation is vested with the status of property because of commercial value of the intellectual creation. Intellectual property right is a right recognised and sanctioned by law. It is an intangible, incorporeal right granted by the statute. The creative intelligence of man is displayed in multiform ways of aesthetic expression but it is often happens that economic systems so operates that the priceless divinity which we call artistic or literary creativity in man is exploited and master, whose works are invaluable are victims of piffling payments.' Therefore, the public opinion in defence of human rights to intellectual property led to declaration of human right and various conventions.

Copyright is a right given by the law to creators of literary, dramatic, musical and artistic works and producers of cinematograph films and sound recordings. In fact, it is a bundle of rights including, *inter alia,* rights of reproduction, communication to the public, adaptation and translation of the work. There could be slight variations in the composition of the rights depending on the work. Like trademarks, a copyright is an intangible property.

A COPYRIGHT OWNER HAS FIVE RIGHTS TO HIS OR HER COPYRIGHTED WORK

Reproduction Right : The reproduction right is the right to copy, duplicate, transcribe, or imitate the work in fixed form.

Modification Right : The modification right (also known as the derivative works right) is the right to modify the work to create a new work. A new work that is based on preexisting work is known as a "derivative work."

Distribution Right : The distribution right is the right to distribute copies of the work to the public by sale, rental, lease, or lending.

Public Performance Right : The public performance right is the right to recite, play, dance, act, or show the work at public place or to transmit it to the public. In the case of a motion picture or other audiovisual work, showing the work's images out of sequence is considered "performance." Sound recordings—recorded versions of music or other sounds—do not have a public performance right.

Public Display Right : The public display right is the right to show a copy of the work directly or by means of film, slide, or television image at a public place or to transmit it to the public. In the case of a motion picture or other audiovisual work, showing the work's images out of sequence is considered "display."

TYPE OF COPYRIGHT ACTS

- General
- Fair use
- Newspaper articles
- Dance
- Sculpture
- Photographs
- Manuscripts
- Images
- Literary, dramatic or musical work
- Computer programmes
- Cinematograph film
- Sound Recording
- Artistic work

Copyright applies to all original literary, dramatic, musical and artistic works. Each of these general categories covers a wide range of creations. Here are just a few examples:

Literary Works : Books, pamphlets, product literature, instruction manuals, operation manuals, poems and other works consisting of text, including computer programs

Dramatic Works : Films, videos, plays, screenplays and scripts

Musical Works : Compositions that consist of both words and music, or music only (note that lyrics only fall into the literary works category)

Artistic Works : Paintings, drawings, maps, photographs, sculptures and architectural works.

Government work : "Government work" means a work which is made or published by or under the direction or control of

- The government or any department of the government
- Any legislature in India, and
- Any court, tribunal or other judicial authority in India.

Keep in mind that copyright also applies to all kinds of recordings, such as records, cassettes, and compact discs, which are called "mechanical contrivances" in the Copyright Act. There is a separate copyright for the musical work, for example, a song, and for the device, such as a cassette that produces the song. Separate protection exists because the song and the sound recording are considered to be two different works.

The word ***original*** is key in defining a work that qualifies for copyright protection. Naturally, you cannot obtain a copyright for someone else's creation. Originality can be tricky to determine, however, and many court cases revolve around the question of whether a work has been copied, even in part, from somebody else's work.

Copyright means the sole right to produce or reproduce a work, or a substantial part of it in any form. It includes the right to perform the work, or any substantial part of it, or in the case of a lecture, to deliver it; if the work is unpublished, it includes the right to publish it, or any substantial part of it.

OTHER FORMS OF COPYRIGHTS

People often confuse copyrights with other forms of intellectual property, particularly trademarks, patents, industrial designs and integrated circuit topographies.

Trademarks : are used to distinguish the goods or services of one person or company from those of another. Slogans, names of products, distinctive packages, or unique product shapes are all examples of features that are eligible for registration as trademarks. Sometimes, one aspect of a work may be subject to copyright protection, and another aspect may be covered by trademark law. For example, if you created a new board game, he may enjoy a copyright on the artwork of the game board and a trademark, for the game's title.

Patents : protect new and useful inventions such as processes, equipment, and manufacturing techniques. They do not cover any artistic or aesthetic qualities of an article. Unlike copyrights, patents can only be obtained by registration.

Industrial Design : are protected for their original shape pattern or ornamentation used to adorn a useful manufactured article. The artwork of your client's game board may be subject to copyright protection. Industrial design protection might be available for the board itself. Like patents, designs are obtained only by registration.

Integrated Circuit Topographies : are protected upon registration. Protection is for the topography of an integrated circuit product, which is a manufactured device made up of a series of layers of semiconductors, metals, insulators and other materials. The three dimensional configuration is a "topography". The original design of the topography is protected.

INFRINGEMENT

A copyright gives you the sole right to produce or reproduce his work, through publication, performances and so on, or to authorize such activities. Anyone who does such things without permission is infringing, that is, violating, and your rights. Naturally, if you publish, perform or copy anyone else's work without their permission, you are infringing their rights.

One specific form of infringement is plagiarism. This is copying someone else's work and claiming it as your own. An obvious example would be taking a novel someone else wrote and publishing it under your own name (or pen name). Plagiarism can also entail using a substantial part of someone else's work. An example would be copying a novel, and simply changing the title and names of the characters. Ironically you do not own your life story. Any information about you that is in the public domain can be the subject of a book about you without consent.

Some activities, if carried out in private, are not considered infringement. For example, if you give a private performance of someone else's song or plays in your own home, this would not be infringement. On the other hand, making a copy of a video cassette movie protected by copyright is infringement, even if you only watch it at home.

If any of the acts specified in Section 14 relating to the work is carried out by a person other than the owner or without licence from the owner or a competent authority under the Act it constitutes infringement of copyright. (Sec.51 of the Act). The type of acts, which will constitute infringement, will depend upon the nature of the work. Secondary infringement such as making for sale or hire of, exhibition in public by way of trade of, distribution - infringing copies - is also prohibited and punishable under the Act.

EXAMPLES OF INFRINGEMENT

- Reprinting an instruction manual or user's manual without the copyright owner's permission.
- Playing music of others as part of your advertisement.
- Giving a public performance of copyright play without permission
- Photocopying information for distribution.

NOT INFRINGEMENT

- Quoting a few lines of the article in a research paper (fair dealing)
- Playing records at home.
- Giving public performance of a play by Shakespeare (no copyright exists)
- Gaining permission from the author and paying him or her fee for a complete list of exceptions to infringement.

FAIR DEALING

A *fair dealing* with a literary, dramatic, musical or artistic work (not being a computer programme) for the purposes of

- For the purpose of research or private study
- For criticism or review
- For reporting current events
- In connection with judicial proceeding
- Performance by an amateur club or society if the performance is given to a non-paying audience
- The making of sound recordings of literary, dramatic or musical works under certain conditions

People such as critics, reviewers and researchers often quote works by other authors in articles, books, and so on. They are not necessarily infringing copyright. The Copyright Act provides that any "fair dealing" with a work for purposes of private study or research, or for criticism, review or newspaper summary, is not infringement. However, in the case of criticism, review, or newspaper summary, the user is required to give the source and authors name, if known.

The line between fair dealing and infringement is a thin one. There are no guidelines that define the number of words or passages that can be used without permission from the author. Only the courts can rule whether fair dealing or infringement is involved.

ADVANTAGES OF COPYRIGHT ACT

The advantages of registering a copyright include the following:

- Establishes a public record of the copyright holder's ownership.
- Enables copyright holders to sue infringers in federal court.
- If made before or within 5 years of publication, establishes sufficient evidence in court concerning the validity of the copyright and the facts stated in the copyright certificate.
- If registration is made within 3 months of publication of the work or at any time prior to an infringement of the work, the copyright owner is entitled to seek statutory damages and attorney's fees in federal court. Without registration, only an award of actual damages and profits will be available, and these can be quite difficult to prove.
- Allows the copyright owner to record the registration to protect against the importation of infringing copies.

Again in addition to above benefits an artist does not have to register his copyright to have protection. However, when he registers he will receive a certificate which can be used to his advantage in the event that his work is infringed. A certificate of registration is evidence that an artist's work is protected by copyright and that he, the person registered, is the owner. In the event of a legal dispute, you do not have to prove ownership; the onus is on his opponent to disprove it. However, registration is no guarantee against infringement. An artist will have to take legal action on his own if he believes his rights have been violated. Also, registration is no guarantee that his claim of ownership will eventually be recognized as legitimate. Note also that the Copyright Office does not check to ensure that an artist's work is indeed original, as was his claim. Verification of claims can only be done through a Court of law.

DISADVANTAGES OF COPYRIGHT ACT

As we know every coin have two sides and therefore this moon of copy right also have a black marks like it restricted to the expression of an ideas; it does not extend to the idea itself. You may have a brilliant idea for an advertising campaign, but until the script is actually written, or the advertisements purchased, there is no copyright protection. In the case of a game, it is not possible to protect the idea of the game, that is, the way the game is played, but the language in which the rules are written would be protected as a literary work.

Other items which are not protected by copyright include names or slogans; short phrases and most titles, methods of procedure, such as a method of teaching or sculpting, etc.; plots, characters, or factual information. In the case of a magazine article including factual information, it is the expression of the information that is protected, and not the facts. Facts, ideas and news are all considered part of the public domain, that is, they are the property of everyone. Note also that you cannot hold a copyright for a work that is in the public domain. However, you can adapt or translate such a work, and hold a copyright of an adaptation or translation.

DIGITIZATION

Digitization is the process of converting analog signals or information of any form into a digital format that can be understood by computer systems or electronic devices. The term is used when converting information, like text, images or voices and sounds, into binary code. Digitized information is easier to store, access and transmit, and digitization is used by a number of consumer electronic devices.

Witten and David (2003) defined Digitization as the process of taking traditional library materials that are in form of books and papers and converting them to the electronic form where they can be stored and manipulated by a computer.

METHODS

- Encoding
- Scanner
- Digital camera
- Digital video camera
- Digital audio recorders
- Analogue device converters with software digital capture

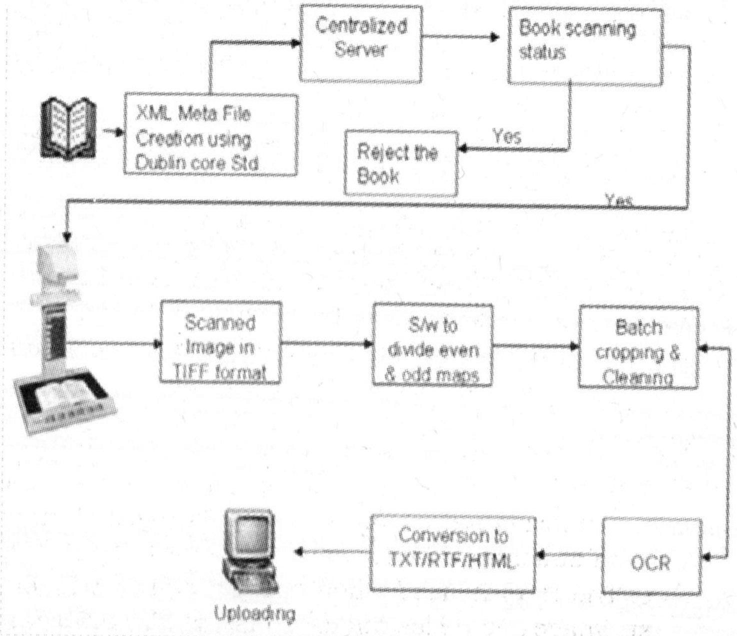

Fig. 1. Diagrammatic presentation of Digitization Process

REASONS FOR GOING TO DIGITIZATION

- To enhance student and faculty research
- To put our collections where our users are – in Google!
- Mass digitization of these materials enhances access. It can make people aware of books they may not have discovered otherwise and lead them, through an internet search, back to our libraries
- To support deeper textual analysis and research. Scholars can trace the evolution of ideas and perform other sophisticated textual analysis when the full text is indexed and searchable by computer, opening scholarship in new ways.
- To fulfill our public service mission
- Many books of enduring general interest – including classic works of literature and more unique items such as early histories of the settlement of California and the West - can now be read by anyone, anywhere, anytime
- To preserve and protect our collections
- In earthquake and fire-prone California, digitizing books in our collections may also help protect the university from catastrophic loss should disaster someday strike our libraries

DIFFERENT STAGES IN DIGITIZING DOCUMENTS

Broadly six stages provides in digitizing documents for a digital library: Registering, Scanning, Optical Character Recognition, Proofreading and formatting and producing the Final Version.

Registering

Before scanning large number of documents, there is the need to first register them and use a filing system to keep their track. If not, you risk misplacing hardcopies, losing files, skipping steps in the process or duplicating work, perhaps without realizing it. There is also the risk of losing electronic versions of files because they have been misnamed or saved in the wrong subdirectory. Moreover, a good filing system is vital, so everyone in the digitizing team knows what he is supposed to do, and he can fill in for another person in case of absence.

Scanning documents

It is necessary to clean and dust off the documents to be scanned; make sure that all the pages are present and in the right order. If the document is in poor condition, try to find a fresh copy. If it is a sheet fed scanner, cut the document open to get individual sheets to feed through the scanner. If necessary, you can rebind the documents later. If you do not want to damage the documents, you can photocopy each page and feed in the photocopy through the scanner, though this uses a lot of paper and reduces the quality of the scan.

To scan a document on a flatbed scanner, place it face down on the scanner platen or put the pages into the sheet feeder. Then, in the software, choose a setting, resolution and colour and scan each page of the document at the settings you have chosen.

Optical Character Recognition (OCR)

Optical Character Recognition (OCR) software converts a scanned image into a text file that a word processor can read. To do this, it must first recognize where the text is on the page. The software breaks the text blocks down into lines or into an individual character. It tries to match the image of each letter against patterns it recognizes as an "a", "b", etc. There is a problem to encounter with languages that use Latin scripts with accented characters. As a solution, you should use the OCR software that is specific for language.

Proofreading

This is the act of making corrections to the document text and layout. This is done in two ways:

a. Comparing the scanned text on the screen with the hardcopy and entering the corrections directly into the computer. The word processor's spellchecker will help in spelling errors quickly.

b. Printing out the scanned text and comparing it with the original copy. Mark any corrections on the printout, and then enter them into the computer. This is a slower method, but may be the best option if there are no enough computers for each proof reader.

Reformatting

The Optical Character Recognition (OCR) software may produce a document that consists of straight text, no columns, no headers and footers. There is the need to reinsert these by hand or correct where they appear on the page. There may be also need to change the typeface, heading styles and so on, to make the document more attractive and readable. Alternatively, you may be able to adjust the settings of your OCR program to preserve the layout of the page.

Final Version

For many documents, there is a need to add some information to the text so that readers can identify it easily. As for a book you must make sure that the book title, the author or the editor, the publisher and the publication date are all included. As for chapter in a book, you should include the title and the author of that chapter and the original page numbers in the printed version of the book. As for the journal articles you should include the journal title, the date, the volume and the issue number, the article title and the authors and the page numbers in the original printed journal. In other words there is the need to add Metadata to describe each document.

BENEFITS OF DIGITIZATION

- Originals can be located in secure place
- Originals can be moved into an archival facility
- Digital copies can be delivered via Internet
- No need for staff/s in check-in or check-out of documents
- No need for frequent inventory
- Copies can be made in minutes with less effort from staff.
- Time savings can be diverted into care and maintenance of originals

Digitizing information makes it easier to preserve, access, and share. For example, an original historical document may only be accessible to people who visit its physical location, but if the document content is digitized, it can be made available to people worldwide. There is a growing trend towards digitization of historically and culturally significant data.

PROBLEMS IN DIGITIZATION

- Improper digitization process is a source of natural deterioration and damage
- Improper use of equipment and facilities can cause more damage than natural elements
- Digitization without clear goals is at risk of failure
- Poor output of digitization is not due to digitization but due to incomplete appreciation of digitization process
- Cost of digitization increases when work efficiency is low

- Quality is determined by the intentions or goals of digitization

CHAPTER OUTCOME

The copyright concept is more related to earnings for the production of literary work. The royalty and copying can be a few sources of earning. The portion of copyrighted items can be copied for fair use and citations. It is also serve as acknowledgment to the previous work seen by the researcher or literature developer. The copyright Act serves as safeguard to unlawful copying and utilisation without acknowledging the main source. The provisions of copyright Act should be scrupulously followed. This is to avoid any unfair use of literature created by the owner.

Digitization has opened up new audiences and services for libraries, and it needs to be integrated into the plans and policies of any institution to maximize its effectiveness. Digitization is a complex process with many crucial dependencies between different stages over time. Utilizing a holistic life-cycle approach for digitization initiatives will help develop sustainable and successful project.

It is hoped that the approach of the issues outlined, the software mentioned in this paper and the references to more detailed source and past project will contribute to the future success of initiating digitization of library resources.

20
NAAC Norms

Keywords : *Accreditation, NAAC, NBA, COA, Higher Education, Quality, Assurance.*

INTRODUCTION

Accreditation is a formal recognition of an educational program by an external body on the basis of an assessment of quality. It is a process of quality assurance and improvement, whereby a programme in an institution is critically appraised to verify that the institution or the programme continues to meet and exceed the norms and standards prescribed by the appropriate designated agency. Accreditation dose not seek to replace the system of award of degree and diplomas by the universities/ autonomous institutions. But, accreditation provides quality assurance that the academic institution and objectives are honestly pursued, and effectively achieved by the resources available. And that the institution has demonstrated capabilities of ensuring effectiveness of the educational programmes over the validity period of accreditation.

Accreditation plays a vital role in higher education because both the higher education community and government use the system to promote and assure quality and protect the public interest. Accreditation is one of the major ways in which the higher education community sets expectations for quality and how government and the public define and communicate the overriding public interest in higher education. The goal of accreditation is to ensure that education provided by institutions of higher education meets acceptable levels of quality. Accreditation is compulsory for all universities in India except those created through an act of Parliament. Without accreditation, It is emphasized that these fake institutions have no legal entity to call themselves as University/ Vishwvidyalaya and to award 'degrees' which are not treated as valid for academic/employment purposes.

The University Grants Commission Act (1956) explains, "The right of conferring or granting degrees shall be exercised only by a University established or incorporated by or under a Central Act, or a State Act, or an Institution deemed to be University or an institution specially empowered by an Act of the Parliament to confer or grant degrees. Thus, any institution which has not been created by an enactment of Parliament or a State Legislature or has not been granted the status of a Deemed-to-be-University is not entitled to award a degree."

WHY ACCREDITATION?

- Education plays a vital role in the development of any nation. Therefore, there is a premium on both quantity (increased access) and quality (relevance and excellence of academic programmes offered) of higher education.
- The Washington Accord (WA): Agreement that establishes equivalence of other countries' accredited professional engineering programs.
- Accredited Engineering Graduates are recognized by other signatory countries - Possible employment as engineers in those countries without further examinations.

WHY ACCREDITATION IS IMPORTANT, SEVERAL REASONS

Academic quality : The primary purpose of accreditation is to ensure that your program fulfils the basic role of providing you with an education. Methods for measuring the quality of the education you are receiving are not widely agreed upon and the definition of "quality education" varies. However, accrediting agencies do review schools and programs with an agreed upon list of standards. These standards vary across accrediting agencies and may be very specific to academic fields.

Transfer credits : If you are planning to transfer credits into an online program or from an online program to another institute, accreditation may help. Since accrediting agencies review courses and programs against common standards, this process can make the similarities of courses easier to identify. Transferring courses is never a sure thing and requests are usually evaluated individually. Transfer of course credit from a non-accredited organisation or program can be very difficult so if you are considering transfer credit as an option, you should consult with all of the institutions involved.

Financial aid : The Government makes a significant amount of financial aid available to students every year. Government organise several ways for good resource for you as you research funding options and requirements.

Employer expectations : Depending on your field of study and career goals, employers may be looking for graduates from programs with accreditation. This may be a general preference or specific requirement for accreditation by a particular agency.

State licensure : There are occupations in which a State license is required in order for you to work in the field. Examples include teaching, nursing, and law, but there are many others. If you need a license to work, a test is often part of the process. Graduating from an accredited program is usually a requirement to sit for the test and to be issued a license. Agencies in each State monitor these areas of work closely and also provide a form of accreditation to institute and programs operating within the state.

MAJOR CHALLENGES TO ACCREDITATION

The new higher education is challenging the very foundations of traditional accreditation and raising questions about whether accreditation must undergo a more fundamental transformation. There are at least five major developments that are posing challenges to the existing accreditation system.

Global competitiveness & Quality

Ability to compete globally and maintain the quality of our higher education systems are mounting. There is an urgent need to strengthen the quality of Indian higher education, especially given the growing tension between institutional and public definitions of quality and rigor. Accreditation must play a key role in influencing higher education to move beyond minimum or adequate quality to performance excellence.

Accountability

There is growing demand for increased accountability to government, consumers and the general public. The public is calling for increased transparency and reporting of consumer-friendly information relating to the performance of higher education. Accreditation can play a major role by changing accreditation standards and placing a strong emphasis on performance outcomes, especially student learning outcomes.

Changing Structure of Higher Education

The changing structure and delivery of higher education includes new types of educational institutions and the use of distance learning, which allows institutions to operate on a global scale and holds the potential for improving value and access. The traditional boundaries of geography, academic disciplines and programs, and modes of delivery are blurring. Students are now attending multiple educational institutions and utilizing different delivery systems, often simultaneously. These new realities require new solutions to ease the transfer process. The accreditation process, while responding to institutional and programmatic interests, may not be equipped to respond to the demands of this new environment.

Transparency

The system of accreditation is very complex and difficult to understand. The public-private system of accreditation must become more open and transparent to provide assurances that it is balancing institutional and public interests in setting standards and accrediting institutions and programs. This will require more consistency in accreditation standards and more involvement of outside stakeholders in the accreditation process.

Value and Affordability

Rising costs and reduced federal and state funding are pressuring higher education institutions to increase affordability and improve the value of and returns on higher education. Shrinking resources for higher education also demand that funds are used wisely and to the benefit of the public interest. Additionally, while accreditors view the accreditation process as an "investment," institutions often view it as a significant cost with little return on investment. The accreditation process rarely lends itself toward efficiency, productivity improvement, or "cost cutting." Specialized accreditors are viewed as a guild designed to protect the guild from the public.

Figure 1: Accredited Governing Bodies

NATIONAL ASSESSMENT AND ACCREDITATION COUNCIL (NAAC)

The core objective of the NAAC as stated in the vision and mission is Quality Assurance in Higher Education. Assessment and Accreditation are the tool in reaching this objective. In the foremost of NAAC academic activities are the nationwide awareness / promotional programmes explaining the policy, directions and guidelines of MHRD and UGC for assessment and accreditation. Secondly, they are helping the accredited institutions for quality sustenance and quality enhancement activities by setting up of Internal Quality Assurance Cell (IQAC) in each of the Colleges and Universities. Most of the academic activities have been sponsored by NAAC in one way or other. In addition to this the academic staff participated in many seminars / workshops / symposia / conferences across the country organized by various Colleges and Universities, as resource persons to highlight the processes of assessment and accreditation methodology and post accreditation initiatives on quality sustenance and quality enhancement. The National Assessment and Accreditation Council (NAAC) is an autonomous institution of the University Grants Commission (UGC) with its prime agenda to assess and accredit institutions of higher learning in the country. The MHRD and UGC have mandated that all colleges should complete the process of assessment and accreditation. The NAAC has been established in the year 1994 is headquartered at Bangalore. The process of assessment and accreditation has created a tremendous momentum among the academia on issues pertaining to quality and this has largely been due to the successful partnership between NAAC and the State governments. Quality Sustenance and Quality Enhancement are the two key words reverberating in most institutions of higher learning in the country today. While the initial phase of the transformation focused on creating phase is now more focused on creating institutions of the future. Also the issue of colleges and universities being adequately prepared for academic life from the perspective of students takes on more importance. NAAC is the member of the International Quality Assurance Agencies in Higher Education (INQAAHE) and a founder-member of Asia-Pacific Quality Network (APQN)

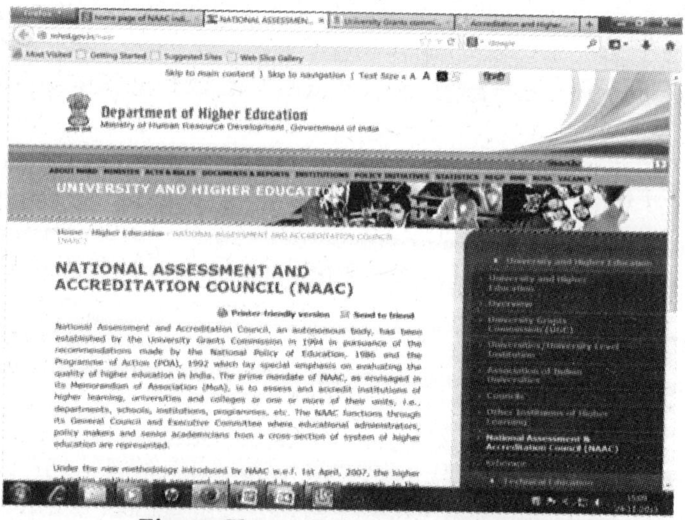

Figure Shows Web page of (NAAC) National Assessment and Accreditation Council

BENEFITS OF ACCREDITATION

- Institution to know its strengths, weaknesses, and opportunities through an informed review process
- Identification of internal areas of planning and resource allocation
- Collegiality on the campus
- Funding agencies look for objective data for performance funding
- Institutions to initiate innovative and modern methods of pedagogy
- New sense of direction and identity for institutions
- The society look for reliable information on quality education offered.
- Employers look for reliable information on the quality of education offered to the prospective recruits
- Intra and inter-institutional interactions.

OBJECTIVES

- To grade institutions of higher education and their programmes
- To stimulate the academic environment and quality of teaching and research in these institutions
- To help institutions realise their academic objectives
- To promote necessary changes, innovations and reforms in all aspects of the institutions working for the above purpose
- To encourage innovations, self evaluation and accountability in higher education

FUNCTIONS OF ACCREDITATION

- Verifying that an institution or program meets established standards
- Assisting prospective students in identifying acceptable institutions

- Assisting institutions in determining the acceptability of transfer credits
- Helping to identify institutions and programs for the investment of public and private funds
- Protecting an institution against harmful internal and external pressure
- Creating goals for self-improvement of weaker programs and stimulating a general raising of standards among educational institutions
- Involving the faculty and staff comprehensively in institutional evaluation and planning
- Establishing criteria for professional certification and licensure and for upgrading courses offering such preparation
- Providing one of several considerations used as a basis for determining eligibility for Federal assistance

THE ACCREDITING PROCEDURE

Standards : The accrediting agency, in collaboration with educational institutions, establishes standards.

Self-study : The institution or program seeking accreditation prepares an in-depth self-evaluation study that measures its performance against the standards established by the accrediting agency.

On-site Evaluation : A team selected by the accrediting agency visits the institution or program to determine first-hand if the applicant meets the established standards.

Publication : Upon being satisfied that the applicant meets its standards, the accrediting agency grants accreditation or pre-accreditation status and lists the institution or program in an official publication with other similarly accredited or pre-accredited institutions or programs.

Monitoring : The accrediting agency monitors each

accredited institution or program throughout the period of accreditation granted to verify that it continues to meet the agency's standards.

Re-evaluation : The accrediting agency periodically re-evaluates each institution or program that it lists to ascertain whether continuation of its accredited or pre-accredited status is warranted.

COUNCIL OF ARCHITECTURE (COA)

The Council of Architecture (COA) has been constituted by the Government of India under the provisions of the Architects Act, 1972, enacted by the Parliament of India, which came into force on 1st September, 1972. The Act provides for registration of Architects, standards of education, recognized qualifications and standards of practice to be complied with by the practicing architects. The Council of Architecture is charged with the responsibility to regulate the education and practice of profession throughout India besides maintaining the register of architects. For this purpose, the Government of India has framed Rules and Council of Architecture has framed Regulations as provided for in the Architects Act, with the approval of Government of India.

Any person desirous of carrying on the profession of 'Architect' must have registered himself with Council of Architecture. The practice of profession of an architect is governed by the Architects (Professional Conduct) Regulations, 1989 (as amended in 2003), which deals with professional ethics and etiquette, conditions of engagement and scale of charges, architectural competition guidelines etc. Pursuant to these Regulations, the Council of Architecture has framed guidelines governing the various aspects of practice.

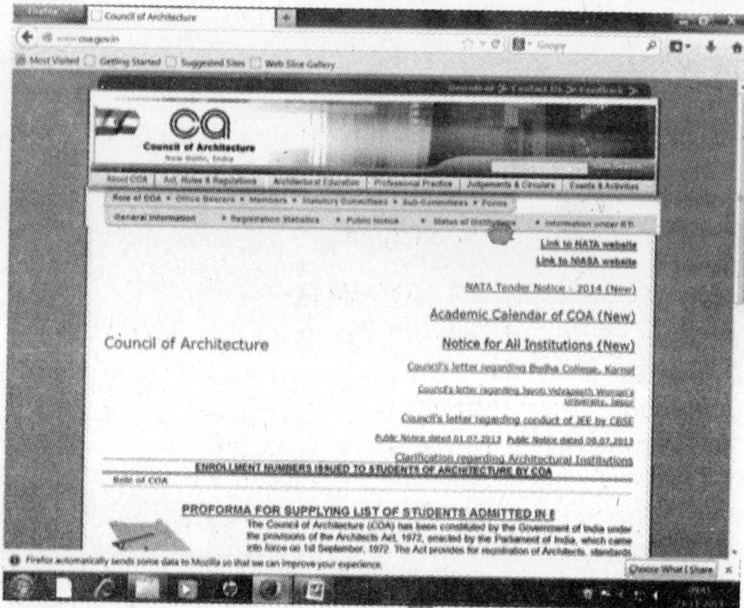

Figure Shows Web page of (COA) Council of Architecture

There are 280 institutions, which impart architectural education in India leading to recognized qualifications. The standards of education being imparted in these institutions (constituent colleges/departments of universities, deemed universities, affiliated colleges/schools, IITs, NITs and autonomous institutions) is governed by Council of Architecture (Minimum Standards of Architectural Education) Regulations, 1983, which set forth the requirement of eligibility for admission, course duration, standards of staff & accommodation, course content, examination etc. These standards as provided in the said Regulations are required to be maintained by the institutions. The COA oversees the maintenance of the standards periodically by way of conducting inspections through Committees of Experts. The COA is required to keep the Central Government informed of the standards being maintained by the institutions and is empowered to make recommendations to the Government of India with regard to recognition and de-recognition of a qualification.

NATIONAL BOARD OF ACCREDITATION (NBA)

The **National Board of Accreditation** (**NBA**), *India* was established by *AICTE* (All India Council of Technical Education) as an autonomous body under section 10(u) of AICTE act, 1987 for periodic evaluations of technical institutions & programmes basis according to specified norms and standards as recommended by AICTE council. It has the full authority to recognize or derecognize institutions and programmes under them. It is the only authorized body in India entrusted with the task of undertaking accreditation of technical education programmes. Following the decision to close down the AICTE in the wake of a corruption scandal, Union Education Minister Kapil Sibal announced that the National Board of Accreditation will be elevated as an independent body and become the nodal agency responsible for *accreditation* in India. The National Board of Accreditation has since become an Independent Society constituted under the Registrar of Cooperative Societies.

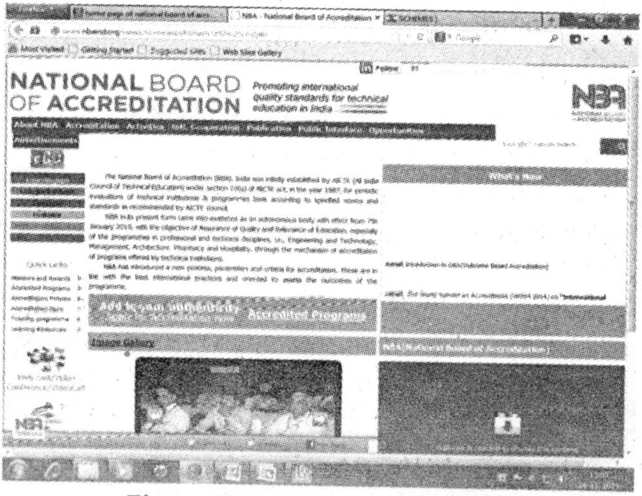

Figure Shows Web page of (NBA) National Board of Accreditation

National Board of Accreditation (NBA) which was set up in 1994 under Section 10(u) of the AICTE Act awards accreditation status to programmes as Accredited for five years, accredited for three years and Not Accredited (NA). Accreditation was based on 8 point criteria which was input-based. NBA has, however, revised the criteria for accreditation of institutes to bring it at par with international parameters. Accreditation is now based on a 1000 point scale and is an outcome based accreditation system. The purpose of the accreditation by NBA is to promote and recognize excellence in technical education in colleges and universities—at both the undergraduate and post graduate levels. Institutions, students, employers, and the public at large all benefit from the external verification of quality provided through the NBA accreditation process. They also benefit from the process of continuous quality improvement that is encouraged by the NBA's developmental approach to promote excellence in technical education.

Through accreditation, the following main purposes may be served

- Support and advice to technical Institutions in the maintenance and enhancement of their quality of provision
- Confidence and assurance on quality to various stakeholders including students
- Assurance of the good standing of an Institution to government departments and other interested bodies
- Enabling an Institution to state publicly that it has voluntarily accepted independent inspection and has satisfied all the requirements for satisfactory operation and maintenance of quality in education

IMPACT OF ACCREDITATION

The purpose and impact of accreditation goes far

beyond quality assurance of an Institution/programme. Major impacts of accreditation system are summarized below

- Encourages quality improvement initiatives by Institutions
- Improves student enrolment both in terms of quality and quantity
- Helps the Institution in securing necessary funds
- Enhances employability of graduates
- Facilitates transnational recognition of degrees and mobility of graduates and professionals
- Motivates faculty to participate actively in academic and related Institutional / departmental activities
- Helps create sound and challenging academic environment in the Institution, and Contributes to social and economic development of the country by producing high quality technical manpower

BENEFITS AND SIGNIFICANCE OF ACCREDITATION

The process of accreditation helps in realizing a number of benefits, such as

- Helps the Institution to know its strengths, weaknesses and opportunities
- Initiates Institutions into innovative and modern methods of pedagogy
- Gives Institutions a new sense of direction and identity
- Provides society with reliable information on quality of education offered
- Promotes intra and inter-Institutional interactions

ACCREDITATION SIGNIFICANCES

Benefits to Institutions

Accreditation is market-driven and has an

international focus. It assesses the characteristics of an Institution and its programmes against a set of criteria established by National Board of Accreditation. NBA's key objective is to contribute to the significant improvement of the Institutions involved in the accreditation process. Accreditation process quantifies the strengths, weaknesses in the processes adopted by the Institution and provides directions and opportunities for future growth. NBA accredited Institutions may be preferred by funding agencies for releasing grants for research as well as expansion etc. It signifies that the Institutional performance is based on assessment carried out through a independent competent body of quality assessors, with strengths and weaknesses emanating as a feedback for policy-making. NBA provides a quality seal or label that differentiates the Institutions from its peers at the national level. This leads to a widespread recognition and greater appreciation of the brand name of Institutions and motivates the Institutions to strive for more.

Benefits to Students

Students studying in NBA accredited Institutions can be assured that they will receive education which is a balance between high academic quality and professional relevance and that the needs of the corporate world are well integrated into programmes, activities and processes. It signifies that he has entered the portals of an Institution, which has the essential and desirable features of quality professional education.

Benefits to Employers

Accreditation assures prospective employers that students come from a programme where the content and quality have been evaluated, satisfying established standards. It also signifies that the students passing out have acquired competence based on well established technical inputs.

Benefits to the Public

Accredited status represents the commitment of the programme and the Institution to quality and continuous improvement.

Catalyst for International Accreditations

Due to accreditation from NBA, the Institution's systems and procedures get aligned with the Institution's Mission and Vision. All essential prerequisites for international accreditation are included in the accreditation process of NBA. Therefore, NBA acts as a catalyst for the Institutions planning to acquire International Accreditation.

Benefits to Industry and Infrastructure Providers

It signifies identification of quality of Institutional capabilities, skills and knowledge.

Benefits to Parents

It signifies that their ward goes through a teaching-learning environment as per accepted good practices.

Benefits to Alumni

It reassures alumni that alumni are products of an institute with a higher standing in terms of learning.

Benefits to Country

Accreditation helps in gaining confidence of stakeholders and in giving a strong message that as a country, our technical manpower is of international standards and can be very useful in enhancing the global mobility for our technical manpower.

NEED OF ACCREDITATION

Accreditation of educational Institutions/ programmes is a global practice and its need has been felt by various developing and developed countries for one or more of the following purposes.

- Funding decisions
- State recognition of qualification/ certification of professionals
- Accountability of Institutions to stakeholders
- Encouraging self improvement initiatives by Institutions
- Quality assurance of educational programme

Accreditation may be summarized as a process, based on professional judgment, for evaluating whether or not an educational Institution or programme meets specified standards of educational quality. Its primary purpose is to assure prospective students and public that graduates of an Institution, conducting various programmes, have achieved a minimum level of competence in their chosen fields of study, thus serving as a form of consumer protection. In many countries, accreditation is the legal responsibility of ministry of education or other governmental agencies.

DEVELOP NATIONAL ACCREDITATION FRAMEWORK

Accreditation should hold higher education accountable for results. In accrediting institutions and programs, all accrediting bodies should place a stronger emphasis on performance outcomes, especially student-learning outcomes, in accreditation decisions. The national accreditation framework would contain following essential components

Performance Outcome Measures

The strongest emphasis would be placed on the demonstration by institutions and programs that they are producing results, especially evidence of student learning. The framework would report student learning based on standards for valid and reliable assessment. The framework would also contain a set of comparable performance measures that include student learning that would be tailored according to institutional mission and program so they can be used for both accreditation and public reporting and consumer profiles.

New Process Standards

The framework would promote more open and flexible process standards that encourage innovation and diversity in higher education and do not prescribe specific input and process standards (e.g., facilities, faculty). They are flexible because they promote creative solutions that are continuously being changed and adapted and are effective in getting results and promoting continuous improvement.

Continuous Improvement

The framework would require institutions and programs to move toward world-class quality and report measurable progress in relationship to their national and international peers. This requirement would be modelled using leading best practices for benchmarking and continuous improvement techniques.

Outcome-Based Approach to Engineering Education

What is OBE?

OBE is a process that involves the restructuring of curriculum, assessment and reporting practices in education (electrical eng education) to reflect the achievement of high order learning and mastery beside the accumulation of course credits.

OBE addresses the following key questions

- What do you want the students to have or able to do?
- How can you best help students achieve it?
- How will you know whether they have achieved it?
- How do you close the loop?
- Anticipation of real benefits
- More directed & coherent curriculum

- Graduates will be more "relevant" to industry & other stakeholders (more well rounded graduates)
- Continuous Quality Improvement (CQI) is an inevitable consequence

OBE Benefits for Students

- Emphasis of course work on more challenging tasks, less memorization.
- Write proposals for projects, analyze case studies, give presentation to demo – Pos
- Develop greater creativity for innovative and economical problem solving
- Synthesize info, analyze for trends and conclusion
- Plan and organize task, work in teams
- Manage projects and funding
- In short, possessing all desirable attributes to work in 21st Century

CHAPTER OUTCOME

In this chapter, we discussed three issues related to accreditation for quality assurance in higher education. Higher education is at the cross roads. New developments in higher education require a major transformation in the accreditation process toward a more public-private system of governance based on national if not global standards and processes that are conducted at arm's length from those are being accredited. The overriding public interest for the 21st century is promoting accountability for moving to world-class quality and performance. In order to survive in the competitive world of globalization, all higher education institutions should pay special attention to quality in higher education. NAAC, NBA & COA has taken a number of steps to promote the quality of Indian higher education.

21

Open Information Products

Keywords : *Open access, LOR, OER, OCW, Information product, Open Education Resources.*

INTRODUCTION

Open Information product plays important role in the education. Education in its broadest sense is man making. This constitutes overall development of human beings therefore, it must be open for everybody wishing to acquire the knowledge in various field as desired. Recognising the importance of education all sort of material required for study of various branches in education must be made available on Internet. Keeping in the mind of the view the "Open Access" term has been introduced. The concept of Open Access (OA) evolved during 1991 due to the realization of the need to facilitate scholarly scientific communication. Open Access (OA) literature is digital, online, free of charge, and free of most copyright and licensing restrictions.

Open Access to scholarly information is a powerful outcome in the web based education and research now-a-days. Open Access holds promise to remove both, price and permission barriers to the scientific communication by using Internet. In fact, 'Open Access' is a step ahead of 'Free Access which removes just the end users. Open Access removes the permission barrier as well.

Open Archives and Open Access Journals are the two Vehicles of open access. Open Courseware (OCW), Open Educational Repositories (OER), and Learning Object Repositories (LOR) are the recent trends in Open Access. Open Access literature are available in open access journals, institutional repositories, subject repositories, digital archives, and so on. This chapter gives an outline of OER, LOR & OCW.

OPEN THINGS

- Open Access
- Open Content
- Open Educational Resources
- Open source Software
- Learning Object Repositories
- Open Course Ware

OPEN EDUCATIONAL RESOURCES (OER)

Open Educational Resources (OER) are an Internet empowered worldwide community effort to create an education commons. The term "Open Educational Resources (OER)" was first adopted at UNESCO's 2002 forum on the impact of Open Courseware for Higher Education in developing countries funded by the William and Flora Hewlett Foundation. Open Educational Resources are educational materials and resources offered freely and openly for anyone to use and under some licenses re-mix, improve and redistribute. OER are teaching & learning material for everyone freely available online. Examples of OER include full courses, course modules, syllabi, lectures, homework assignments, quizzes, lab and classroom activities, games, etc and these resources contained digital collections around the world. Open Educational Resources include

Learning Content : full courses, course materials,

content modules, learning objects, collections and journals.

Tools : Software to support the creation, delivery, use and improvement of open learning content including searching and organization of content, content and learning communities.

Implementation Resources : Intellectual property licenses to promote open publishing of materials, design principles and localization of content.

Benefits of OER

- Higher Quality Learning
- Improved Access
- Lower Costs & Reliable
- Diversified Curriculum
- Affordable courses & Programmes
- Time consumable

Successful OER in India

- National Repository of Open Educational Resources
- National Institute of Open Schooling
- National Programme on Technology Enhance Learning
- Commonwealth of Learning
- National Knowledge Commission

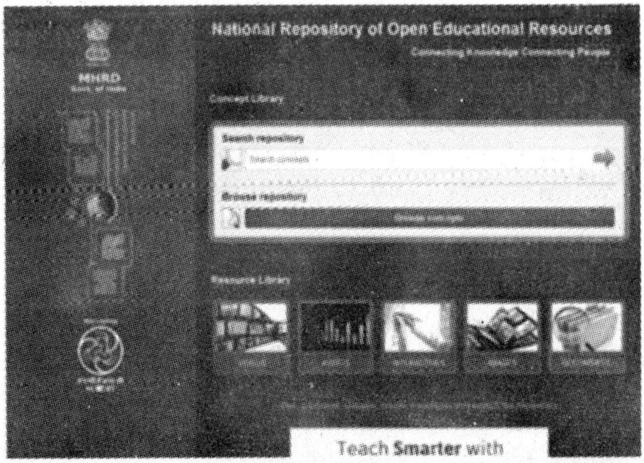

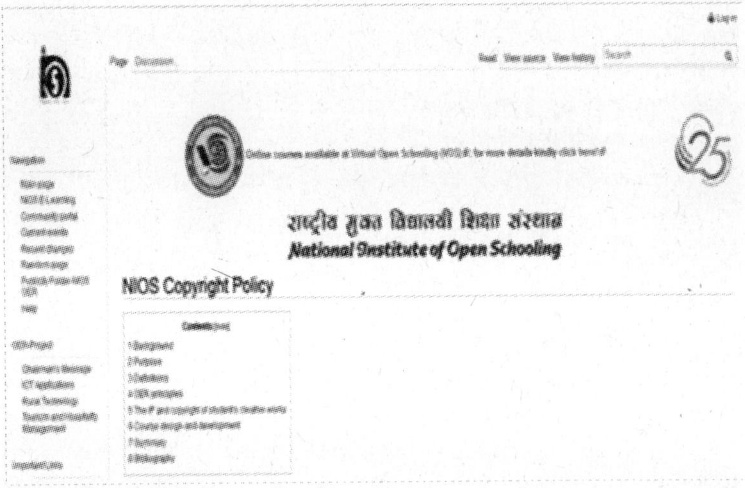
राष्ट्रीय मुक्त विद्यालयी शिक्षा संस्थान
National Institute of Open Schooling
NIOS Copyright Policy

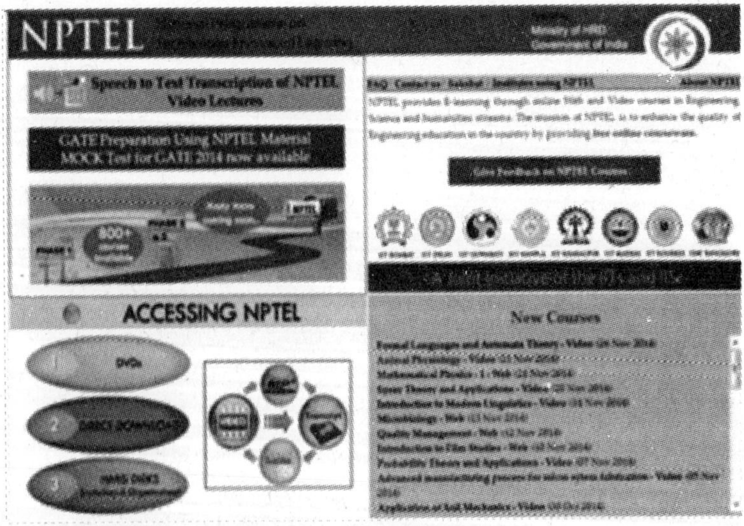
NPTEL
Speech to Text Transcription of NPTEL Video Lectures
GATE Preparation Using NPTEL Material
MOCK Test for GATE 2014 now available
ACCESSING NPTEL
New Courses

National Knowledge Commission
Report to the Nation
2006 - 2009

COMMONWEALTH of LEARNING
We're Moving

LEARNING OBJECT REPOSITORIES (LOR)

The Increasing use of Information technologies to create new learning resources, to manage existing learning resources, and to aggregate learning content from a wide variety of academic and publishing sources has completely altered expectations for teaching and learning. Around the world, Academic Institutions, Professional associations and corporations are striving to make better use of networks and databases to efficiently and effectively achieve learning and professional development goals. One of the way they have chosen to pursue these goal is to make learning resources readily accessible to educators and learners through learning object repositories.

Object repositories are seen as key enablers for bringing increased value to learning resources by providing opportunities for reuse, repurposing or reengineering to suit a variety of purposes and end-users needs. Creating learning resources in object formats is seen as way to bring about increased flexibility, customizations, ease of update, search ability and manageability to rich stores of content and learning resources that are available from publishers or that have been created by faculty members or teachers.

Characteristics of Learning Object

- Learning Object Repositories have tremendous potential to become powerful teaching and learning tools that can be used inside and outside the classroom
- Learning objects are at the heart of the learning technology
- Learning objects have generated excitement because of their potential reusability
- A learning object can be simultaneously shared, reused and placed into multiple courses, and course management systems

- Digital resources available on networks are non-rival resources as many people can use these simultaneously

Benefits of Learning Objects for LIS Education

The following are the benefits of learning object in LIS education

- The repository certainly benefits instructors who are teaching a particular subject for the first time. It can show the different perspectives/approaches that other instructors have taken in teaching the subject, the level of details covered for different topics, amount of materials that can be covered in a certain amount of time, types of activities used to enhanced learning and evaluation methods. Course development time is reduced when learning objects are re-used, after customizing them to the local context and the instructor's personal preferences and style
- The repositories are also useful to instructors who are already teaching a particular subject. It can serve to alert the instructor about new developments and emerging topics that are being covered by other instructors. Instructors can also search for supplementary materials, e.g. diagrams, illustrations, exercise/tutorials and class activities
- For students, the repository can provide supplementary readings, tutorials and practice exam questions to enhance learning
- For researchers, the repository can provide raw data for research on LIS curriculum across Asia, teaching styles and methods, and national and cultural differences
- LIS professionals can use the repository for e-learning in new and emerging areas, if the learning objects are detailed and comprehensive enough

- The repository can be useful both for traditional topics in LIS as well as for new and emerging areas
- With learning object on the same topics from different countries, the repository can help educators to appreciate the different national and cultural contexts of LIS, e.g. topics and concepts that receive different emphases in different countries, different terminologies, different applications, different examples scenarios used different approaches to teaching and learning, and different presentation styles
- The repository can be most useful in new and emerging subject areas to facilitate "pollination". A new subject developed in one school can help other school to start courses in the same subject. It can also serve to identify experts in new areas who can be engaged as consultants or invited as resource persons

Challenges in Developing Learning Object Repositories for LIS Education

The development and maintenance of a learning object repositories present unique challenges in three areas

- Content Creation and Development
- Content Management and Organization
- Repository systems

Major Learning Object Repositories

There are several online repositories or collections of learning objects that target Higher Education faculty needs. A learning object can be as small as a paragraph as a large as a complete online cause and come in the form of HTML/Text files, simulations, JAVA, Flash, QuickTime movies etc. Learning objects have arisen in response to the faculty need for high-quality, reusable instructional materials that are organized to be easily searchable. Online search engines that search the whole web simply bring back too many results. Instructional materials like policy guides, assignments, simulations, websites, tutorials, matrices, and other kinds of formats and media expressions are easier to find from within a contained collection. Following are the popular LORs

OPEN COURSEWARE

Another service has gained momentum after establishment of different institutional repositories or open access archives is the metadata harvester. The Open access idea has now expanded to the area of learning resources. "Open Courseware" is a prominent factor exposing information freely on web in selected fields. OCW is an innovative and bold idea. It aims to support learning & teaching programme significantly learning material contained in an OCW Provides learners an opportunity to gain knowledge beyond their routine classroom environments.

Concept of Open Courseware

The Open Courseware concept is a part of the larger movement that promotes free and unrestricted access to knowledge. An OCW site provides open access to the primary teaching materials for courses taught at educational institutions, enabling educators to draw on the materials for the development of their own personal knowledge. The materials are in the digital form which can be accessed online, thus breaking the barriers of time and distance. Indian academies can play a significant role in creating OCW materials for the students to propagate the teaching and learning process. An Open Courseware is a free and open digital publication of high quality educational materials, organized as courses.

Advantages of Open Courseware

- OCW provides open access to high quality

educational content to educators and learners

- Provides a model demonstrating the value of openness
- Institutional benefits
- Advances knowledge by unlocking information for the benefit of all
- Easy to retrieve appropriate course material
- Providing multiple accesses
- OCW providing the facilities of downloading and printing the appropriate course material
- OCW materials are free of charge and free of copyright
- It helps to improve recruitment
- Provides a resource for students, faculty and alumni that support learning and collaboration

Table Shows Some Important Indian Initiative OCW Websites

Sr. No.	Name of the Websites	URL
1	Consortium for Educational Communication (CEC)	http://www.cec-ugc.org/
2	IGNOU – eGyankosh	http://www.egyankosh.ac.in/
3	IITs: National Programme on Technology Enhanced Learning (NPTEL)	http://www.nptel.iitm.ac.in/index.php
4	MHRD – Shakshat	http://www.sakshat.ac.in/
5	Free textbooks from NCERT, on web	http://hindionweb.debashish.com/free-texbooks-from-ncert-on-web
6	MIT Massachusetts Institute of Technology OCW	http://ocw.mit.edu/OcwWeb/web/home/home/index.htm

Consortium for Educational Communication (CEC)

One of the innovations in higher education carried

out by the UGC in early eighties was using powerful medium of films for knowledge communication. As early as in 1984 UGC launched countrywide classroom (CWCR) and Production facilities at 6 universities. Initially the coordination with these centres was done from UGC office with the support of a consultant. Subsequently an inter-university Centre named as 'Consortium for Educational Communication' was set up in the year 1993. The CEC coordinates the development of Centers, ensuring the quality of software, coordination of telecasting of the selected films, inspiring and encouraging innovations. During the two decades of CWCR and a decade of CEC, considerable progress has been made. CEC's Learning Object Repository (LOR) is an OCW initiative having educational resources in different subjects like Archeology, Biology, Botany, Chemistry, Commerce, Computer Science, Economics, Education, English, Fine Arts, etc. Users have the facility to browse the LOR by using various options such as Topic, Subject, Learning Object, Keywords, etc.

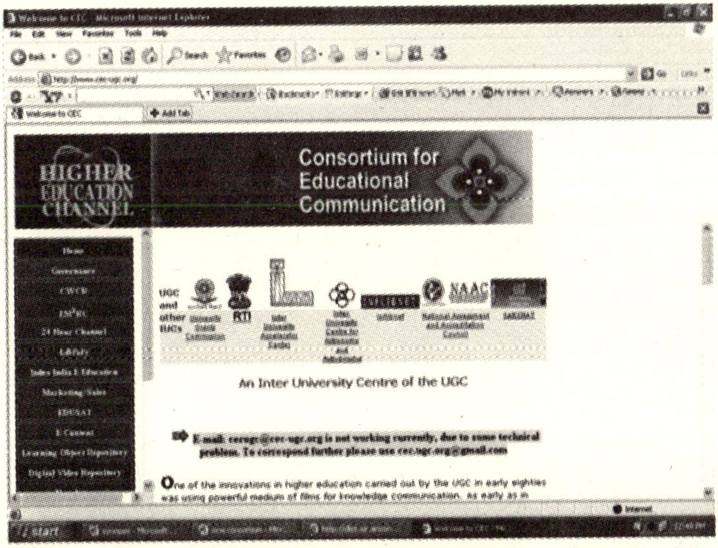

Figure Shows Home Page of Consortium for Educational Communication http://www.cec-ugc.org/

IGNOU – eGyankosh

National digital Repository is a major initiative of the Indira Gandhi National Open University to provide just – in – time access to learning resources among educational institutions in the country. It has been developed with an objective of long – term preservation of learning materials available in various formats.

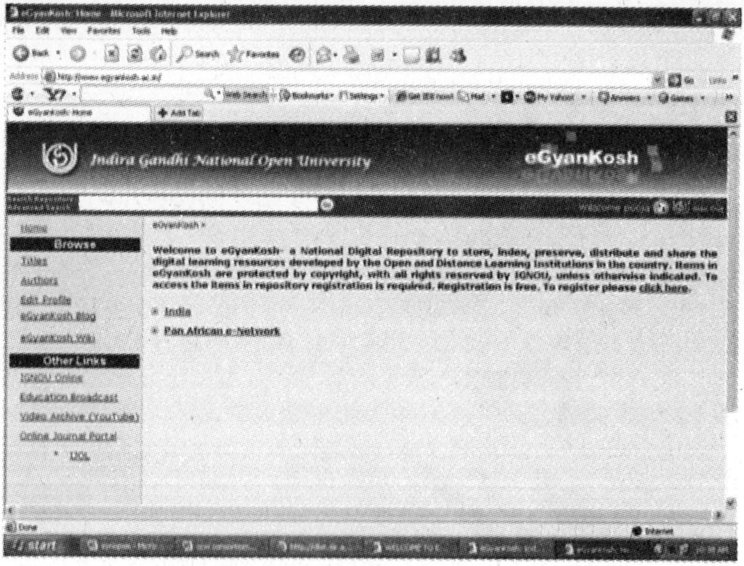

Figure Shows Home Page of IGNOU eGyankosh
http://www.egyankosh.ac.in/

IITs: National Programme on Technology Enhanced Learning (NPTEL)

It is a joint venture by seven Indian Institutes of Technology (IITs) and Indian Institute of Science (IISc). It is funded by Ministry of Human Resource Development (MHRD), Government of India. Six major engineering disciplines have been covered in this project so far (NPTEL Phase I) at the undergraduate (BE/B.Tech) Level.

- Civil Engineering

- Computer Science and Engineering
- Electronic Engineering
- Electronics and Communication Engineering
- Information Technology
- Mechanical Engineering

In addition, a number of core curriculum courses common to all engineering programmes such as Mathematics, Physics, Chemistry, Management, Electronics, Language, etc. have also been included. Video Courses provided through Technology channel TV, Eklavya.

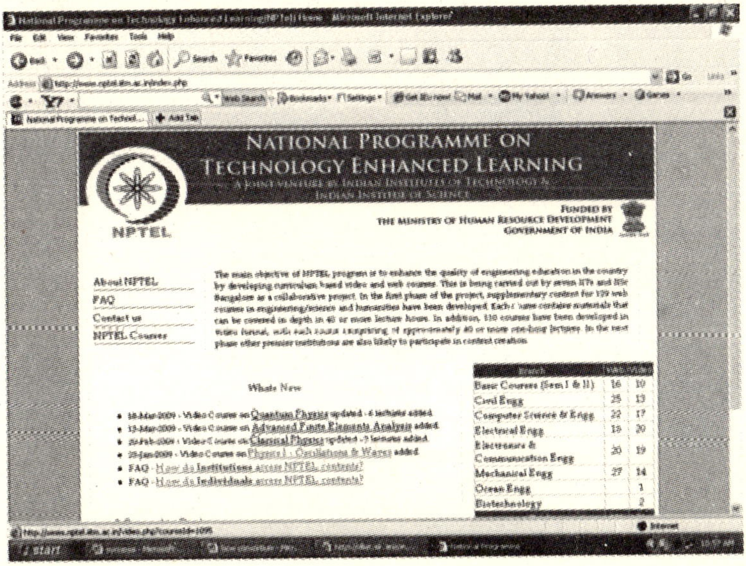

Figure Shows Home Page of National Programme on Technology Enhanced Learning http://www.nptl.iitm.ac.in/index.php

MHRD – Sakshat

Sakshat has been designed and developed be IGNOU for the Ministry of HRD, offers e - Books, e - Journals, Digital Repository, Scholarship, Audio/Video

Library having electronic resources (animation), Reference Material Created by various educational bodies such as NIOS, IGNOU, etc. and Virtual class. The study material are mostly been classified on the basis of class, subject and topics.

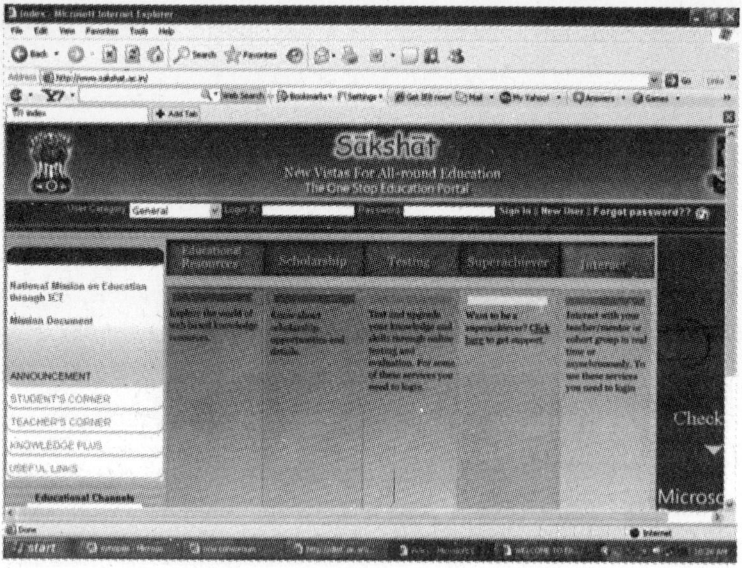

Figure Shows Home Page of Sakshat
http://www.sakshat.ac.in/

NCERT Textbooks

NCERT has initiated the step towards making school textbooks available on the Internet for students and teachers. We hope through this endeavour a variety of pedagogical possibilities would open up for students and teachers throughout the country. We also hope that this effort will lead to a situation where teachers begin to adopt a more modular approach, rather than a sequential approach to teaching and learning through access to a variety of teaching and reference material. These Textbooks are based on National Curriculum Framework 2005.

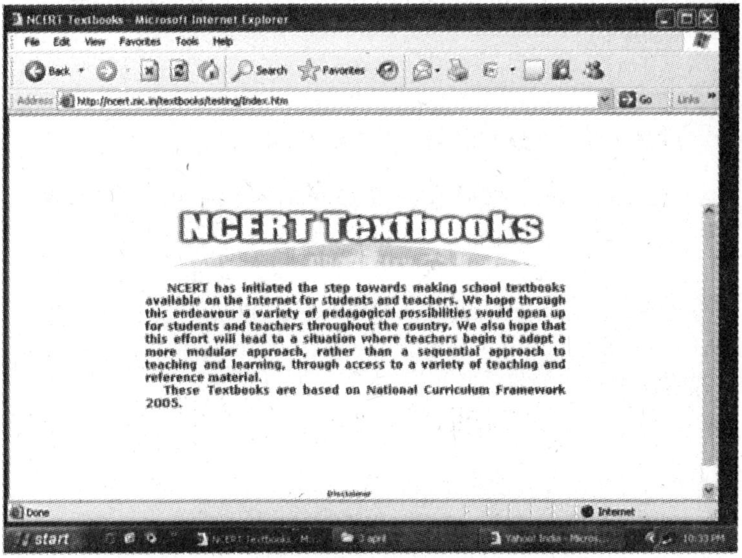

Figure Shows Home Page of NCERT Books
http://ncert.nic.in/textbooks/testing/Index.htm

MIT (Massachusetts Institute of Technology) OCW

MIT OCW is an initiative of the Massachusetts Institute of Technology (MIT) to put all of the educational material from its undergraduate – graduate – level courses online, free and openly available to anyone, anywhere, by end of year 2009. MIT OCW can be considered as a large-scale, web-based publication of MIT Course materials. The project was announced in Oct 2002.

MIT OCW offers over 2603 Courses were available online. OCW is a free publication of course materials used at MIT student can

- Get lecture notes, problem sets, labs and more
- Watch lecture videos and demonstrations
- Study a wide variety of subjects

Figure Shows Home Page of MIT Open Courseware http://ocw.mit.edu/OcwWeb/web/home/home/index.htm

NEED OF OCW

Now a day's Distance education and e-learning are buzz words. Open Access plays vital role for students to find out Course Material which is free of cost online. The OCW's can also greatly contribute in strengthening the educational infrastructure of the institute providing distance education. It supports e-learning and distance education. Such initiatives are established by developing countries. Indian OCW's should be the responsibility of the educational organizations including Universities, Colleges, and Technical Institutions. These organisations may be imparting education in both regular and distance educations. It is in infant stage at present. However introducing OCW will be helpful in upgrading national educational level.

CHAPTER OUTCOMES

This chapter clears the increasing use of Information technologies to create new learning resources, to manage existing learning resources, and to aggregate learning content from a wide variety of academic and publishing sources has completely altered expectations for teaching and learning. In the broadest sense, Open Access are playing important role in the educational field. Internet is the major resource of these LOR, OER, and OCW etc. Whole World can access on one click of the mouse, is the identity of the internet. Fruitful information is the only source to make a man in real sense. Study of these learning object is anything that has an educational purpose. In the case of an online course, it is given that a learning object is a digital object that is used in order to achieve the desired learning outcomes or educational objectives.

These all new technologies make it more practical that teaching materials are shared among faculty to save time for course development and content creation. Effective teaching of new subjects and modules to cover topics related to knowledge management, Information systems, and digital media requires that LIS faculty look for new teaching methodologies and learning styles and introduce new modes of assessment suitable for collaborative learning. Open Educational Resources & Open Courseware's are beginning to draw much interest, especially in the context of e-learning. They have tremendous potentials to become powerful teaching and learning tools that can be used inside and outside the classroom. i-DLR, a learning object repository serves as an educational "hub" for students and beginning professionals to learn about Digital Libraries.

22
Visual Thesaurus

Keywords : *The Visual Thesaurus, Thinkmap, Vocabulary Control, Brainstorming, Information Product*

INTRODUCTION

All the students, researchers, scientists and professionals need new terms, relevant to their study or working field. It is an essential aspect of our life to collect information to fulfil their requirements. So, to get or to provide better terms it is necessary to arrange information in a systematic form. A Thesaurus and other reference materials help users gain more from the richness of information. Users learn new vocabulary, understand how words are interrelated and inspired to incorporate a wide range of words into writing. Good word choice improves writing by adding interest and clarity. Users gain the ability to describe things more specifically or with more detail. The Thesaurus used for generation of keyword lists which form the basis for planning, priority setting and other research management tasks. The Thesaurus is also useful in computer assisted indexing and abstracting. Thesaurus can be used for three basic purposes.

- In indexing but not in searching
- In searching but not in indexing
- In both indexing and searching

Day by day the number of online Language and Subject Thesaurus including the internet is increasing. The online Thesaurus systems are making more and more information available in the full text format. The Thesaurus plays a vital role in retrieving relevant information.

PREAMBLE OF VISUAL THESAURUS

The Visual Thesaurus (VT) is one way to explore words and their meaning. The Visual Thesaurus is a tremendous resource for improving reading, writing and communication skills. Users find the Visual Thesaurus captivating and playful and are quickly engaged in learning new words and concepts. It is a reference tool, powered by Thinkmap, which gets users of all ages excited about words. Using our visualization technology, the Visual Thesaurus takes a unique and remarkably beautiful, approach to presenting the results of a word lookup.

The Visual Thesaurus creates an animated display of words and meanings. The Thinkmap visualization places word in the center of the display, connected to related words and meaning. The Visual Thesaurus moves beyond strictly synonyms to display and animated connections among word definitions, multiple word meanings and even antonyms. A user can broader and narrow search interactively by selecting parts of speech or type of relationship among the words displayed. It's provides guidance and inspiration for anyone interested in words and conversion- writers, professionals, researchers and students. Through its emphasis on exploration and vocabulary building, the Visual Thesaurus improves reading, writing and communication skills.

The Visual Thesaurus are controlled vocabularies constructed to provide a unified way for cataloguers and indexers to identify and describe visual materials such as pictures, illustrations and photographs, thereby increasing their accessibility for researchers. A large part of librarianship consists of crafting methods by which patrons can successfully navigate collections of materials to find the items they need. By creating standard and uniform ways of referring to concepts which can be named any number of ways, such vocabularies hone in on the essence of materials and decrease wasted time by simplifying the task of catalogue users in formulating their queries. The need for analogous resources for processing visual materials led to the creation of the Library of Congress's Thesaurus for Graphic Materials and the Getty Research Institute's Art and Architecture Thesaurus over the last two decades. The recent rises in demand for images and concurrent technological advances have greatly expanded the need for effective retrieval strategies to avoid endless searching through mountains of data.

The Visual Thesaurus are finding their way into digital libraries as well as in to a wide range of information retrieval systems. The Visual Thesaurus could be used to display the relationship of the selected terms to other terms. Visual interfaces enhanced with a thesaurus can be designed to support a variety of information seeking tasks, namely searching, browsing and navigation. More specifically depending on the level of sophistication that can be offered in the interface, visual thesaurus has the potential to support such interactive tasks as quarry formulation, modification or expansion. The Visual Thesaurus that will support user's information search support retrieval experience within the context of digital libraries.

More recently, metadata-enhanced digital library Visual interfaces form the following perspectives:

- Information access and retrieval features supported
- Metadata elements used
- Visualization techniques and metaphors utilized.

THE CONCEPTS

Thesaurus

"Thesaurus is a controlled vocabulary arranged in a known order and structured so that the various relationships among terms are displayed clearly and identified by standardized relationship indicators."

According to Merriam Webster dictionary

"Thesaurus is a book of words or of information about a particular field or set of concepts. It is a list of subject headings or descriptors usually with a cross-reference system for use in the organization of a collection of documents for reference and retrieval."

Visual Thesaurus

- It's a dictionary! It's a thesaurus!
- It's a reference tool, powered by Thinkmap that gets users of all ages excited about words.
- Great for writers, journalists, students, teachers, and artists.

"The Visual Thesaurus is an interactive dictionary and thesaurus which creates word maps that blossom with meanings and branch to related words. It's an innovative display that encourages exploration and learning."

Vocabulary Controlled

"A controlled vocabulary is an established list of standardized terminology for use in indexing and retrieval of information. An example of a controlled vocabulary is subject headings used to describe library resources".

Thinkmap

"Thinkmap is designed to improve the ability of users to browse through complex information. It allows for interactive, dynamic filtering and the display of structured information without overwhelming the user or undermining the depth of the information resource".

BENEFIT OF VISUAL THESAURUS

- Displays word entries using visual map
- Allows for interactive navigation of both words and meanings
- Colour coded parts of speech for grammar usage
- Promotes enthusiasm for word meanings and relationships
- Introduces 16 kinds of semantic relationships (antonyms, "type of", "see also")
- Allows access from anywhere via online subscription

USE THE VISUAL THESAURUS

Find the right word : The Visual Thesaurus over 145,000 words and 115,000 meaning. Find the word user need and discover related meanings.

Develop a better vocabulary : See how words are used in different parts of speech.

Use words precisely : The intuitive interface helps users find words through their semantic relationship with other words and meanings.

Master word usage : Roll over a meaning to see its definition and example sentences that express that meaning.

Improve our grammar : Meanings are colour-coded to indicate parts of speech.

Unlimited access to our magazine : Read features about language and the creative process and join a community passionate about words, language and creativity.

Explore 39,000 proper nouns : Historical figures, phrases and trademarks and included Look up Mozart Manda or simply, 'M'

Check our spelling : The Visual Thesaurus suggests a

word if you spell it wrong. Hear word pronounced correctly. The Visual Thesaurus offers both American and British pronunciations.

Hear words pronounced correctly : The Visual Thesaurus offers both American and British pronunciations.

Personalize our experience : Use the Settings Panel to control font size, filter content, display up to 17 semantic relationships and more.

Email word maps to friends : Share your favourite words with friends and family.

Make word lists : Construct lists of favourite words or organize them by theme.

Play our spelling quiz : Take a spelling challenge that is both vocabulary-expanding and downright addictive.

Access the Visual Thesaurus anywhere : No software to install, access from virtually any computer with an Internet connection.

Explore five additional languages : Search for words in Spanish, German, Italian, French and Dutch, as well as English.

VISUAL THESAURUS IS A BRAINSTORMING TOOLS

The Visual Thesaurus is an interactive dictionary and thesaurus which creates words maps that blossom with meanings and branch to related words. Its innovative display encourages exploration and learning. Users will understand language in a powerful new way. Through the Visual Thesaurus innovative interfaces, users will immediately see all the words and meanings that are related to their word in the brain. The Visual Thesaurus as a vocabulary builder and will benefit from using more descriptive words in their creative writing, poetry writing and essay writing. Professionals in writing and creative fields like advertising praise the Visual Thesaurus for its ability to spark creativity and the brainstorming processes.

The Visual Thesaurus's are freely online available on internet. The Visual Thesaurus becomes an fluid, dynamic and important tool to help these youngsters increase and refine their writing and speaking vocabularies. Word maps blossom with meaning, helping find just the right word. You will write more descriptively and precisely, discover new ideas, and expand your vocabulary. This site includes some great information and knowledge to useful for users. These some searching tools are given bellows.

Synonyms to Early Writers

The users introduces to the basic concept of a synonym and how varying vocabulary usage through synonyms can enhance their writing. Users will also synthesize their understanding of synonyms and the Visual Thesaurus by paying "Synonym Charades' a fun guessing game where users will figure out original book. Prepare a list of synonyms for the word 'Money' (e.g. dough, jack, simoleons, long green, bucks, cabbage, shekels, yellow boys, hard cash, and bank). Explain that our English language has a large, richer vocabulary than most other languages. A strategy to use in order to take advantage of our colourful language is to practice thesaurus skills. A Visual Thesaurus is a book of synonyms and antonyms. Writers look up common and overused words in a thesaurus in order to find synonym. These synonyms help make compositions more interesting and less repetitive.

Learning Grammar through Wordplay

In this area users master some of the more interesting and challenging vocabulary words from a New York Times article by analysing the writer's use of nouns and verbs in the article and then constructing original sentences using those words in different contexts. The Visual Thesaurus has multiple objectives-to teach the grammatical components of a sentence, to help users broaden their vocabularies, and to use wordplay as a means of teaching sentence structure.

Effective use of Transition Words

Users explore and understand the use of transition words in context and write their own persuasive essay using transition words. The Visual Thesaurus goal is to get users to replace overused words with more interesting, higher-level synonyms.

Using Descriptive Language

Informative features explore everything from how writers find inspiration to how words and phrases become part of our lexicon. Hear from experts in fields ranging from teaching to copyright and learn how to make language work for users.

Exploring the Power of Puns

Users are asked to analyse various Shakespearean and contemporary puns and how particular words make these puns possible. They will use the Visual Thesaurus to examine the subjects of this wordplay and to help them create original puns in small groups.

Seeing Words in New Way

Users are introduced to the basic functions of the Visual Thesaurus by comparing and contrasting the use of a traditional dictionary and the use of the Visual Thesaurus to explore a word's meaning.

Words have Multiple Meanings

People will have a better understanding of some common words, including an understanding that simple words have multiple meanings. Users also learn of the value of using a thesaurus as part of their writing process.

By learning more of the options for word choice to better express themselves.

Exploring Different Parts of Speech

Users gain experience writing, choosing appropriate language and understanding parts of speech. Each word's part of speech, definition and a sample sentence are present. They learn that words have multiple functions when used in different contexts. Through these exercise, they gain practice in writing and learn how word choice affect both meaning and intent.

USING THE VISUAL THESAURUS

The Visual Thesaurus is dynamic graphical interface shows relationship among words. Search on a word and the display that pops up in the center of the screen makes it quite clear how the words relate to each other. Closely related words are grouped. Solid lines indicate a direct relationship, while a dotted line means that the central word is a type of the other.

- For example, type the word in the search box at the top of the window and press the "LOOK IT UP" button.

- Try typing the word "Design" into the search box and pressing the "LOOK IT UP" button.
- After searching for a word, the main display will populate with many words and meanings.
- The word searched for will appear in the center of the display and will be surrounded with words and meanings that are related to it. "Design" is a direct synonym of "Plan".

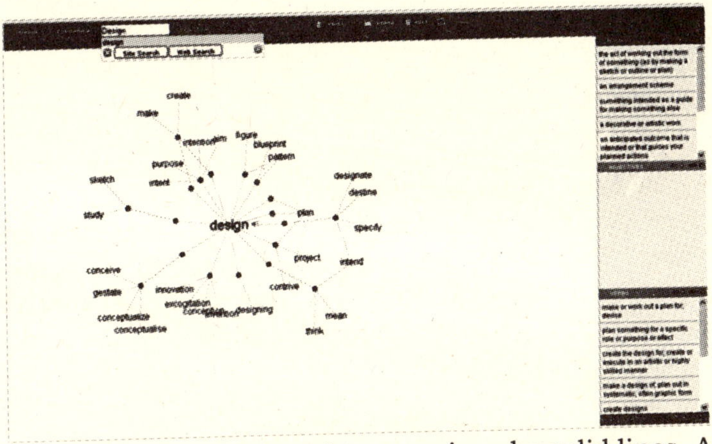

- Words are connected to meanings by solid lines. All the words connected to the same meaning are synonyms.
- The circle representing those meanings in the Visual Thesaurus display area will highlight and their definition will be shown.

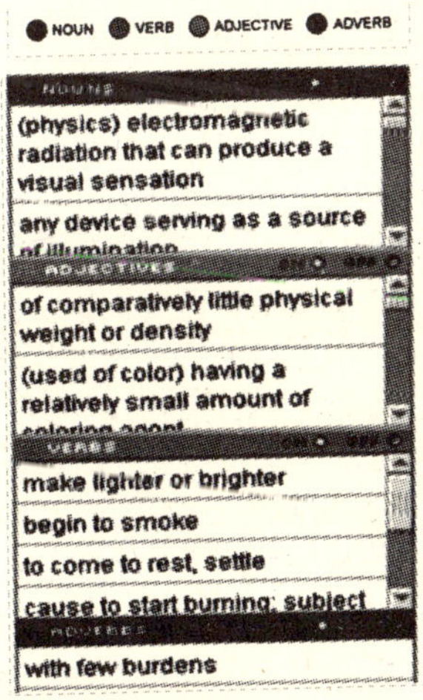

The right of the Visual Thesaurus display are the meaning lists. Meanings are divided into the four parts of speech Nouns, Verbs, Adjectives and Adverbs. Each part of speech is colour coded to match the circle representing meanings in the Visual Thesaurus display.

- Antonyms, pairs of words that express opposite concepts are connected by dashed red lines.

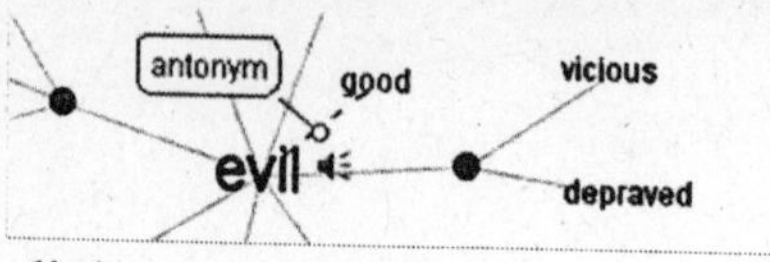

- If right click on a word or meaning in the Visual Thesaurus display, see a "pop-up" menu that shows the various actions that can be taken on that word, such as Pronounce word, Search Internet, Search for Images, Expand Selection, and Make Center. Not all actions will be available on every word and meaning.

CHAPTER OUTCOME

The Visual Thesaurus is a powerful way to combine text and image for presentation but also a great memory aide for helping consolidate the knowledge for future use. In this chapter described the idea of a visual thesaurus, a tool for recognizing visually similar events, visual synonyms using colour, texture, pattern and other user defined features. Users gain experience writing, choosing appropriate language and understanding parts of speech.

The Visual Thesaurus is a useful information product for all type of fields to improve reading, writing and communication skills. The Visual Thesaurus helps the users to gain more from the richness of information. Users learn new vocabulary, understand how words are interrelated and inspired to incorporate a wide range of words into writing. It is helpful product for specially LIS professionals to improve their skills for providing better services to the users.

Bibliography

The following is a brief list of sources of information referred in these comprehensive chapters.

- Ambati, V. Sankar, P.; Pratha, L. and Jawahar, C. 2005. "Quality management in digital libraries." In Proceedings of 1st ICUDL.
- Amberkat, B.W. & Rehpade, S. "Changing dimensions of library management: Challenges and Opportunity" Sausar, 3 February 2013. Pg.no. 112-113.
- Arambam Hileima Devi "Human Resource Development for Digital Environment: A Case Study of the Libraries of Manipur", http://www.ifla.org.
- Balague, N. "Managing your library and its quality: the iso 9001 way", *Woodhead publishing limited, Cambrige"* UK, 2011. http://www.woodheadpublishing.com/en/book.aspx?bookID=2479&ChandosTitle=1
- Beloglazov, Anton & Rajkumar Buyya "Energy Efficient Resource Management in Virtualized Cloud Data Centres" *10th IEEE/ACM International Conference on Cluster, Cloud and Grid Computing*, 2010. http://www.cs.binghamton.edu/~millerti/cs680r/papers/Cloud/EnergyEfficientResourceManagementCloudCenters.pdf
- Benefits of Ebooks. 2008 http://epublishersweekly.blogspot.in/2008/02/30-benefits-of-ebooks.html

- Benefits of Cloud computing, http://blogs.sap.com/innovation/cloud-computing/risks-and-benefits-of-cloudcomputing-020025
- Bhandarkar, P. L. & T. S. Wilkinson *Methodology and Techniques of Social Research,* Mumbai: Himalaya Publishing House, 2009.
- Boss, Richard W. "*RFID Technology for Libraries*" http://www.ala.org/ala/pla/plapubs/technotes/rfidtechnology.htm
- Breeding, Marshall "The Many Facets of Managing Electronic Resources" *Magazine Computers in Library,* 2004. 24, 01 http://www.infotoday.com/cilmag/jan04/breeding.shtml
- Careo (Campus Albert Repository of Educational Objects) http://www.careo.org/
- Chandrasekar, M. "Leading roles of library and information science professionals in current era" International Journal of Library Science, 2013
- Chappell, Marcia H. "The place of reference service in Ranganathan's theory of librarianship". http://www.jstor.org/discover/10.2307/4306718?uid=3738256&uid= 2129&uid=2&uid=70&uid=4&sid=21102472723191
- Chaudhry, A.S. and Khoo, C.S.G. issues in developing a Repository of learning Objects for LIS Education in India. http://www.ifla.org/IV/ifla72/index.html
- Das, Sarama and Srijib Patra "Ranganathan's Five Laws in the Light of ICT" 2008. http://ir.inflibnet.ac.in/dxml/bitstream/handle/1944/1290/41.pdf?sequence=1
- Department of Higher Education, Ministry of Human Resource Development, Government of India, http://mhrd.gov.in/schemes_technical_eng
- Deshpande, R. M. "Study of Customer Satisfaction

Management in Libraries and Information Centres of Regional Engineering Colleges in India", Ph. D Thesis, 2002.

- Deshpande, Ravikant M., Rahangdale, Bharati, & Bhoskar, Ranjana "Factors Responsible for Current Status of Libraries of National Institute of Technology in India", *2nd International Conference on Academic Libraries* (pp.208-213) New Delhi: indo American Books Publication. 2013.
- Dhawan, S. M. Basic of Information Dissemination. http://www.unesco.org/education/Aladin/paldin/pdf/course02/unit_05.pdf
- Dspace, http://www.dspace.org
- E-book. http://en.wikipedia.org/wiki/E-book
- Electronic resource management http://en.wikipedia.org/wiki/Electronic_resource_management
- Electronic resource management http://en.wikipedia.org/wiki/Electronic_resource_management
- E-literacy, The Impact of ICT on the Development of Information Literacy by Students in Further Education http://www.jelit.org/53/01/JeLit_Paper_8.pdf
- Eprints, http://www.eprints.org
- Fedora, http://www.fedora.org
- File of Library Automation, Barcode, LIBSYS 7, RFID Technology (Gates EAS Built in Electronic Control Unit, Scanners/ LSmart work station, Kiosk, RFID Tags, Self Adhesive, RFID Reader, WI-Fi Library inventory Reader from TAGSYS) implemented in VNIT LIRC Nagpur.
- File of TEQIP, INDEST Consortium, Library Automation, Digital Library Project, Training of Human Resources, RFID Technology, and

Awareness Programme for faculty and students of various technologies implemented in all RECs / NITs.

- Five laws of library science http://en.wikipedia.org/wiki/Five_laws_of_library_science
- Fostering, Anu L. "Intrapreneurship - The new Competitive Edge". http://dspace.iimk.ac.in/bitstream/2259/471/1/149-156+.pdf
- Frederick, Friend J. The future of libraries in the work of S. R. Ranganathn, 2007 http://drtc.isibang.ac.in:8080/bitstream/handle/1849/310/064_p3_frederick-friend-on-r ranganatha_formatted.pdf [Accessed on 01/07/2013].
- Gaylord Images http://www.gaylord.com/litsting.asp?H=8&PCI=132467
- Golnessa Galyani Moghaddam and V.G. Talawar. "Library Consortia in Developing Countries: An Overview" *Program : electronic library and information systems*, 2009, vol. Vol.43, n. No.1, pp. 94-104. http://liswiki.org/wiki/Alphabetical_List_of_Library_Consortia
- Greenstone, http://www.greenstone.org
- Halder, Sambhu Nath "Multimodal roles of library and information science professionals in present era" 2011 http://www.academicjournals.org
- Hirwade Mangala, and Hirwade Anil *Information Technology: A Practical Manual,* Mumbai: Himalaya Publishing House, 2007.
- http://21stcenturylibrary.wordpress.com/2010/08/24/21st-century-library-skills-need-to-support-21st-century-workforce-demands/
- http://alalearning.org/2011/09/27/this-is-the-21st-century/
- http://en.wikipedia.org/wiki/Tattle-Tape

- http://etips.sulekha.com/cctv-cameras-advantages-disdavandates_1903
- http://en.wikipedia.org/wiki/Consumer-electronics
- http://library.oglethorpe.edu/services/orientation_plan.pdf
- http://www.academicjournals.org/ijlis/pdf/pdf2009/nov/halder.pdf
- http://www.businessdictionary.com/definition/tacit-knowledge.html#ixzz2JunUe24f
- http://www.ceserp.com/cpjour/index.php?journal=ijls&page=article&op=view&path[]=4
- http://www.imls.gov/assets/1/AssetManager/21stCenturySkills.pdf
- http://www.knowledgeboard.com/download/3512/Tacit-vs-Explicit.pdf
- http://www.slideshare.net/badamikk/kkb
- http://www.tlainc.com/articl139.htm
- http://www.uky.edu/~gmswan3/575/KM_roles.pdf
- I-DLR Interactive Digital Library Resource Information System http://www.coe.missouri.edu/~DL/iDLR/index.php
- INDEST-AICTE Consortium http://paniit.iitd.ac.in/indest/downloads/brochureforcoremembers.pdf
- Information Explosion, http://en.wikipedia.org/wiki/Information_explosion
- Introduction to Visual Thesaurus http://www.visualthesaurus.com/webmasters/
- Introduction of VNIT http://en.wikipedia.org/wiki/Visvesvaraya_National_Institute_of_Technology
- Krubu, D. E. and Osawaru K. E. (2011) "The Impact of Information and Communication Technology (ICT) in Nigerian University Libraries" *Library Philosophy*

and Practice http://www.webpages.uidaho.edu/~mbolin/krubu-osawaru.htm

- Kude, N. S. "Quality management through library and information science education in India: issues and trends' ,*UGC sponsored national seminar on quality assessment and quality indicators for lis education*, Organising secretary golden jubilee celebration, Nagpur: 2006, pp. 190-1.
- Kulshrestha, Raman Prakash "Marketing Strategy of Information Services in IIM Libraries and Information Centres in India" http://dspace.jgu.edu.in:8080/dspace/bitstream/10739/170/1/Marketing%20Strategy% 20of%20 Information% 20Services% 20in%20Today%20Hi%5B1%5D%2012.pdf
- Kumar, Ranjit *Research Methodology: A Step by Step Guide for Beginners*, New Delhi: Pearson, 2005.
- Kumbar, R. D. "The importance of marketing and total quality management in libraries', *Electronic journal of academic and special librarianship*, v.5 no.2-3. http://southernlibrarianship.icaap.org/content/v05n02/kumbar_r01.htm
- Kunwar Singh V, and Bhaskar Rao, *An Overview of the Library Consortia in India: planner* 2008. Pg.140-149.
- Laamanen, I. "Quality management in the information service centre of the fioh", *Health information management:what strategies?*, proceedings of the 5th *European conference of medical and health libraries*, Coimbra: Porpugal, 1996, pp. 57-4.
- LIBSYS, RFID technology Web site: http://www.tagsysrfid.com
- LIS Professionals Skills, http://www.isrj.net/Pdf_files/Ghante_LIB.pdf

- Maricopa Centre for Learning and Instruction (MCLI) http://www.mcli.dist.maricopa.edu/
- Massachusetts Institute of Technology (MIT), http://ocw.mit.edu/index.html
- Metadata, The Metadata Challenge: Promoting Discovery, Access, and Usability for Online Books http://works.bepress.com/john_mark_ockerbloom/13/
- McGreal, R. Learning Objects: A practical definition. http://www.itdl.org/journal/sep_04/article02.htm
- Mendhe R.M. and Taksande P.G. *Consortia: A new trends in LIS. III conference of VLA on Librarian and ICT,* Shegaon: 2008
- MERLOT – Multimedia Educational Resources for online Learning and Teaching http://www.merlot.org/
- Moodle, http://www.moodle.org
- Mitchell, Erik "Using Cloud Services for Library IT Infrastructure" http://journal.code4lib.org/articles/2510
- Nageswara Yogi, A.M., Leelavathi, S.H. & Sunderrajan, K. "Resource Sharing Using Information Communication Technology with Knowledge Centre, ADE : A Case Study". http://ir.inflibnet.ac.in/bitstream/handle/1944/950/11.pdf?sequence=1
- National Programme on Technology Enhanced Learning (NPTEL) http://www.nptel.iitm.ac.in/
- New Skills for LIS Professionals in Technology-Intensive Environment, S.P. Singh http://crl.du.ac.in/ical09/papers/index_files/ical-55_200_422_3_RV.pdf
- Noruzi, Alireza "Application of Ranganathan's Laws to the Web". 2004 http://www.webology.org/2004/v1n2/a8.html

- Open Access, http://www.en.wikipedia.org/wiki/open_access
- Open Courseware Study, http://www.edufive.com/studyOCW.html
- Open Course Ware, http://www.ocw.uci.edu
- Open Course Ware Consortium, http://ocwconsortium.org/
- Patle Bharati V. "Creation of Man in Essence through Libraries" *International Conference on Entrepreneurial Approaches to Librarianship* (pp.198-205) (New Delhi: Bookwell Delhi, 2013.
- Pendam, G. W. "Quality assessment and quality indicators of library and information services in academic libraries' ,*UGC sponsored national seminar on quality assessment and quality indicators for lis education*, Organising secretary golden jubilee celebration, Nagpur: 2006, pp. 210-4.
- PLA Library Association, http://www.ala.org/pla/tools/technotes/rfidtechnology
- Portal, http://searchcio-midmarket.techtarget.com/definition/portal
- Project Gutenberg, http://www.gutenberg.org/wiki/Main_Page
- Rajendra K. Kumbhar, *Thesaurus of Library and Information Science Terms* New Delhi: Ess Ess Publication, 2005
- Ranganathan, S. R. father of Indian library science http://libraryforall.tripod.com/sr.html
- Role of COA Council of Architecture, (2002) New Delhi India http://www.coa.gov.in/#top
- Salwsky, Donna "Building a keyword library for description of visual assets: Thesaurus basics Journal of Digital Asset Management" *Journal of Digital Asset Management*, 2007 Pg. 130–138. http://www.palgrave.com

- Sarma, Gautam Kumar and Apurba Mujumdar : Open Courseware (OCW) initiative for e-learners in India., http://www.apurba.110mb.com/open%20courseware%20initiatives.pdf
- Sasson, R. The Benefits and Advantages of eBooks. http://www.successconsciousness.com/ebooks_benefits.htm
- Schray, Vickie, "Assuring Quality in Higher Education: Recommendations for Improving Accreditation" http://www2.ed.gov/about/bdscomm/list/hiedfuture/reports/schray2.pdf
- Shalu Bedi and Kiran Sharma. *"Library Consortia: A Step forwards the Information Society.* Chandigarh: 2008.
- Sharma, Sumati and Ashok Kumar Mohinder Singh "Digital Reference Service" *DESIDOC Bulletin of Information Technology* 2004 Vol. 24 (issue. no. 6), pp.11-18
- Shepherd, M. "Library Collaboration: What makes it Work?" http://www.iatul.org/doclibrary/public/conf_proceedings/2004/murray20sheperd.pdf
- Selected files of LIRC, VNIT, Nagpur.
- Stafford Amy, Shiri Ali and others "Searching: User-Centered Evaluation of a Visual Thesurus-Enhanced Interface for Bilingual Digital Libraries" http://www.mendeley.com/research/searching-usercentrer...rusenhanced-interface-for-bilingual-digital-libraries/#
- Subject Gateways, The clever way to information by Pankaj Kumar Das http://ir.inflibnet.ac.in/dxml/bitstream/handle/1944/107/cali_26.pdf?sequence=1
- Teaching and Learning on the Web http://www.mcli.dist.maricopa.edu/tl/index.html
- Technical Education, http://www.aicte-india.org/teqip.htm.

- The concerned files of the LIRC, VNIT, Nagpur.
- The expertise of Human resources in LIRC, VNIT, Nagpur.
- Top 5 Benefits of Collaboration Technology for Businesses. http://www.parklandchamber.com/the-top-5-benefits-of-collaboration-technology-for-businesses
- Turner, Amos "Visual Thesaurus Pathfinder Introduction" 2000 http://www.ischool.utexas.edu/%7Evmuseum/turner/pathfinder.html
- Venable, Melissa. "Accreditation and Higher Education: What do you need to know? " 2011 http://www.onlinecollege.org/2011/05/03/accreditation-and-higher-education-what-do-you-need-to-know/
- Villanueva, Benevieve D. and Joanna Opena, "Problem Formulation and Hypothesis Testing: A Module for AERS 282-Social Research Design" http://coweb.org/benevieve/Problem%20 Formulation% 20and% 20Hypothesis% 20Testing.pdf
- Visual Thesaurus, http://www.thinkmap.com/;jsessionid=E2A9632DA9EF20508224F19A494387B9
- Vortal, http://oxforddictionaries.com/definition/vortal
- Warren, Gabriela "The Benefits of Online Collaboration Tools". http://www.parklandchamber.com/the-top-5-benefits-of-collaboration-technology-for-businesses
- What are the Characteristics of Entrepreneurs? http://www.bookfresh.com/resources/article/what-are-the-characteristics-of-entrepreneurs
- Wikipedia, the free encyclopaedia, National Board of Accreditation http://en.wikipedia.org/wiki/National_Board_of_Accreditation